From SPHINX to CHRIST

An Occult History

From SPHINX *to* CHRIST

An Occult History

By
EDOUARD SCHURÉ

RUDOLF STEINER PUBLICATIONS
151 North Moison Road
Blauvelt, New York 10913, U.S.A.
1970

FOREWORD

THE reader of the following pages is privileged to witness spiritual adventure of a depth and intensity rarely equalled by creative human beings, even in their most exalted moments. The aliveness, the freshness, the excitement of spiritual discovery which motivated the author will find response in wide circles today.

To Edouard Schure in a moment of extra-sensory perception appeared the esoteric Light flowing from one Mystery Center to another, from the mighty Himalayas to the plateau of Iran, from the heights of Sinai to the summit of Tabor, from the secret sanctuaries of Egypt to the sacred groves of Eleusis. As in a lightning-flash he saw the divinely Illuminated Ones whom we know as Rama, Krishna, Hermes, Moses, Orpheus, Pythagoras and Plato, and recognized that through them all moved the impulse of the eternal, Secret Wisdom.

In that instant of cosmic consciousness Schure experienced the continuity of inspiration as historical fact. He discovered the key to the Secret History of man's striving for the spirit in all ages of time. From that recognition he wrote this book.

Schure was convinced that the Secret Wisdom not only can enlighten us concerning our own spiritual past, but can provide the insight necessary if we are to share in shaping a constructive future for humanity.

Rudolf Steiner considered Schure to be " one of the best guides for finding the path to the spirit in our day," stating that the ideas expressed in his writings " can awaken within every human being a premonition of the solution of the riddles of existence."

Edouard Schure is a master in depicting for modern readers the engrossing story of man's eternal search for the esoteric knowledge of his origin, evolution and destiny in the light of the eternal spirit. His books therefore are of paramount importance today.

—PAUL M. ALLEN.

Botton Village,
Danby/Whitby,
Yorkshire, England.
May, 1970.

CONTENT

BOOK I

PLANETARY EVOLUTION AND THE ORIGIN OF MAN

BOOK II

ATLANTIS AND THE ATLANTEANS

CONTENTS

BOOK III

THE MYSTERY OF INDIA

BOOK IV

MANIFESTATIONS OF THE SOLAR WORD

I

ZOROASTER

BOOK V

MANIFESTATIONS OF THE SOLAR WORD

II

A CHALDEAN PRIEST IN THE TIME OF THE PROPHET DANIEL

CONTENTS

BOOK VI

MANIFESTATIONS OF THE SOLAR WORD

III

THE DEATH OF CAMBYSES AND THE SUN OF OSIRIS

BOOK VII

THE HELLENIC MIRACLE

APOLLO AND DIONYSUS—THE ELEUSINIAN MYSTERIES—THE BASIS OF TRAGEDY

BOOK VIII

THE COSMIC CHRIST AND THE HISTORICAL JESUS

CONTENTS

BOOK I

PLANETARY EVOLUTION AND THE ORIGIN OF MAN

> Gods do not think as men think. The thoughts of men are images; the thoughts of Gods are living beings.
> RUDOLF STEINER,

CHAPTER I

THE RIDDLE OF THE SPHINX AND THE PRIMORDIAL WISDOM

THE aim of all wisdom is to solve the problem of man, the last word in planetary evolution. This problem comprises that of the whole world, for the small universe of man, the microcosm, is a reflection and miniature synthesis of the universe, or macrocosm. Founded on the same principles, they are diverse but concordant expressions of the invisible Creator, visible in His works; of the sovereign Spirit Whom we call God.

No symbol expresses more eloquently the interlinked problem of Nature and Man than the Sphinx of immemorial Egypt, whose meaning human thought has long striven to decipher.

For about ten thousand years, that is to say, ever since the beginnings of the first civilisations of Africa and Asia that preceded our European civilisations, the colossal Sphinx of Gizeh, carved from the rock and couched in the tawny desert sand, has propounded this formidable problem to every passer-by. For from that dumb form, with its haughty countenance, there issues a superhuman language more impressive than any speech.

"Behold me," it says. "I am the Nature-Sphinx. Angel, eagle, lion and bull, I have the august visage of a god, and the body of a winged and roaring beast. You have neither my croup, my claws, nor my wings, but your bust resembles mine. Who are you? Whence come you? Whither do you go? Have you risen from the slime of earth, or did you descend from the glowing disk of the sun that now rises gloriously above the mountains of Arabia? As to myself, *I am, I see, I know*—from everlasting. For I am one of the eternal Archetypes that exist in the Light Unmanifest, but . . . it is forbidden to me to speak otherwise than by my presence. As to you, ephemeral being, obscure voyager, fleeting shadow—seek and discover !—or else, despair ! "

To the piercing question, the imperious command, of the winged beast, mythologies, religions and philosophies have responded in innumerable ways throughout the course of history.

They have allayed without assuaging the thirst for truth that burns in the heart of man. In spite of wide diversity of rites and dogmas, they are in accord upon one essential point ; for, by means of symbols, sacrifices, disciplines and promises, these spiritual guides ceaselessly assure man of the fact that he came from a divine world and can return to it if he so wills ; that there is in him something ephemeral and something eternal, and that the former should be used only for the purpose of developing the latter.

Since the dawn of Christianity, which offers truth to the most humble and causes the whole human race to thrill with hope, the legend of a paradise lost through the sin of the first man, and of salvation offered to degenerate humanity through a divine sacrifice, has solaced souls for nearly two thousand years. But the popular and suggestive story, in its childish form, no longer satisfies an adult humanity that has mastered the forces of nature —a humanity that desires to penetrate all mysteries by means of reason, and that believes, like doubting Thomas, only in the tangible.

Thus man finds himself standing to-day before the ancient Sphinx, whose ever-repeated question troubles him in spite of himself. Weary at last, he cries : " O Eternal Sphinx, foolish and vain is your riddle ! There is no God. Even if He exists in some region inaccessible to my senses, I do not wish to know of Him—I can do without Him. The gods are dead. There is no Absolute, no supreme God, no First Cause. There is only an unending torrent of phenomena that follow one another like waves around the fatal circle of the universe. O deluding Sphinx, torment of wise men, scarecrow of the masses, I fear you no longer ! It matters not to me by what strange chance I issued from your loins, but, since I have been born, I can escape from your talons, for I call myself Will, Reason, Analysis—and all things bow down before my power. Thus I am your master, and you become purposeless. Vain symbol of the past, phantom of the vanished gods, sink now into the sand and leave to me the earth, which I will fill at last with liberty and bliss ! "

So speaks the new man, the superman of a science which is only the science of matter. The Sphinx is silent : the Sphinx uncomprehended by man, deprived of its aureole and of its golden disk, symbol of the winged sun ; deprived of its power to bring the word of the gods to human souls in the silence of the temples— the Sphinx, drained of life amid the desert sands, is silent. And the triumphant superman beholds himself in the mirror of science.

Then he starts back in fear. For he sees himself in the form of a gorilla, with hairy body and prognathous countenance, which

sneers at him : " Behold your ancestor ! Salute your new god ! "
Confronted by this vision, the superman tries in vain to stiffen his
pride ; he shudders with horror, and feels himself humiliated by
implacable science. And in the depths of his heart he hears a
voice which seems to be that of the distant Sphinx, for it is subtle
as an aerial whisper, and harmonious as the murmur which issues
from the statue of Memnon under the first sun-rays. " Foolish
man," it says ; " believing yourself to have descended from the
apes, you would deserve never to rise. Know that your greatest
crime is to have murdered God ! "

Such is the state of mind which science without soul, science
without God, produces in humanity. Thence arise the two doctrines of agnosticism and materialism which rule the mentality
of the present day. Agnosticism says : " *Ignorabimus*, we shall
never know the cause of things ; let us cease to trouble about it."
Materialism says : " There is nothing beyond matter and instinct ;
let us make the best of it." These two doctrines have the same
result : fatalism in history and philosophy, realism in art, suppression of religious feeling and of the idea of divinity. The
effort to free man by liberating him from God ends in making
him the slave of matter. The decapitation of the universe is
the decapitation of the human being.

I am, of course, not confusing here true science, so admirable
in its work of observation and classification, with its fanatic vul-
garisers, the theorists of agnosticism and materialism. It is they
who shroud thought in a black veil through which the whole
world resembles a cemetery. There are, indeed, many who
have long protested against this veil with its innumerable
folds that suffocate thought and hide the living universe.
But where is to be found the sword of light that will
rend it ?

Some have recourse to ancient metaphysics, but these abstract
conceptions, divorced from living nature, furnish only blunted
weapons. Others resign themselves to a philosophy of water-
tight compartments, which places science in one compartment
and religion in another—a philosophy leading to radical im-
potence, for it cuts man into two halves. Others again
return to the dogmas of the Church, and, without understanding them, seek consolation in her rites, whose evocative
magic has been lost, together with their sublime significance.
These rites can still allay uneasiness, but they cannot bestow
truth.

Where is the sword of light that will penetrate the darkness
of the soul and the deeps of nature, and rediscover God? Is
murderous science the mistress of the world? Is life-giving

wisdom but an empty name? Many have said it, and many more believe it.

Nevertheless . . . there is a primordial wisdom, a wisdom eternal and transcendent, in which the fulness of knowledge abides. Once it flowed level-banked, like the Ganges from the Himalayan snows. To-day it seems merely a thin stream of water trickling over a bed of pebbles. But it has never completely dried up. This wisdom proceeds from faculties other than those used by contemporary science. Intuition is but a glimmering of it, a first step towards it. It is called Vision, Contemplation of the Divine, Communion with the Eternal. It is derived from the inner light which is kindled in man at a certain stage of his development. It penetrates through the astral world, the laboratory of creative forces, to the spiritual world where all things have their origin. Pure and radiant is the source of this wisdom; obscure and imperfect the translations of it into human art and language. For it springs from the direct influx of the Spiritual Powers that created the world. Not only did the early sages perceive these Powers, but they inwardly contemplated the great Mysteries of Creation; that is, the successive aspects assumed by the solar system before the earth was made. They beheld the eternal forms that float in the astral light before the eye of pure vision, and they gave the same names to the planets as to the cosmic forces that shaped them. That is why the planets became the gods of mythology[1].

The great occultists and mystics of the sixteenth and seventeenth centuries had some gleams of this primordial wisdom. Henry Kunrath tried to condense it in his *Teatrum sapientiæ æternæ;* Jacob Boehme approached it in his *Aurora;* Paracelsus studied

---

[1] The great astronomers of the sixteenth and seventeenth centuries, such as Copernicus, Galileo and Kepler, who formulated the laws of celestial mechanics and opened up for us the depths of space, regarded the stars very much as did the magi of Chaldea and the priests of Egypt.

They believed in a hierarchic *dynamism*, a universal *animism*, but differentiated and graduated. For to them the stars, though governed by mathematical laws, were alive. They looked upon them not only intellectually, but spiritually. In the stars they saw the gods, and in the cosmos the Creative Spirit. Hear this passage from Kepler: "The whole of creation forms a marvellous symphony, in the order of ideas and of spirit, as well as in that of material beings. All is held and linked together by mutual indissoluble affinities : all forms a harmonious whole. In God, there is the same harmony, a harmony supreme; for God has created us in His image, and has given us the idea and feeling of harmony. All that exists is living and animated, because all is linked together; there is no star that is not "animal," that has not a soul. The souls of the stars are the cause of their movements and of the sympathy that unites them one to another; this explains the regularity of natural phenomena."—Kepler, *Harmonices Mundi,* 1619.

it in his treatise on *Astronomia Magna ;* Leibnitz had a presentiment of it when he spoke of *perennis quædam philosophia.* The Theosophical leader, Rudolf Steiner, called it *Urweltweisheit,* an untranslatable word which can merely be paraphrased as " primordial world-wisdom. [1]

---

[1] That which is acquired by man through inspiration and vision is merely a reflection from the spiritual powers that made the world. The watchmaker has the idea of a watch, and constructs it according to his plan. When the watch is made one can, by taking the works to pieces, trace the idea which presided at its construction. Such is the position of man with regard to the divine creative wisdom. Before our world was born this wisdom existed ; it was the plan of the world, and was later communicated to man. In it are expressed the ideas of the gods.—Rudolf Steiner, *From a lecture delivered in* 1909.

CHAPTER II

THE FIRE-PRINCIPLE AND THE HIERARCHY OF POWERS

THE central doctrine of the ancient occult science, first formulated by the Rishis of India, was that of the Fire-Principle, substance of the universe and instrument of the gods.

Agni, the Fire hidden in all things, the original and invisible Fire, whose smoke, flame and light are but external manifestations —*Agni*, the creative Fire, is truly the universal agent and substance. For, on the one hand, Fire is the elemental form of matter; on the other, it is the garment and, in a sense, the body of the gods, the medium through which they act upon the world. Road of Flame, whereby Spirit descends into matter : Road of Light, whereby matter remounts to Spirit.

This ancient doctrine of the Fire-Principle, whose divine poetry illumines the Vedas, is later formulated scientifically by Heraclitus, the greatest of the Greek philosophers of the Ionian school. Heraclitus saw in Fire the main principle of the visible universe. " Fire is the generative element, and from its transformations all things are born. Condensed fire becomes steam ; steam becomes water ; water, through a further condensation, becomes earth." This is what Heraclitus calls *the movement from above downwards*. Inversely, earth, in becoming rarefied, is changed into water, from which nearly all the rest follows by means of evaporation from its surface. This is *the movement from below upwards*. Let us add that fire is not only the vivifying principle, but also the destroying principle. The universe was produced by fire, and by fire it will be dissolved. [1]

---

[1] The above is a resumé of the philosophy of Heraclitus according to the fragments that we possess.

It is interesting to compare this old idea of the whole visible world having emanated from Fire—that is to say Heat—with the discoveries of modern astronomy through spectroscopy. Here is an extract from a remarkable article by Charles Nordmann on *The Metamorphoses of Stars and their Temperature* (" Revue des deux Mondes," June, 1910). " The essential differences which exist between diverse types of stars, from the point of view of their chemical composition, are due to the different temperatures that prevail. When the temperature rises, the atoms of the chemical elements indicated by the ordinary rays of the spectrum are broken up, and give place to simpler forms indicated by ' reinforced rays,' which Lockyer has named ' proto-elements.' These proto-elements, when

20

Let us say at once that in these two movements, from above downwards and from below upwards, and in these two phenomena of condensation and rarefaction, the whole cosmogony of our planetary system is summed up. For these accompany the descent of Spirit into matter, and the return of matter to Spirit. Heraclitus deposited his book on the Fire-Principle in the temple of Diana at Ephesus, meaning to imply by this act that his knowledge was derived from initiation and from the gods; that is to say, through inspiration, not merely from reason and reflection. At this epoch philosophy was mainly intuitive and synthetic. It became analytical with the Eleatics, and dialectical with Socrates, Plato and Aristotle.

We will now quote some words of that wise theosophical thinker, Rudolf Steiner, in which the occult doctrines of the four elements and the Fire-Principle are combined with those of contemporary science.

" In order to understand this ancient and sacred teaching which has come to us from the East, we must consider Fire in relation to the four elements. The meaning of the four elements is no longer understood by present-day materialism. In the esoteric sense, the elements do not signify simple and irreducible substances, according to the conception of modern chemistry, but successive states of matter. 1. Earth signifies the solid state (in this sense ice is Earth). 2. Water signifies the liquid state (in this sense mercury and molten iron are Water). Fire or Heat is a subtler and finer state than Air. It might be called ' radiant matter,' a term used by Crookes. Fire differs from the three other elements, firstly, because it interpenetrates them and all things, while they are separated from one another. Further, one can touch that which is solid, liquid or gaseous, and feel it, through a certain degree of outward resistance. One can even touch a burning substance; but the heat is felt from within as well as outwardly. Fire is an element at once internal and external, with regard to man and to all things. The ancient wisdom knew

the temperature rises still further, are re-formed into other elements, ever lighter and simpler, and the process finally ends in transmutation into hydrogen and helium. The stars of Orion are therefore the hottest of all, and the greater or lesser simplicity of the stellar spectrum, together with the importance of the part played therein by the reinforced rays, would indicate the temperatures of the stars. Two important philosophical ideas emerge from these researches : that of a chemical and thermal evolution of the stars, and that of the transmutation of chemical elements through the action of heat. . . . Thus is demonstrated for the first time the possibility of that transmutation of the elements so sought after by mediæval alchemists and so scoffed at by nineteenth-century chemists. . . . The stars offer us a complete demonstration of transmutation in the alchemistical sense, since the heavier metals never appear until the lighter elements have become sufficiently cooled."

this. The sages said : *With fire matter becomes soul. There is soul in fire, there is fire in soul.*

" Fire is then the door by which we enter from the exterior to the interior of things. When we regard a burning object, we see two things as well as fire : smoke and light. Light is born of fire—but do we see it ? We think so, but it is not true. We see solid, liquid or gaseous substances illuminated by light. We do not see light itself. Light is in reality invisible. Passing from fire to light, we enter the invisible, the etheric, the spiritual. With smoke, the opposite takes place. When a thing burns, we behold the transference from material to spiritual, which produces light. But this transference is accompanied by smoke. With smoke, fire encloses a spiritual element in matter. Nothing is born in isolation. All progress is paid for by a proportionate recoil. When light is born, shadows are also born. Air is born from fire that becomes smoke, water from air condensed into liquid, earth from liquid solidified. From this point of view, the whole universe is concentrated fire, spirit enchanted in matter." [1]

When we thus penetrate into the laboratory of the universe, and behold circulating in its veins the agent of life, subtle and all-powerful Fire, we gain a wider comprehension of the strength and majesty of the primitive Aryan religion. The Aryans worshipped Fire, for they saw in it the throne, the substance, and the vestment of the gods.

But, before considering planetary evolution, we must form some idea of the Hierarchy of Powers engaged in the cosmic drama. The sages of old enthroned their gods upon Fire and Light, because these forces are their elements. Let us try to enumerate them from below upwards, in the ascending order of the human intelligence. We shall next see them acting from above downwards, in the descending order of creation. The Old Testament sums up the Hierarchy of Powers, which are the divine faculties in action, in the dream of Jacob, who saw the angels descending and ascending the ladder of the universe. This dream represented symbolically the Hierarchy of the invisible world which animates and sustains the visible world. Esoterically interpreted, it reveals a

---

[1] Notes taken from lectures delivered by Dr. Steiner in April, 1909. We may recall here that the latest theories of contemporary science concerning the constitution of matter regard atoms as composed of electrons, that is to say, of electrical atoms grouped in a certain manner. On this hypothesis the whole universe would be merely an electrical phenomenon, and we seem to come very near to the conception of *Agni*, the ' hidden fire ' of the Vedic hymns. So do extreme analysis and extreme synthesis meet together, and so does modern science rejoin the ancient wisdom.

knowledge more profound than that obtained from our microscopes and telescopes.

Mount the steps of matter, and you find Spirit. Mount the steps of human consciousness, and you find God. Just as there exist, above the four elements, other elements more subtle, so above the four kingdoms of visible nature—mineral, vegetable, animal and human—there exist other kingdoms corresponding to the different states of imponderable matter. These are the spheres of the Devas and Asuras of India, identical with the Elohim of Moses ; and the Greek gods were anthropomorphic forms of the same. The esoteric Christian tradition, which can be traced back to Dionysius the Areopagite, divides them into nine categories, arranged in groups of three, and forming an organic whole.

Above man—as all prophets have said, and all peoples have believed—there are the Angels, the Feroher of the Persians, the Genii of the Latins, who have sometimes been identified with the higher and immortal Self of man. But the Angel is not the same as the higher self which it is destined to awaken. Every man has his Guardian Angel whose duty it is to follow him and guide him, from one incarnation to another. Esoterically, these angels are called ' Sons of Life,' and their element is the Air. Above the Angels are the Archangels, the Asuras of Hinduism, who rule the souls of nations. Fire is their element, and occult tradition looks upon them as the most active agents in the general life of humanity, whose main lines and movements are traced and guided by them. Above the Archangels reign the Archaï (called Αρχαι by Dionysius the Areopagite), the Spirits of Personality and Initiative, whose rôle may be defined by giving them the title : ' the Beginners.' For it was they who gave the first impulsion to the Archangels in the saturnian and solar periods. It is they who preside over all human movements and revolutions, and over the entry upon the world-scene of great personalities who change the face of history. Such is the first group of spiritual Powers that rises above man, and that may be called the chief group of workers in the planetary laboratory, because their ardent and complex influence reaches both to the depths of matter and to the secret places of human individuality.

Above these comes the second triad of Powers, the Devas of the Hindus. Dionysius the Areopagite has named them the Virtues, ἐξουσίαι ; the Dominions, δυνάμεις ; and the Principalities, χειρίοτες. In them we see the rulers and ordainers of the whole planetary system. Intermediaries between the inferior and superior Powers, these sovereign spirits are nearer to divinity than to man. They might be called ' the Infallibles,' for they cannot, like the Archangels, descend into matter ; neither can they, like them, ove man to whom they have given breath and life. It is these Powers who create in space the planetary spheres wherein the forces of the infinite are precipitated. They hold the balance of the whole system, and establish its norm. They are the Elohim of Moses, and the Creators of the earth.

Far above all human conception or imagination rises the third triad of Powers in the ascending order.

The Thrones are the supreme Powers of Self-giving and Sacrifice. We shall see presently the great part they played in the origin of our planetary system. The Seraphim (whose Chaldean name signifies Love) and the Cherubim (meaning Wisdom and Infinite Force) are so near to God that they directly reflect His Light, whose blinding and devastating splendour cannot be borne by the lesser Powers. The Seraphim and Cherubim transmit it to them, softened and condensed into radiant forms. They themselves assume these forms, suffused with Love and Wisdom. They plunge into the heart of the Divine Trinity, and emerge brilliant as lightning, with the thoughts of God embodied in their spiritual essence. They do not labour, they shine; they do not create, they awaken; they are living rays of the impenetrable Godhead.

To sum up, the INFERIOR TRIAD (Angels, Archangels and Archaï) is that of the Combative Powers, to whose lot the hardest labour falls, who have the earth for battle-field, and man for object. The MIDDLE TRIAD (Virtues, Dominions and Principalities) is that of the Ordaining and Balancing Powers, who act upon the whole of the planetary system. The SUPERIOR TRIAD (Thrones, Cherubim and Seraphim) is that of the Radiating and Inspiring Powers, who act upon the whole Cosmos. They form a part of the so-called Divine Sphere, for they are essentially, like God Himself, above Time and Space, though they make God manifest in Time and Space.

In this vast hierarchy, each order of Powers is influenced by those superior to it, and acts upon those below it, but not upon those above.

It should be noted that the Spheres of activity of the Powers interpenetrate one another without intermingling, and that the conditions of Space and Time vary with each Triad of the hierarchy. The sphere of Angels, Archangels and Archaï, which comes immediately above man, and which man enters during sleep, is the *astral sphere*, also called the sphere of penetrability. Here reigns the fourth dimension; that is to say, beings can interpenetrate one another without mingling. Distance is modified, or does not exist. All things are at once united by sympathy or antipathy. The sphere of the Powers of the second Triad is the *spiritual sphere*, which might also be called the sphere of expansion and concentration. Here rule the fifth and sixth dimensions ; that is to say, creation in the void by the afflux of the forces of infinity. With the third Triad we enter the highest *divine sphere*, that of the Infinite and Eternal, which transcends Space and Time, but commands them.

The table on p. 26 represents the ladder of the Powers, having for throne the Fire-Principle, for centre the Divine Trinity, and for crown the Seraphic Triad. Light, Life and Truth are projected from above by the effluence of the Three Words, and pass through the spheres of the Elohim and the Archangels to penetrate the heart of man with the fire of Lucifer. All the divine rays are concentrated upon man, that from him may spring forth a new being, a new light, and a new word.

By means of this chain, God, the Gods, the Elements and Man, form a conjoint and indivisible Whole, which generates and organises itself, and evolves steadily and integrally along parallel lines. The superior Gods engender the inferior Gods, who engender the Elements, of which Matter is only the appearance, and of which Man, existing in germ since the beginning, gradually becomes the centre and pivot.

Seen from above downwards, this table shows the ray by means of which the Gods see the World and Man ; that is the side of Light. Seen from below upwards, it represents the prism by means of which Man sees the World and the Gods ; that is the side of Shadow.

Let us now see the Powers at work in the Creation.

SYNTHETIC TABLE OF THE HIERARCHY OF POWERS

COSMIC POWERS

Seraphim Love
Cherubim Harmony
Thrones Will

6th DIMENSION
(Sphere of Influx from Infinity)

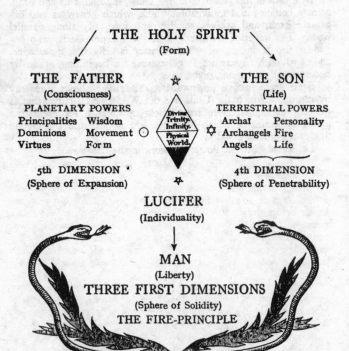

THE HOLY SPIRIT
(Form)

THE FATHER		THE SON
(Consciousness)		(Life)

PLANETARY POWERS		TERRESTRIAL POWERS	
Principalities	Wisdom	Archaï	Personality
Dominions	Movement	Archangels	Fire
Virtues	Form	Angels	Life

Divine Trinity. Infinity. Physical World.

5th DIMENSION
(Sphere of Expansion)

4th DIMENSION
(Sphere of Penetrability)

LUCIFER
(Individuality)

MAN
(Liberty)
THREE FIRST DIMENSIONS
(Sphere of Solidity)
THE FIRE-PRINCIPLE

CHAPTER III

THROUGHOUT the whole universe are manifested the law of
eternal movement, the law of rotation, and the law of metamorphosis or reincarnation. The law of the rebirth of worlds in new
but related forms, after long periods of cosmic sleep, applies
equally to stars and planets, gods and men. It is the necessary
condition for the manifestation of the Divine Word, the radiation
of the Universal Soul by means of stars and men.

Our earth had three incarnations before becoming the actual
Earth. It first formed an indistinguishable part of the primeval
nebula of our system, called Saturn in occult cosmogony. We
shall call this ' the first Saturn,' to differentiate it from the actual
Saturn that survived it. Next the Earth formed part of the primeval Sun, which stretched as far as the actual Jupiter ; and finally,
forming with the Moon a single star, it disengaged itself from the
Sun. This star is known as the Moon in occult cosmogony, but
we shall call it the primeval moon, or Earth-Moon, to distinguish
it from the actual Moon. In the end the Earth threw off the Moon,
and became the Earth as we know it.

The germ of the human being existed in the primeval Sun,
in the form of an etheric embryo, but it only began to exist as a
living being, possessing an astral body like a fiery cloud, in the
primeval Moon or Earth-Moon ; while only on the actual Earth
has the human being acquired self-consciousness through developing its spiritual and physical organs. In Book II, we shall indicate
the stages of this development, when speaking of Atlantis and the
Atlanteans.

During the successive metamorphoses of the planetary system,
the Elohim of the Superior Hierarchies evolved the Gods of the
Inferior Triad—Archaï, Archangels and Angels—who, with their
aid, became the generators of the Earth and of Man.

The planetary periods of which we shall next speak extend
over many millions of years. Ever since the time of the Rishis,
the vision of great Adepts has deciphered these world-epochs

whose reflections still quiver in the astral light,' seeing them
unrolled in vast panorama before the inner senses.   These seers
have from age to age transmitted their visions to mankind in
mythological forms adapted to the human understanding.

The Hindus call these astral panoramas ' the Akashic record.'
In the Jewish-Christian tradition they are called ' the Book of
God.' And it is remarkable that Joan of Arc, the saint of Domrémy,
the ignorant but inspired peasant-girl, used this same term when
she replied to the scholastic quibbles of the doctors of Poitiers
with these superb words : " There are more things in the Book
of God than in your books ! "

It is scarcely necessary to say how imperfect the success of all
visionaries must be when they strive to describe in earthly language
the superhuman images which are presented to them in the ' astral
light,' not in dead and motionless forms, but in living masses,
and like overflowing rivers. The difficulty is to give them meaning
and connection, to regulate and classify these overwhelming
visions.

The Saturnian nebula, the first form of our planetary system,
was a mass of heat without light.   Heat is the first form of fire ;
hence the saying of Heraclitus that the world was born from fire.
This nebula was in the shape of a sphere whose radius covered the
distance between the actual Saturn and the Sun. But no star
gleamed in its shadowy depths ; no ray of light emerged from it.
Through its substance there passed shudderings of cold and waves
of heat, from the activities of the Powers that were working within
it.   Upon its surface there arose from time to time ovoid fountains
of heat, drawn upwards by the attraction of the Elohim from
immeasurable space.

The second verse of Genesis describes this first planetary
phase : " And the earth was without form and void ; and darkness
was upon the face of the deep.   And the Spirit of God [1] moved
upon the face of the waters."

Now the Elohim who, at the birth of our world, represented
the Spirit of God, belonged to the supreme hierarchy of the Powers.
It is they who are called ' the Thrones' in Christian tradition, which
affirms that they gave their bodies as a sacrifice for the renaissance
of the Archaï. These bodies consisted only of vital heat, the
breath of love. As to the Archaï, or Spirits of the Beginning,
these were beings belonging to a former cosmic evolution, who

---

[1] The term Elohim, used by Moses in the Book of Genesis to signify God,
means He-of-the-Gods, or God-of-Gods. God is conceived simultaneously as
both singular and plural—singular, as the divine Universal Principle ; plural
as power in action in the Elohim.

had long been passive, and, as it were, merged in divinity. But their nature was such as to render them capable of becoming, in a new cosmic period, pre-eminently Creative Gods, subject to a renewal of personality. This personality was given them by the Thrones, who sacrificed their bodies in pouring out all their forces upon the Archaï. Hence the fountains of heat which issued from the primitive Saturn, and seemed to inhale the divine life of the Thrones, just as in a waterspout one sees the water uplifted towards the clouds, while the sky inhales the ocean.

Like a living creature, the immense Saturnian nebula had its inspiration and expiration. The inspiration produced cold, and the expiration, heat. During the inspiration, the Archaï withdrew to its centre; during the expiration they approached nearer to the Thrones and inhaled their essence. Thus by degrees they regained self-consciousness, and became detached from the Saturnian mass. But as they became purified, and discarded the inferior elements, they left behind them a gaseous vapour. At the same time, the Elohim of the second hierarchy, who were working within the nebula, had caused it to start rotating. Thus there was formed on its circumference a gaseous ring, which, when later broken up, became the first planet—the actual Saturn with its rings and its eight satellites.

The Archaï, the Gods of Personality, the Great Beginners, aspired to create a world. They dreamed its outlines; they felt within themselves its first shapings. But they could not create this world in the darkness of Saturn, region of smoke and vapour; they must have Light . . . physical Light. . . . the creative agent. Amid the shadows which enveloped them, this presentiment of Creative Light grew within them. Presentiment —or remembrance? Remembrance perhaps, of a former world, of some other cosmic period; memory of far-off glory and splendour in the Saturnian night. Presentiment also; for already in the soul of the Archaï, there trembled, like the herald gleam of future daybreaks, the majesty of the Archangel, the beauty of the Angel, the sorrow of Man ! . . . But, to embody this dream, there must be a Sun in the heart of Saturn, there must be a revolution in the nebula, brought about by the influence of the Supreme Powers.

The dark night of Saturn was nearing its close. The Thrones cast the Archaï into a deep slumber. Then they plunged like a hurricane into the whirling, stifling smoke of the Saturnian chaos, in order to condense it, and to re-form it, with the aid of the Fire-Principle and the other Powers, into a Star of Light. For how many centuries, for how many millenia, must this cosmic cyclone have lasted, where heat and cold strove together and terrific many-coloured lightnings spurted forth from the tortured darkness !

There was then neither Sun nor Earth by which to measure the years; neither clepsydra nor clock to count the hours. . . . But, when the Archaï awoke from their profound sleep, they were floating upon a fiery globe crowned with ethereal light, above a nucleus of smoky vapour.

The first Sun had been born. With its dark centre and its photosphere, it occupied the space that now stretches between the actual Sun and the planet Jupiter. The Archaï, its young masters, the new Gods, floated upon an ocean of flame and hailed the surrounding Light. Then, beyond the fluid veils of these luminous waves, for the first time they perceived the Thrones, like winged spheres, mounting in the direction of a far-distant star, which grew smaller and smaller till it was lost in the Infinite —and with it the Thrones also vanished.

Then the Archaï cried: " The Saturnian night is ended. Behold, we are robed in fire; we are Kings of Light! Now can we create according to our desire, for our desire is the thought of God ! "

But as they observed the ethereal photosphere that enveloped them, they became aware of something sinister in space, beyond their luminous abode. A great ring of smoke, inhabited by elemental beings of a lower order, surrounded the new-born sun as with a fatal circle—the black necklace of the radiant star. From this vaguely outlined ring would be born later the actual Saturn —Saturn, the waste-matter of creation, the ransom paid for the Sun. Thus, through Saturn, was the new universe weighed down by an inevitable Fate, which the Elohim must conquer, but which they could not remove; thus was manifested from the beginning the tragic law that there can be no creation without waste, no light without shadow, no progress without recoil, no good without evil.

Such was the transition from the Saturnian to the Solar period, which is summed up in the fourth verse of the Book of Genesis : " And God (Elohim, He-of-the-Gods) divided the light from the darkness."

CHAPTER IV

THE SOLAR PERIOD—FECUNDATION OF THE ARCHANGELS BY THE CHERUBIM—OCCULT SIGNIFICANCE OF THE ZODIAC

THE sphere of the first Sun reached as far as the actual Jupiter. To a greater extent than any of the planets that would be born from it, this Sun had life. It consisted of a dark, smoky nucleus, and a vast photosphere ; not of metals in a state of fusion, as in the actual Sun, but of more subtle matter—of an ethereal and transparent fire. An observer placed in Sirius would have seen this Sun from time to time wax and wane, now glowing with a greater brilliance, now almost extinguished. Astronomers have discovered similar stars to-day. The first sun had its regular inspiration and expiration. Its inspiration seemed to draw all its life inwards, and to cause it to become almost as dark as Saturn ; but its expiration was a marvellous radiation which flung a wheel of light into Infinity. These alternations of light and darkness proceeded from the life of the Gods, from the Elohim who reigned over this star.

The Archaï, or ' Beginners,' had already conceived Archangels upon the nebulous Saturn, but they were merely thought-forms clothed in etheric bodies, organs of vitality. Upon the Sun, the Fathers of the Archangels bestowed on them astral bodies, radiant organs of sensation. For the Archaï are the most powerful magicians of all the Elohim. By the force of their will they can give personality and life to their thought-forms. Moses, rebeholding this process, reliving it in himself, exclaimed : " And God said, Let there be light—and there was light." By the creative breath of the Archaï, the Archangels arose, and became the life, light, and soul of the first Sun.

Rudolf Steiner has said : " Such is the conception of a fixed star. All things in the universe derive their life from that of the Archaï. A Sun is created by them, and the Archangels are their messengers, announcing to the universe the actions of the Spirits of the Beginning."

The Archangels were the men of the first Sun. They ruled this star, and, rising into space above their natal Fire, they—who were of the essence of ecstasy and light—sought the Divine Source from which they themselves had emanated. In the immensity of the universe they could see at first only the constellations, the messengers of other Archangels, their distant brothers. The constellations! . . . flaming script of the firmament, where the thoughts of the Universal Spirit are traced in hieroglyphics blazing with myriads of suns! . . . But as their spiritual sight developed, they beheld an army of sublime Spirits in diverse majestic forms encamped in a vast circle in the path of the zodiac. These were the Cherubim, inhabitants of spiritual space, the Elohim of Harmony, the first to plunge into the mysterious heart of Divinity with the Seraphim, the Spirits of Love. Gathered from the deeps of heaven on every side, in twelve groups which drew gradually nearer together, the army of the Cherubim finally concentrated itself circle-wise around the Solar world for the incubation and fecundation of the Archangels.

This fact, of which the Chaldean magi were aware, was the origin of the names of the twelve zodiacal signs, still preserved in modern astronomy. Each constellation was identified with a category of Cherubim, represented in occult tradition by *sacred animals*. The Chaldeans, Egyptians and Hebrews symbolised the Cherubim under the forms of the Bull, the Lion, the Eagle and the Angel (or the Man). These were the four sacred animals of the Ark of Moses, of the four Evangelists, and of the Apocalypse of St. John. The Egyptian sphinx summarises them in a single form which is a symbol, marvellously adapted from visible and invisible nature, of the whole course of evolution, human and divine. These four essential forms of the world of life are again found in the four cardinal points of the zodiac, with one exception : the Eagle has been replaced by the scorpion. The Eagle deals death with its beak and talons, but its wings signify the sunward flight, the resurrection. In sacred symbology—which interprets the soul of things—the Eagle signifies both death and resurrection. The Scorpion, which has taken its place in the zodiac between Libra and Sagittarius, signifies only death. This substitution may in itself be a symbol, for through its descent into matter humanity has preserved the meaning of death and forgotten that of resurrection.

No earthly forms could suggest the splendour and beauty of the Cherubim, ranged in a vast circle in the signs of the zodiac around the solar world, for the inspiration and fecundation of the Archangels. No earthly language could express the ecstasies and transports of the Archangels as they received this influx and felt themselves impregnated by divine thought. But, as we have said, this first solar world had its periodical eclipses, its brilliant days and its sombre nights. From time to time the Archangels withdrew with the solar rays into the dark centre of the star, and fell into a semi-slumber. The wild soaring into cosmic space, under the burning gaze of the Cherubim, was accompanied by a terrific outpouring of light, by a vast, harmonious " music of the spheres." Now came the decrease of sound and of brilliance, the darkness and silence in the hidden depths of the star. Without, in their ecstasy, the Archangels had been conscious of the angelic world. Within, in the dark shadows, they still thought of the Cherubim, but the appearances of these became contracted, in their memory, into forms of anguish, anger and desire. These Thought-Forms, generated during the troubled sleep of the Archangels, became the prototypes of the animal world which would later be developed upon earth. The animals are distorted copies, and in a sense caricatures, of divine beings.

It might be said that if Angels (and consequently men) are generated from the Archangelic ecstasy in Light, then the animals are generated from their nightmares in Darkness. The animal world is thus the counterpart of the angelic world, and the ransom paid for it. Here again is seen the law of the evolution of worlds and beings by the discarding of their lower elements. We shall see this law exemplified down the whole ladder of creation, even to the smallest details of human life. The discarding of these elements is not only necessary for the purification of the higher elements, but also as counterbalance and leaven in the totality of evolution. Their temporary regression may seem like an injustice, but it is not so in the infinitude of time, for they will eventually be caught up again and carried forward on a new life-wave.

CHAPTER V

THE FORMATION OF JUPITER AND MARS—THE WAR IN HEAVEN—LUCIFER AND THE FALL OF THE ARCHANGELS

MEANWHILE the Powers of the Middle Triad (Virtues, Dominions and Principalities) who play the rôle of organisers in the planetary system, and regulate the distribution of forces—Powers who act chiefly through expansion and contraction—were working upon the solar world from within. Through their efforts, the primeval Sun underwent two new contractions, which caused two new planets to be thrown out from its dark nucleus—Jupiter and Mars.

To the sight of a man observing the formation of these new bodies, from the planet Saturn, the sole indication of such a cosmic event would have been the appearance of two new spheres turning around the Sun—one self-luminous (Jupiter), the other opaque (Mars) At the same time such an observer would have seen the photosphere of the Sun contract, and then shine unintermittently, and with greater brilliance than before. This was all that could be remarked on the physical plane.

But the vision of a seer would have taken note of a much greater event which was transpiring on the astral plane. This event, one of the most decisive in the whole of planetary evolution, is called in occult tradition the War in Heaven. In all mythologies there are legendary traces of it: for instance, in the Combat of Gods and Titans in the theogony of Hesiod, with which is connected the story of Prometheus ; and in the Fall of Lucifer in the Judo-Christian tradition. This event, which preceded and brought about the creation of the Earth, was not an accident. It was a part of the Divine plan, but its determination was left to the initiative of the Powers. Empedocles has said : " The world was born of two forces, Love and War (Eros and Polemos) " —a profound thought which finds confirmation in the Christian esoteric tradition of the struggle of the Elohim among themselves. Lucifer is not Satan, the Spirit of Evil, as the popular, orthodox belief declares. He is one of the Elohim, and his name of *Light-Bearer* ensures his indestructible archangelic dignity. We shall see later why Lucifer, Spirit of Knowledge and Individuality, was as necessary to the world as Christ, Spirit of Love and Sacrifice ;

how all human evolution is the result of their conflict; and how their final and supreme reconciliation will be the crown of man's ultimate return to divinity. For the moment we must follow Lucifer in his earthward descent and his work of creation.

Of all the Archangels, Lucifer, representative and chief patronymic of a whole class of angels and spirits, was the one who had penetrated most deeply and boldly into the secrets of the Divine Wisdom and the celestial Plan. He was also the proudest and the most indomitable, desiring to obey no God save himself. The other Archangels had already created Angels out of their thought-forms, pure prototypes of divine man. These angels had only a diaphanous etheric body and a radiant astral body, in which were united in perfect harmony the Eternal-Masculine and the Eternal-Feminine. They experienced Love as a spiritual radiation, without pain and without egoistic desire of possession, because they were astrally and spiritually androgynous. Lucifer, however, saw that in order to make man independent, desirous and rebellious, the sexes must be separated; and, in order to persuade the Angels to his own way of thinking, he moulded in the astral light a dazzling image of the future Woman, the ideal Eve, and displayed it to them. Large numbers of them were filled with enthusiasm for the image, which seemed to promise the world delights hitherto unknown, and these grouped themselves around the rebel Archangel.[1]

Now there then existed an intermediate star between Mars and Jupiter. It was still only a ring, destined to be condensed into a planet when broken. Lucifer chose it in order to create, with his Angels, a world which, without passing through terrestrial ordeals, should find its own joy and strength within itself, and taste the fruits of life and knowledge without the aid of the All-Powerful.

The other Archangels and all the Elohim were ordered to prevent this, because such a world would have brought disorder into the plan of creation and broken the chain of the divine and planetary hierarchies. The long and heated strife which then ensued between the armies of the rebellious Archangel and his peers, as well as his superiors, ended in the defeat of Lucifer, and had a double result: (1) the destruction of the partly formed planet, whose debris became the planetoids; (2) the banishment of Lucifer and his Angels to an inferior world, another planet

---

[1] This is, without doubt, the primitive conception of the occult tradition in which the union of Lucifer and Lilith (the first Eve) is said to have given birth to Cain—*i.e.*, man descended into matter, condemned to crime, suffering and expiation. But it must be remembered that all accounts of events taking place on the astral plane are merely imperfect translations of the reality.

which had been drawn out from the Sun's centre by the Principalities and Dominions. This planet was the Earth ; not the Earth of to-day, but the primeval Earth which was still one with the Moon.[1]

Such was the cosmogonic happening which provides one of the chief features in our planetary history—a kind of astral conflagration whose reflection trails comet-like through all mythologies, and darts fiery rays into the secret depths of the human soul.

First lightning-flash of Desire, Knowledge and Freedom, the torch of Lucifer can be rekindled in all its splendour only at the Sun of Love and Life Divine—that is, the Christ.

---

[1] Esoteric tradition holds that, at this same period, a certain number of Elohim, who did not wish to take part in the creation of the Earth and of other worlds subject to the laws of condensed matter, left the Sun in order to create Uranus, Neptune and other planets beyond the Saturnian region. According to ancient teachings, which is confirmed by modern science, our solar system was originally evolved from the Saturnian nebula. Therefore is Saturn the oldest of the gods, and the one with whom Time began.

CHAPTER VI

THE PRIMEVAL EARTH OR EARTH-MOON—DEVELOPMENT OF THE ANGELS—THE BIRTH OF MAN

THE separation of the primeval Earth from the Sun (brought about by the Powers of the Middle Triad (Virtues, Dominions, Principalities) had a double object. Firstly, to provide a field of action for the Luciferian spirits, and a testing-place for nascent humanity, by making use of the dark, dense matter drawn from the Sun ; secondly, to free the Sun in this way of its lower elements, and to allow it to shine out in all its purity and strength as throne of the Archangels and of the Creative Word. The Earth and the Sun thus constituted the two poles of the physical and moral worlds, and lent a greater intensity to planetary evolution through their combined action and opposition.

The primeval Earth was in the form of a star with a liquid nucleus and an outer envelope of burning gas. Within it, all the metals and minerals were fermenting in a state of fusion ; but on its surface was formed a vegetable crust, a kind of ligneous and spongy tufa, where grew, parasitically, enormous semi-vegetable, semi-molluscan creatures, waving their branch-like arms in the warm atmosphere like tentacled trees. In the gaseous vapour which eddied around the Earth-Moon, there already floated, like small fiery clouds, the first germs of future men. These embryonic beings had no physical body, but they had etheric bodies, or interior vitality, and astral bodies, or a radiant aura by means of which they perceived the surrounding atmosphere. Thus they had sensation without self-consciousness. They had no sex, and they were not subject to death. They re-formed themselves ceaselessly from within, and drew nourishment from the effluvia of the humid, burning vapours around them.

The Archangels were the rulers of the first Sun ; their sons, the Angels, were the rulers of the Earth-Moon. They attained to consciousness of self by beholding themselves reflected in the human germs that peopled this star, and by instilling into these their own thoughts which were then returned to them revivified. Without such reflection and duplication no being, human or divine, can attain self-consciousness.[1]   The special function of the Angels was to become guides and inspirers of men in the succeeding cosmic period, that is to say, upon our Earth.   Upon the Earth-Moon they were the awakeners of the nascent human beings.   They aroused sensations in them, and in so doing became conscious of themselves, and of their lofty mission.   Having fallen with Lucifer into the troubled depths of matter, they must re-ascend to their divine source through loving man, suffering with him, sustaining him on his slow upward journey; while man must strive to reach and understand God through the Angels. The Angel is the Archetype of the future Man; and through the raising of man to angelic stature there will be born, at the end of planetary time, a new God, the free, creative Individuality.

But before that there must be the descent of the shadowy spiral, the painful labour in the darkness of animalism. And who can say which shall suffer most, the man ever more humiliated, more tormented, as he attains wider self-consciousness, or the invisible Angel who strives and suffers with him?

[1] It is because division or duplication is the primal condition of consciousness that the Rosicrucian wisdom states: "Where there is a self, there are two selves."

CHAPTER VII

THE SEPARATION OF THE MOON FROM THE EARTH—ORIGIN OF THE
ACTUAL EARTH—THE LEMURIAN RACE—DEVELOPMENT OF THE
SEXES—THE FALL OF THE ANGELS—DESTRUCTION OF THE
LEMURIAN CONTINENT

IN the formation of a planetary world there is a correspondence
between the above and the below; all is linked together; all
things progress on parallel lines—gods, men and elements.
Materialistic philosophy claims to deduce biology from chemistry
and to cause self-consciousness to spring from purely physiological reactions; here, on the contrary, all things are evolved
from the Invisible, and take form and shape in the Visible. According to the Divine Plan, the spiritual world expresses itself
with increasing splendour in the material world. First, the
involution of Spirit into Matter; then the evolution of Matter
back to Spirit through ceaseless individualisation. At each new
metamorphosis of the planetary world, at the birth of each new
planet, all beings mount one step of the ladder, while preserving
the same distances apart. But these upward steps can never
take place without an immense throwing-off of waste matter—
matter which will be made use of in the future by new
life-waves.

We have seen these laws exemplified in the Saturnian period,
in the Solar period, and in the period of the Earth-Moon. The
development of the actual Earth will furnish us with still more
striking examples.

The Earth that we inhabit, the Adama of Moses, the Demeter
of Orpheus and Homer, seems very old to us by reason of the
long life of the human race and the shortness of each human incarnation; but it is still a young star as regards the duration of
its actual organism, and has yet to pass through three more metamorphoses in the distant future, according to the great Adepts.
Its establishment as the Earth-Planet, with which we are solely
concerned in this chapter, was due to the last great cosmic upheaval, namely, the separation between the Earth and the
Moon.

39

The actual Moon was originally an integral part of the Earth, its densest and heaviest portion. The Spiritual Powers who separated the Earth from the Moon were the same who had formerly separated the Earth-Moon from the Sun. The principal object of this separation was the descent of man from the astral to the physical plane, where he was to acquire personal consciousness through the development of new organs. But this important event in human evolution was only made possible by separating the Earth and the Moon to form two poles, the Earth being the masculine pole and the Moon the feminine.[1] The corresponding physiological development resulted in the appearance of two sexes in the animal and human kingdoms. The human species could only free itself from animalism by the division of living beings into opposite sexes, and with bi-sexuality three new forces came into play—sex-love, death and reincarnation. These three were forceful agents of action, dissociation and renewal ; charms and terrors, goads and spurs, in human evolution.

Before attaining its present form, however, the human being, fallen from the astral to the physical plane, had to pass through the principal phases of animal life (fish, reptile, quadruped, anthropoid). But, contrary to the theories of Darwin and Haeckel, the main factors in human evolution were neither natural selection nor adaptation to environment, but an inner urge brought about by the action of the Spiritual Powers who guided man step by step and gradually developed him. Man would never have succeeded in crossing the vast spaces that stretch between instinctive animalism and conscious humanity without the higher beings who worked upon him and moulded him from generation to generation, from century to century, throughout millions of years. It was creation and co-operation combined ; a mingling, a fusion, a continual remodelling. These guiding spirits acted upon evolving humanity in two ways, by incarnating in human bodies, and by spiritual influence ; so that the human being was shaped, as it were, both from within and from without. It may be said that man is at the same time self-created and God-created. From himself came the effort, but from the Gods the divine spark, the germ of his immortal soul.

Let us try to imagine the human being before the separation of the sexes, in the period called by geologists the primary epoch.

At this time, the surface of the earth was still burning. In

---

[1] On the contrary, the Earth in relation to the Sun represents the feminine element.

place of what are now the oceans, there rolled around the planet semi-liquid, semi-vaporous masses, seething in the shadowy depths, gaseous and transparent on the heights, and traversed by a myriad currents of heat or cold. And through these dark or translucent vapours there already floated beings endowed with strange vitality and singular mobility.

However disquieting this unfamiliar ancestor may seem to us now, it had its own beauty. It resembled less a fish than a long blue-green serpent, whose gelatinous and transparent body, reflecting all the colours of the rainbow, left the inner organs visible. In place of a head, there issued from the upper part a phosphorescent fan-shaped plume, containing the protoplasm which eventually became the brain of man. This plume served as an organ of perception and of reproduction—of perception because, thanks to its extreme sensitiveness, the primitive creature, having neither eyes nor ears, was aware of everything that approached it, whether harmful or friendly; of reproduction, because this great flower, luminous like a sea-medusa, also fulfilled the function of a male organ of fecundation. For concealed within the creature's agile, undulating body there was a female organ, a matrix. At certain seasons, these hermaphroditic beings were drawn to the upper and less dense regions of their ocean-vapours by the rays of the sun, under whose influence fecundation took place—that is to say, self-fecundation, unconscious and involuntary, as in the case of many plants to-day whose pollen falls from the stamens and fertilises the stigmata. Then the new being, which was formed within the old one, gradually took its place, drawing life from it until, having attained to full growth, the old shell could be thrown off, as the serpent throws off its skin. There was thus a periodical renewal, but there was neither death nor rebirth. The creature did not yet possess a 'self.' It lacked what the Hindus call *manas*, the germ of mind, the divine spark, the crystallising centre of the immortal soul. It possessed, like all animals, only a physical body, an etheric, or vital, body, and an astral, or radiant, body ; and by means of this last it experienced what resembled a mixture of tactual, auditory and visual sensations. Its mode of perception was something like a rudimentary form of what we to-day call the sixth, or divinatory, sense, in a few specially endowed individuals.

Let us now advance through several millions of years to the eocene and miocene periods. The appearance of the earth has changed. The fire has withdrawn to its centre, while the watery masses have extended. Part of the vaporous envelope of the globe has been condensed, to spread over its surface in the form of oceans. In the southern hemisphere a continent has emerged. This is Lemuria.[1]

Upon the surface of this continent, composed of granite and solidified lava, there grew gigantic ferns. The atmosphere was always full of clouds, through which a vague light penetrated. Everything that existed on the Earth-Moon, germs of plants and animals, had now reappeared in more advanced form, swimming in the oceans, crawling or walking on the earth, flying in the heavy air. The being destined to become man, the hermaphrodite of the primary epoch, half-fish, half-serpent, had assumed the form of a quadruped, a kind of saurian, but very different from the present saurians, its degenerate offspring. The cerebro-spinal system, which had been scarcely indicated in the primitive human medusa, was now considerably developed. The pineal gland was enclosed in a skull, and had grown into a brain, though it still protruded, like a mobile crest, through an orifice in the upper part of the cranium. Two eyes had appeared, eyes whose sight was as yet dim and clouded; but the pineal crest had preserved its gift of astral sensitiveness, so that this disconcerting and hybrid creature had two modes of perception: one on the astral plane, still strong, but steadily diminishing, and one on the physical plane, very weak, but steadily increasing. The fish-like gills had become lungs; the fins had become paws. As to the head, it was like the head of a dolphin with frontal bones like those of a lion.

In order to transform this half-crawling, half-walking creature, so miserable, so deeply humiliated, yet endowed with such vast potentialities, into an upright human being, with head lifted

---

[1] Naturalists who study the terrestrial globe from the paleontological and anthropological standpoints have long indicated the existence of a continent, now submerged, in the southern hemisphere. It comprised Australia, part of Asia, and Central Africa, and reached as far as South America. At this epoch, part of Central and Northern Asia, all Europe, and the greater portions of Africa and America, were still under water. The Englishman, Slater, named this ancient continent Lemuria, after the anthropoid lemurs, for according to Haeckel, the German naturalist, animals of a lemurian type inhabited it. (See Haeckel's *Natural History of Creation.*) Blandfort, writing on ' the former existence of an Indo-Oceanic continent,' says that paleontology, physical geography, and observations of the distribution of fauna and flora all bear witness to a prehistoric connection between Africa, India and the Malay Archipelago ; that this primitive Australia must have existed from the beginning of the permian to the end of the miocene period ; and that South Africa and the Indian peninsula are the remains of it. Scott Elliott, in *Lost Lemuria,* says that this continent existed for four or five millions of years. Its flora included coniferæ and giant ferns, and there were many steaming swamps. Its fauna consisted of all kinds of reptiles—ichthyosauria, plesiosauridæ, dinosaurs (dragons), and pterodactyls with bat-like wings. There were flying lizards of all sizes from that of a sparrow up to those with wings five yards broad. The dragons, or dinosaurs, were terrible beasts of prey, ten to fifteen yards in length.

towards the sky, capable of speech and of thought, there were required greater forces, more subtle and ingenious processes, than any of those imagined by our learned naturalists. There were required miracles—that is to say, concentration of spiritual forces upon a given point. There were required Spirits from above, Gods appearing under the lightest veils of matter, to cause these rudimentary beings to mount towards Spirit. In a word, it was necessary to remould them, and to mark them with the divine seal. The Book of Genesis says simply : " God created man in his own image " (Gen. I, 27) ; and again : " The Lord God breathed into his nostrils the breath of life, and man became a living soul " (Gen. II, 7). Further, (Gen. VI, 1-4), we read that the sons of God took for wives the daughters of men, of whom were born mighty men, or giants. All these statements represent profound truths, upon which esoteric wisdom can throw light, linking up the words of Moses with the discoveries of modern science.

Firstly, esotericism defines the complex part played by the ' sons of God.'

There remained upon the Moon a class of Angels of the lowest order of the Luciferians, Angels who aspired not only to be guides to men, but also to experience life themselves by assuming physical bodies and plunging into the violent sensations of matter. These incarnated in large numbers in the bodies of the dolphin-headed saurians, destined for future men, and through their action the circulatory and nervous systems were developed. In thus entering nascent humanity they brought to it, together with insatiable desire, the divine spark, .immortal principle of the ' self.' But it was still necessary for this self to be illuminated and impregnated by a higher order of spirits who were truly divine.

The planet Venus was then inhabited by the Archaï ('Aρχαί) of whom we have already spoken, the teachers of the Archangels, and the most powerful of all those whom Hindu mythology designates as Asuras. Above all others, these chiefs of the third divine hierarchy, charged with the creation and education of man, deserve the name of Gods. For they cannot assume physical bodies, nor be in any way connected with matter. They disdain fire, and live only in light. But they can make themselves visible to inferior beings by assuming astral and etheric bodies which they can mould at will by the power of thought. Such were the beings who came to inhabit the earth for a time, during the Lemurian age. It is of them that Hesiod seems to speak when he says : " The Gods, robed in air, walked among men."

Here we touch, so to speak, upon the divine energies that

laboured at the formation of man. The plastic genius of the
Greeks gathered up all this evolutionary history into the symbol
of Prometheus bringing fire with which to mould the human clay.
It was he who set man upright, aspiring towards heaven, and who,
together with the Gods, taught him to control the powers of fire.

We must now describe, according to true history, how primitive
man first became aware of the Gods from on high, the Archaï,
Lords of the Beginning and of Light.

Let us imagine the ever-moving, fire-tormented surface of
the Lemurian continent. As far as eye can see there stretch
immense swamps, from which rise numberless volcanoes of
varying heights. The sky is darkened by thick masses of cloud
through which the sun never penetrates. Here and there extend
mountain-chains covered with giant forests. Upon one bare
summit, where great masses of granite rocks have burst through
the hardened lava, are gathered large numbers of the lion-headed,
vaguely human, saurians, attracted by a strange light that issues
from a cave. For here appears from time to time the Master,
the God, whom they fear and venerate through some invincible
instinct.

At all periods the Gods, in order to manifest themselves to
living beings, have been obliged to assume a form similar to theirs.
Therefore the Teacher who appears to this assembly is clothed
in the form of a winged and luminous dragon. His body is
merely an etheric body, surrounded by an astral nimbus like a
radiant aureole, but to those who behold him he seems more
living than themselves—as in truth he is. He speaks in no articulate
language, but by means of gestures and radiations of light. His
eyes flash, and his body, his wings, and the plume upon his head
are all glowing. The rays that proceed from him seem to illumine
the inmost parts of all things, and the watching saurians begin to
understand the souls of all beings, even to hear their voices and
their cries, to which they strive to respond. Suddenly the divine
creature raises itself, with moving wings and blazing crest, and
an opening appears in the dark clouds overhead, through which
is seen an army of the Gods enveloped in light—sublime countenances, innumerable, unknown. And above them there shines
for an instant a golden disk. . . . Then the gliding, crawling
creatures imitate the gestures of their Master, raise themselves
in a transport of delight, and, uplifting their rudimentary arms,
adore the Supreme Deity in the form of the Sun, ere it is once
more veiled from them.

In this way the worship of the Gods, and the religious instinct,
were instilled into what was to become humanity. These early
glimmerings in the Lemurian age were most powerful factors in

the physical evolution of man. Through them the vital organs became more refined and the limbs more supple, while from the chaos of tactual sensations sight and hearing were developed. They brought about, successively, vertical stature, voice, and the rudiments of language ; and in proportion to man's progress, the Archaï assumed ever more noble forms, and finally appeared as Archangels with human faces. But the memory of the first Masters of humanity, in pterodactyl form, never ceased to haunt man's mind. This was partly due, it is true, to a confused remembrance of antediluvian monsters who had similar forms ; but nevertheless, in the oldest mythologies the dragon is never a malevolent being, but rather a god, or more often still, an all-wise magician. In Japan, China and India, in Germanic and Celtic mythology, the dragon is a sacred animal. The ' King of the Serpents,' in the Hindu epic *Naal and Damayanti*, provides a curious example of this. Veneration of the dragon as a god arose from a memory of the first Teachers of humanity.

As man gradually freed himself from animal forms, and approached human form, the separation of the sexes became more pronounced. In the following epochs, the opposition of the sexes and sexual attraction were to be the strongest forces underlying human progress ; but their first results were appalling. They brought about such disturbances, and an upheaval so extensive, that the whole planet was thrown into a state bordering on chaos. In the animal world, as in the human, the new pleasure of dual creation acted like an intoxicant, and the whole world of living beings was seized with a kind of madness. The various species showed a tendency to become mixed. Pterodactyls and serpents produced birds of prey. The sea became a breeding-place for monsters. The lower ranks of humanity, uniting with mammals, gave birth to apes. But man is, nevertheless, not a perfected ape. On the contrary, the ape is a degenerate and degraded form of primitive man, a caricature, a result and a reminder of his first sin.[1] At the sight of an ape man is rightly filled with horror, for it says to him : " Take care lest you descend towards instinct, instead of mounting towards conscience, and become like unto me ! "

Never had there been so frightful a scourge upon the planet.

---

[1] In his fine book, *Creative Evolution*, M. Bergson recognises a ' breath of life,' an *élan vital*, in the animal species. His intuition, applied to a detailed study of their physiology, convinces him that man is not the product of an inferior species, but that these species are the off-shoots of a single stem of which man forms the summit.

From this generative disorder sprang all the evil passions : uncontrolled desires, envy, hatred, wrath, war between men and animals, war among men themselves. These passions spread to the astral atmosphere of the earth like poisonous fumes, heavier than the thick clouds that enveloped it.

The Greek genius, which humanises all that it touches and encloses the horrors of nature in lines of redemptive beauty, presents this period to us in the legend of Pandora. The Gods were jealous of Prometheus, who had stolen the divine fire, and so sent to earth the phantom seducer, Woman, decked in all her charms, whom Epimetheus imprudently accepted. But when Pandora lifted the cover of the vase which she carried, a swarm of diseases, plagues and evils escaped from it, and spread over the earth like a black cloud, to overwhelm the human race. Quickly she replaced the cover ; within the vase there remained only Hope. This is a marvellous symbol of the disorders engendered by the first unchaining of sexual love—and of the infinite desire of the imprisoned soul which, in spite of all, trembles before the Eternal Feminine manifested in the flesh.

Disaster was inevitable. A great part of the Lemurian continent [1] would have to be destroyed by a cataclysm which would change the surface of the globe and uplift the survivors on a new life-wave. For there is a close and constant correlation between the passions reigning in the world and the forces smouldering within the earth. The Fire-Princip e, or Creative Fire, enclosed and condensed in one of the earth's concentric spheres, is the force which upheaves the submerged strata of the terrestrial crust, and causes volcanic eruptions. It is an element not conscious, but passional, endowed with extreme vitality and energy, and capable of reacting violently to magnetic impulses, animal or human. Such is the luciferian element concealed within the shell of the earth ; and, considering this astral correspondence between the animistic life of the globe and of its inhabitants, it is not surprising that the volcanic activity of the southern continent reached its height at the end of this period.

Terrific seismic convulsions shook Lemuria from end to end. Its numberless volcanoes began to vomit forth torrents of lava. New eruptive centres broke out everywhere, emitting fountains of flames and mountains of ashes. Millions of monsters, crouching in the gulfs or clinging to the summits, were suffocated by the fiery air or swallowed up in the boiling seas ; but some few escaped, to reappear in the succeeding period. As to the degener-

---

[1] Australia, India, Indo-China, Madagascar, part of Africa and of South America, are the remnants of it.

ate men, they were swept to destruction with the continent, which, after a series of eruptions, gradually sank and disappeared beneath the ocean ; but a chosen remnant of the Lemurian race took refuge upon its western extremity, under the leadership of a Manu or divine Guide. From this point they were able to reach Atlantis, the green and virgin land which had recently emerged from the waters, whereon was to be developed a new race and the first human civilisation.

In this rapid sketch of esoteric cosmogony we have seen our solar system formed by means of successive condensations, similar to those discovered by Laplace in his " World System." But behind the physical laws which work through matter, we have discerned the Spiritual Powers that animate them. Through the efforts of these Powers we have seen Saturn emerge from the nebula, and the Sun kindled in its centre ; we have seen the birth of the planets, one after another, and the War among the Gods. Each of these stages is a separate world, a long cosmic dream, in which one thought of Divinity is expressed, one aspect revealed. Through the Archaï, the Word of the Beginning. Through the Archangels, the Cosmic Ecstasy in the solar Light. Through Lucifer, the creative Lightning in the darkness of the Abyss. Through the Angels, divine compassion. Through Man, desire and suffering.

Shall then this trembling light-spark, fallen from the heart of God, retrace its steps, rejoin the Powers that gave it birth, and become in its turn some kind of god, while still retaining freedom and selfhood? O hazardous journey, along an endless road, whose first turnings are lost in shadow, whose goal is veiled in blinding splendour !

Let us essay to follow it up some few steps of the ladder that stretches to Infinity.

BOOK II

ATLANTIS AND THE ATLANTEANS

.

In the golden age the Gods, robed in air,
walked among men.

HESIOD.

CHAPTER I

THE TRADITION CONCERNING ATLANTIS—ITS CONFIGURATION AND ITS GEOLOGICAL PERIODS

THE priests of Ancient Egypt carefully preserved the tradition of a vast continent which had formerly occupied a great part of the Atlantic Ocean, and of a powerful civilisation engulfed with the continent in some pre-historic catastrophe.

Plato records this tradition as told by Solon, who claimed to have heard it from the Egyptian priests. " The Atlantic sea was then navigable, and had an island fronting that strait which you call the Pillars of Hercules ; and this island was larger than Libya and Asia together ; and there was a passage thence for the seafarers of that day to the other islands, as well as from those islands to all the opposite continent which bounds that ocean truly named. For these regions which lie within the aforesaid strait seem to be but a bay with a narrow entrance ; but the other is truly ocean, and the land surrounding it may truly and most correctly be called a continent. In this Atlantic Island, then, was formed a great and marvellous league of Kings, ruling over the entire island itself and many others, and over parts of the continent also ; and besides these, of the lands east of the strait they governed Libya as far as Egypt and Europe as far as Tyrrhenia." Such is the account given by Plato at the beginning of his celebrated dialogue, the *Timæus*.

In another dialogue, the *Critias*, of which only the first part has been preserved, there will be found a long description of the island of Poseidonis, with its golden-gated town encircled by narrow water-courses, its temple, and its assembly of priest-kings, hereditary sovereigns united by a constitution received from a divine Founder whom Plato calls Neptune. This interesting fragment breaks off at the moment when the nation, which had long remained prosperous and faithful to its inherited virtues, falls into a state of irremediable decadence due to perversity and overwhelming ambition.

Although so short, this fragment is infinitely suggestive, for it gives us a glimpse of a far-off past which has been concealed from us by the passage of time and the absence of historical records. Despite the obviously Hellenised form of the story, one is struck by the strangeness of these rites and customs, in which a patriarchal simplicity seems mingled with the pomp of Babylon and the splendour of the Pharaohs. Plato recounts that the island of Poseidonis, the last remnant of the great Atlantean continent, was destroyed and submerged nine thousand years before the time of Solon Strabo and Proclus give the same facts. It may be added that the Egyptian priests, who imparted this information to Greek travellers, claimed to have received it from the Atlanteans themselves through some far-back connection, and that they said to Solon : " You Greeks speak of a single deluge, although there were several before "—a statement confirmed by modern geology, which has found traces of three successive deluges in the buried strata of the earth. The skeletons of mammoths and other animals, and of fossilised men, found in the tertiary and quaternary strata, are up till now the sole evidence of these far-distant epochs of our globe.

But, while awaiting the researches of a more wonderful science, the discoveries of oceanography help to corroborate the ancient tradition. They have mapped out the contours of the backbone of Atlantis in the ocean depths, while soundings of the Atlantic have proved the existence of an immense chain of submarine mountains, covered with volcanic débris, and extending from north to south.[1] They rise abruptly from the ocean-bed to a height of nine thousand feet, the Azores, Saint Paul, Tristan da Cunha, and Ascension Island being the highest points, which still rise above the waves. Further, the researches of Le Plongeon, Quatrefages and Bancroft, in anthropology and comparative ethnology, have proved that all the races of the globe (black, red, yellow and white) formerly inhabited America, part of which already existed in the time of Atlantis and was attached thereto. Striking resemblances have also been remarked between the ancient monuments of Mexico and Peru and the architecture of India and

---

[1] " Has Atlantis, the mysterious continent which formerly joined Africa to America, and according to legend was one day engulfed by the ocean, ever existed save in the minds of poets ? M. Edmond Perrier announces that a naturalist, M. Germain, has applied himself to finding a solution of this problem based on exclusively scientific data. He has studied minutely the living fauna and flora of the Canary and Cape Verde Islands, as well as the fossilised fauna and flora of the peaks of the lost continent which still rise above the ocean. These fossils are identical everywhere, on all the island-peaks from Mauretania to America. The corals of the island of St. Thomas are the same as those of Florida. Everything goes to prove that there was a connection between the two existing continents, and that Atlantis disappeared at the end of the tertiary period. A gulf must first have been produced between the coast of Venezuela and the still existing archipelago. Mauretania and the Cape Verde Islands must have been separated later."—*Le Temps*, 11 November, 1911.

Egypt. With the aid of all these facts, and by combining the traditions concerning the deluge that exist among the Indians of North, South and Central America, with those of other nations, Mr. Scott Elliott has constructed a history of Atlantis which, while including a considerable amount of hypothesis, yet forms a homogeneous and conclusive whole.[1] On the other hand, Dr. Rudolf Steiner, endowed with esoteric knowledge and highly-developed clairvoyance, has furnished us with many novel and striking glimpses of the physical and psychical constitution of the Atlanteans in relation to anterior and posterior human evolution.[2]

Let us first study the geological story of Atlantis according to Scott Elliott.

A million years ago Atlantis was joined to a portion of Eastern America which had already emerged from the ocean. It occupied not only the place of the present Gulf of Mexico, but stretched far out to the North-East in a vast promontory which included the British Isles of to-day. Curving round towards the south, it formed another promontory in the direction of Africa, of which only the northern portion existed. An arm of the sea separated the two, so that the human races born and developed on this continent might move towards England, and later, Norway. They had, however, only a narrow channel to cross before reaching North Africa, and thence Central Asia, formerly a part of Lemuria.

After a first inundation, eight hundred thousand years ago, Atlantis split apart and was separated from America by a narrow strait. On the eastern side it retained the shape of an open shell, while Ireland and England formed one large island together with the newly arisen Scandinavia.

By a second cataclysm, two hundred thousand years ago, Atlantis was broken up into two islands, a large one to the north called Routa, and a smaller southern one called Daitya. At this time Europe already existed, and during all these three periods there was easy communication between Atlantis, North Africa and Europe.

This was interrupted, eighty thousand years ago, by a new upheaval, after which there remained only the island called Poseidonis by Plato, the last fragment of the great isle of Routa, equidistant from America and from Europe.

The island of Poseidonis was engulfed in its turn, in the

---

[1] *History of Atlantis.* By W. Scott Elliott. (See also the much fuller accounts given by Lewis Spence in *The Problem of Atlantis* and *The History of Atlantis* (Rider and Co.) Tr.)

[2] *Our Atlantean Forebears*, by Rudolf Steiner. See also the chapter on *World Evolution* in his *Outline of the Secret Wisdom.*—(Leipzig, 1910.)

year 9564 B.C., according to the information given to Solon by the Egyptian priests.

Thus, slowly but surely, ancient Atlantis arises from the ocean depths. It is as though we saw the veils of millennia withdrawn, and a lost civilisation come into view, growing ever more distinct in colour and outline. First, a tremendous efflorescence of life in the tropical Eden of a primitive humanity, still half-blinded, as it were, by divinity, from which it has not yet fully emerged. Then a long series of wars, followed by a federation of Initiate-Kings—a fertile oasis in this *mêlée* of races, this human furnace whence was to issue the pure gold of the Aryan type. Finally, decadence and the reign of Black Magic, launching upon the world a host of passions, and unchaining the powers of darkness.

We will now try to give an outline of these rapid visions.

CHAPTER II

PRIMITIVE ATLANTIS—COMMUNION WITH NATURE AND SPON-
TANEOUS CLAIRVOYANCE—THE PARADISE OF DREAMS AND THE REIGN
OF THE GODS

THE Atlantean period, whose geological stages we have just surveyed, represents historically the transition from animalism to
humanity, properly so-called ; in a word, the development of the
conscious ' I,' the bud from which the higher human faculties
were to flower. But if the primitive Atlantean was, physically,
nearer to the animal than to the man of to-day, we must not think
of him as a degraded being like our present-day savage, his degenerate offspring. It is true that he possessed analysis, reason and
synthesis, as acquired by us, only in a rudimentary form ; but, on
the other hand, he had certain psychic faculties highly developed,
which became atrophied in later humanity ; an instinctive perception of the souls of things, ' second sight ' in both waking and
sleeping states, senses of an extraordinary acuteness, a tenacious
memory, and an impulsive will that acted magnetically upon
all living things, and even upon the elements.

The primitive Atlantean, who used stone-pointed arrows, had
a slender body, more elastic and less dense than ours, with more
supple and flexible limbs. His sparkling, serpent-like eye seemed
to see through the soil and the bark of trees, and to penetrate into
the souls of animals. His ear could hear the grass growing and
the ants walking. His narrow brow and horse-like profile, like
that of certain American-Indian tribes, resembled the sculptures of
Peruvian temples.[1]

---

[1] With regard to the narrow brow of the Atlantean, and the shape of his skull,
it is necessary to add an important note ; for the observations of occult science
tend to complete those of anthropology. In the adult man of to-day, the etheric
or vital body is completely absorbed in the physical body. In the Atlantean
it stretched beyond it to a distance of a foot or more ; and it is still the same with
children. The etheric body being the seat of memory, and the brain the organ
of self-perception, in a waking state, it follows that full self-consciousness is only
possible when the etheric body is completely identified with the physical, and when
its upper portion is exactly contained within the skull. In the Atlantean race
this phenomenon came about gradually, but not until about the middle of its
evolution. The memory of the primitive Atlantean floated, so to speak, above
him, in his etheric body. He could recall every smallest image that it contained,

Very different from that known to us was the natural setting of Atlantean life. A heavy canopy of clouds,[1] through which the sun only began to penetrate after the atmospheric convulsions of the first cataclysms, overhung the entire globe. Deprived of the rays of the sun, man, ruler of animals, raiser of plants, lived in intimate communion with the gigantic and exuberant flora and the savage fauna of the earth. All these were, in a way, transparent to him. He saw the souls of things as changing lights and coloured vapours. The water of the springs and rivers was much lighter and more fluid than now, as well as more vivifying, and in drinking it man imbibed powerful influences from the earth and the vegetable world. The air was warmer and heavier than our crystalline, azure atmosphere, but the Fire-Principle, circulating through all things, animated it with thousands of meteors. Threatening storm-clouds would sometimes move above the crests of the mountains and the forests, without actual thunder, but with a kind of crackling, like long, fiery serpents veiled in darkness ; and the Atlantean, sheltering in caverns or in the hollow trunks of trees, believed that he saw in them the changing forms of living spirits. By contemplating these phenomena, he discovered that he had a certain power over them, that he could attract these clouds filled with latent fire, and make use of them to scare the forest monsters, the gigantic deer and the terrible winged dragons, survivors from the Lemurian age. Much later, when black magic had become the sole religion of the greater part of Atlantis, man abused this power to the extent of making it a dread instrument of destruction.

The primitive Atlantean was thus endowed with a kind of natural magic, the remains of which yet survive among various savage tribes. He had power over nature, through the eye and through the voice. His early speech, composed of imitative cries and passionate interjections, was a continual appeal to invisible forces. He charmed the serpents ; he tamed the deer. His power over the vegetable kingdom was particularly strong. He knew how to draw magnetically the vital force from plants ; to accelerate their growth by giving them his own life-forces ; and to curb and train by will-power the flexible branches of the young

but for him past and present were alike. He could scarcely distinguish one from the other, for he lived only in the actual moment. He had only a vague self-consciousness, and spoke of himself in the third person. When he began to say ' I,' he confused this ' I ' with that of his family, his tribe, and his ancestors. He lived immersed in nature, but his inner life was intense. His unreflective self acted with so much the greater force upon his surroundings, and by turns exercised its will in lightning-flashes, or received violent impressions from without.

[1] Scandinavian mythology has preserved the memory of this epoch in what it terms *Nibelheim*, the region of clouds, inhabited by dwarfs who cast metals.

trees. The first Atlantean villages were indeed constructed of trees ingeniously interlaced, living and leafy retreats which formed the habitation of numerous tribes.

When the Atlantean, weary from the hunt and the chase, reposed on the outskirts of his virgin forests, or on the river-banks, his soul seemed to be immersed in the luxuriance of nature, and a kind of religious sentiment awoke in him, and took instinctively a musical form. For at the close of the day, at the advent of the dark, mysterious night, all sounds were extinguished. No more humming of insects, or hissing of reptiles ; the bird-cries were suddenly silenced ; the bellowings of the great deer were stilled. No sound remained save the monotonous voice of the wide river, over which hovered, like airy smoke, the murmur of the distant cataract. These voices were sweet as those of the shell which the hunter on the sea-shore had once lifted to his ear. And so the Atlantean listened . . . and still listened. At first he heard only the silence. . . . Then, withdrawn into himself and become reverberant like the sea-shell, he heard another voice, which seemed to echo behind and through all others, from beyond the silence. It seemed to issue from the river, from the cataract, from the forest and from the air ; and resolved itself into two ascending notes— ceaselessly repeated—a rhythmic chant like that of the waves ever breaking and re-forming on the shore. These two notes said : " Ta-ô ! . . . Ta-ô ! " . . . Then the Atlantean had a confused sensation that this was the voice of a great Being that breathed in all beings—and in naïve adoration he repeated : " Ta-ô ! . . . Ta-ô ! " This was his whole prayer, but it expressed in one breath a fore-consciousness of all that is most profound and most sublime in religion.[1]

With the night a new life began for the Atlantean, a life of dream and vision, a voyage through strange regions. His etheric and astral bodies, less closely linked to the physical than ours, allowed him to rise more easily to super-physical spheres. And the spiritual world, which is the centre of the universe, flowed into the soul of primitive man in torrents of light. In his waking state the Atlantean saw neither sun, nor planets, nor the blue firmament which was ever concealed from him by heavy clouds. In sleep he did not see their material forms, but his soul, freed from the body, bathed itself in the World-Soul, while the Cosmic Powers that ensoul the earth and the planets appeared to him in impressive

---

[1] From this primitive fact, handed down by tradition, is derived the name of the supreme divinity among certain peoples. Taô was the name of God among the early Egyptians, and became that of the initiator of their religion, Hermes-Tot ; as Wod or Wotan became that of Odin-Sieg, the teacher of the Scandinavian race.

and majestic forms. Sometimes he saw the Manu, the guide and father of the race, in the form of an old man with a traveller's staff, and, led by him, the sleeper felt himself pass through the heavy curtain of clouds and rise ever upwards. All at once he found himself at the centre of a fiery sphere, encircled by streams of luminous spirits, some of whom leaned towards him and offered him the Cup of Life or the Bow of Combat. "You are at the heart of the Earth-Spirit," said the Manu ; "but there are yet other higher Gods." And the sphere widened and grew larger, while the fiery beings that moved around it became so transparent that through them, as through a diaphanous veil, could be seen five other spheres, enormously distant from one another, the last of which shone like a brilliant point of light. Moving in this vision with the speed of an arrow, the Atlantean plunged from sphere to sphere. He saw august countenances, with flaming hair and immense unfathomable eyes, but he could never reach that last sphere of all, with its effulgent lightnings—the sphere from whence, the Manu told him, all things had descended. At last the divine Guide brought the astral traveller back to earth. For an instant he had been merged in the World-Soul, where shine the Archetypes in all their splendour. Now he passed again through the vaporous garment of the Earth, and his Guide showed him, in passing, her sister-stars, which were still invisible to his physical eyes—here, the sinister Moon, stranded among black clouds like a shipwrecked vessel among rocks—there, the Sun emerging from a sea of vapours like a burning volcano.

On awaking from his dreams, the Atlantean was convinced of having entered a higher world and of having held intercourse with the Gods. For he remembered, although he often confused his dream-life with his waking life. To him the Gods were protectors and companions whom he met on a footing of friendship. Not only was he their guest at night, but they often appeared to him in the daytime also. He heard their voices in the winds and in the waters ; he received advice from them ; his soul was so suffused with their influence that he sometimes felt them within himself, attributed his actions to them, and believed himself to be one of them.

We must therefore picture to ourselves this savage being, by day hunter of the mammoth and the aurochs, slayer of the flying dragon, becoming by night an innocent child, a young, wandering soul, *animula vagula, blandula*, caught up in the currents of another world.

Such was the dream-paradise of the primitive man of Atlantis. At night he drank deep of the waters of Lethe, forgetting the days of sweat and blood ; but throughout the day he remembered fragments of his splendid visions, and still pursued them in the chase. These visions were to him as a sun bringing rays of light into the confusion of his tenebrous forests. After death he recommenced his dream on a vaster scale, from one incarnation to another; and when after many centuries he was reborn in a cradle of creepers under the leafy boughs of his scented, suffocating forests, there remained with him vague memories of his cosmic voyage, which haunted him like an intoxicating dream.

So, in these primitive ages, night and day, sleep and waking, vision and actuality, life and death, the here and the beyond, were all mingled for man into one vast dream, like a moving panorama of transparent tissue which seemed to stretch to infinity. Neither sun nor stars could penetrate the cloudy atmosphere, but man, guarded by invisible powers, sensed the Gods everywhere.

All the legends of an earthly paradise are based on distant memories of this epoch. From age to age the confused recollection of it has been transmitted and transformed into the mythologies of various races. The Egyptians called it the Reign of the Gods, which preceded the reign of the solar or initiate-kings. In the Bible it was the Eden of Adam and Eve guarded by the Cherubim. Hesiod named it the Golden Age, when the Gods robed in air walked upon the earth. Humanity was to develop new faculties and make new conquests, but throughout successive races, throughout æons, throughout cataclysms and world-changes, it still preserved the indelible memory of a time when it could communicate directly with the universal powers. This memory might change its form, but it always represented man's inextinguishable longing for the divine.

CHAPTER III

ACCORDING to esoteric tradition, the Atlantean civilisation, if
traced back to its origin, covers about a million years. This first
human society, from which our own, so different and so distant,
is derived, represents fabulous humanity before the deluge of
which all mythologies speak. As we have said, four great deluges,
or cataclysms, separated by millions of years, devastated the ancient
continent, whose last vestige disappeared with the isle of Poseidonis. Meanwhile America, which had originally been joined to
it, was growing larger on the Pacific side at the same time as Atlantis, shattered by subterranean fires, crumbled away beneath the
ocean.

During these millions of centuries several glacial periods,
caused by a slight oscillation of the earth's axis, drove the peoples
of the north towards the equator, whence they were frequently
driven back again. There was a continual sequence of exodus,
war, and conquest. Each geological upheaval was preceded by a
period of prosperity and a period of decadence, in which similar
causes produced similar effects. Seven sub-races, or variations,
of the great Atlantean root-race were formed successively, and
each in turn dominated the others. Among them can be recognised the prototypes of all the races that now exist : the red, the
yellow, and the white, who founded the great new root-race of
Semitic Aryans, that was to be separated from the others in order
to start a new cycle. The black race, though of a subordinate
type, is also found. It is a retrogressive remnant of the old
Lemurians, and has produced through cross-breeding the negroes
and the Malayans.

The tradition of the adepts has retained only the main lines and
chief events of the troubled history of these peoples. It takes
note first, with Plato, of the leading characteristic of a spontaneous theocracy and common system of government, dominating
this mixture of races, not by brute force, but by a kind of natural
and beneficent magic. The peaceful rule of a federation of
Initiate-Kings endured for centuries, and the hierarchy of divine

powers seemed to be more or less reflected in these impulsive, yet docile, human masses, in whom the consciousness of self had not yet awakened pride. As soon as that developed, black magic was ranged against white, its fatal shadow and eternal adversary, the tortuous serpent with poisoned breath which, from that moment, has never ceased to threaten man in his quest for power. Both sides then possessed a natural influence over the elements which man has since lost ; and there ensued in consequence a fierce struggle, ending in the triumph of black magic and the total disappearance of Atlantis. We will give a rapid summary of these events.

The first Atlantean sub-race was called the Rmoahalls. It was born upon a promontory of Lemuria, and established itself on the southern portion of Atlantis, in a warm and humid region inhabited by enormous antediluvian animals who lived in vast swamps and dark forests. Some fossil remains of these have been found in coal-mines. It was a race of giants and warriors, of a mahogany-brown colour, acted upon by strong collective impulses. Its name was derived from the war-cry which assembled its tribes together and put fear into its enemies. Its chiefs seemed to act under strong impressions from without, which swept over them and drove them to the conquest of new territories. But, such expeditions accomplished, these temporary leaders retired into the mass, and all was forgotten. Having little memory and no powers of combination, the Rmoahalls were soon conquered, driven away, or subjugated by other branches of the Atlantean race.

The Tlavatlis were a race of the same colour as their rivals, active, supple and cunning. They preferred the rugged mountains to the luxuriant plains, and established themselves in them as in fortresses, making them the starting-point for their raids and excursions. These people developed memory, ambition, skilled leaders, and a rudimentary ancestor-worship. But, despite these innovations, they played only a secondary part in the Atlantean civilisation, though, by reason of their cohesion and tenacity, they inhabited the continent for a longer period than any others. The isle of Poseidonis was peopled chiefly by their descendants. In the Tlavatlis Scott Elliott sees the ancestors of the Dravidian race that still exists in the south of India.

It was left to the Toltecs, whose name appears again among the Mexicans, to carry the civilisation of Atlantis to its highest point of development. These were a tall, copper-coloured people, with strong, regular features. To the courage of the Rmoahalls and the suppleness of the Tlavatlis they added a more accurate memory and a profound veneration for their chiefs. Honour was

paid to the ancient sage, the successful leader, the fearless warrior.
Qualities transmitted from father to son formed the principle of
a patriarchal life, whose tradition became deeply implanted in the
race. Thus there was established a sacerdotal royalty, founded
upon a divine wisdom expressed through higher beings who were
spiritual heirs of the Manu of the race, and endowed with powers of
vision and divination. These royal priests may thus be called
Initiate-Kings, and great was their power for many centuries.
It was derived from a peculiar harmony which existed among them,
and from an instinctive communion with the invisible hierarchies,
and for a long time was benevolently exercised. Veiled in mystery, it was surrounded by a religious pomp and majesty suitable
to this epoch of primitive feelings and strong sensations.

About fifteen degrees north of the equator the Toltec kings
had built their capital, a queenly city, at the same time fortress,
temple and sea-port. Nature and art vied with one another to
render it unique. It rose above a fertile plain on a wooded height,
the last spur of a great chain of mountains that encircled it. The
city was crowned by a temple with thick, square pillars. Its
walls and roofs were covered with the metal called orichalcum by
Plato, a kind of bronze, or copper, favoured by the Atlanteans,
mixed with gold and silver. From far off the glittering gates of
this temple could be seen ; hence the name of the " golden-gated
city." The most striking feature of the Atlantean metropolis,
as described by the author of the *Timæus*, was its system of irrigation. In a wood behind the temple a spring of clear water gushed
from the earth. It issued from a subterranean channel which
brought this volume of water from a lake in the mountains. Falling in sheets and cascades, this spring formed around the city
three circles of canals, which served as both water-supply and
defence, and which were linked up by a system of lagoons to the
harbour, where ships brought the products of distant countries.
The city lay between the canals, at the foot of the temple, and, if
we can believe Plato, there were race-courses and gymnasiums
built upon the great cyclopean dykes which enclosed the canals,
as well as special quarters for foreign visitors.[1]

As long as the flowering-time of Atlantis lasted, the City of
the Golden Gates was the main gathering-place for all her peoples,

---

[1] See the detailed description of the Golden-Gated City in Plato's dialogue
Critias or Concerning Atlantis. He speaks of the capital of Poseidonis which
survived the rest of the continent, but everything points to the belief that his
description applies to the Atlantean metropolis. It is probable that the Egyptian
priests from whom Plato received his information had confused the two cities
through condensing and simplifying past history, as was the custom in ancient
times.

and its temple the glorious symbol and life-centre of their religion. In this temple the federated kings met every year, convoked by the ruler of the metropolis, to settle disputes among the various tribes, to deliberate as to their common interests, and to decide on peace or war with those who were the federation's enemies. War between the kings themselves was strictly forbidden, and all were expected to unite against any who might seek to break the peace.[1]   These deliberations were accompanied by solemn religious rites. Within the temple was a column of steel on which were engraved in sacred language the teachings of the Manu, founder of the race, and the laws laid down by his successors throughout the centuries. This column was surmounted by a golden disk, image of the sun and symbol of the supreme divinity. At that time the sun rarely penetrated through the earth's cloudy curtains, but the Star-King was venerated all the more because his beams so seldom touched the mountain-summits or the brow of man. In calling themselves Sons of the Sun, the federated Kings indicated that their power and wisdom were derived from the Sun-sphere. All sorts of solemn purifications preceded their convocations. After uniting in prayer, the Kings drank from a golden cup water impregnated with the perfume of the rarest flowers. This water was called 'the liquor of the Gods,' and symbolised communal inspiration. Before pronouncing a decision or formulating a law, they slept for a night in the sanctuary. In the morning each recounted his dream, and the ruler of the city, combining these dreams together, sought to draw guidance from them. Not until all were in accord was the new decree promulgated.

Thus, at the apogee of the Atlantean race, a pure and intuitive wisdom was shed from on high upon this primitive people, spreading itself abroad like the mountain-river whose limpid waters enclosed the city and passed from one canal to another across the fertile plain. When one of the Initiate-Kings shared with his chosen subjects the golden cup of inspiration, these felt as though they quaffed a divine nectar which vivified their whole being. When the voyager, nearing the shore, saw the metal roof of the solar temple gleaming afar off, it seemed to him as though a ray of invisible sunlight issued from the building that crowned this City of the Golden Gates.

---

[1] See Plato's *Critias*, which describes, however, a decadent period when black magic had long invaded the cult. Instead of drinking the pure water of inspiration, the kings drank the blood of a sacrificed bull, but the federative constitution remained the same.

CHAPTER IV

**THE ASCENDANCY OF THE SELF—DECADENCE AND BLACK MAGIC—
CATACLYSM AND DELUGE**

THE development of material wealth under the rule of the Toltec pontiff-kings had inevitably a fatal reaction. With the growing consciousness of self there awoke also pride and the spirit of domination. The first outbreak of evil passions took place in a tribe allied to the Toltecs, a cross-bred people of Lemurian ancestry, dark yellow in colour. These Atlantean Turanians were the forbears of the Asiatic Turanians, and the fathers of black magic— the force, born of ambition, which calls to its aid the lower powers of nature, and is opposed to white magic, the force through which man works disinterestedly in harmony with the higher powers. The Turanian kings desired to dominate by conquering their neighbours. They broke the fraternal pact which united them to the Toltec kings, and brought about changes in the religion. Blood-sacrifices were instituted, and instead of the pure draught of divine inspiration they drank the blood of bulls, thus invoking demoniacal influences.[1] Rupture with the hierarchy above, and the forming of a compact with the powers below, brought about the first organisation of evil. Such an organisation can only give birth to anarchy and destruction, since it is an alliance with a sphere whose main principle consists in anarchy and destruction. Each man desires to abase the rest for his own profit. It is a war of all against all, an empire of lust, violence and terror. The black magician not only puts himself in touch with pernicious forces that are the waste-matter of the Cosmos, but he also creates new ones through his thought-forms, which eventually haunt him and tyrannise over him. He pays for his criminal joy in oppressing and exploiting his fellows by becoming the blind slave of tormentors more implacable than himself—the demoniacal illusions, horrible phantoms and false gods that he has made. Such was the nature of the black magic which developed during the decline of Atlantis to an extent greater than has ever since been reached.

---

[1] This also happened in Poseidonis in the last Atlantean period. See Plato's *Critias*.

There were monstrous cults; temples dedicated to gigantic serpents, or live pterodactyls, who devoured human victims; while the men who had attained power were worshipped by troops of slaves and women.

Since in this time of corruption woman had become an instrument of pleasure, sensual excesses increased by leaps and bounds. Polygamy became widespread; hence the degeneration of the human type seen in the lower races and among some of the Atlanteans. Insensate self-worship took a naïve form when the wealthy began to place their own statues, made of orichalcum, gold or basalt, in the temples, and special priests paid homage to them. This was indeed the only kind of sculpture known to the later Atlanteans.

From one century to another, the evil grew, and at last the outbreak of vice, egoism and anarchy attained such dimensions that the whole population was divided into two camps. A minority grouped itself around the Toltec kings who had remained faithful to the old tradition; the rest adopted the religion of the Turanians. Very eventful was this struggle between the enfeebled white magic and the ever-growing black magic, and the same phases repeated themselves desperately again and again. Long before the first catastrophe overtook the continent, the Turanian kings had conquered the City of the Golden Gates. The chief of the solar kings took refuge in the north with an ally, the king of the Tlavatlis, where he established himself with a few adherents; and from this time dated the first of the great eastward migrations, while the genuine Atlantean civilisation continued to decay. The Turanians occupied the metropolis, and blood-rites profaned the Temple of the Sun. Black magic triumphed. Corruption and perversion spread appallingly among this impulsive people who lacked the guiding-rein of reason; and the ferocity of man even infected the animal world. The great felines, whom the primitive Atlanteans had tamed, became jaguars, tigers and lions. At last the elements and the whole of nature were affected—the inevitable Nemesis of black magic—and a first cataclysm separated Atlantis from the beginnings of America. Others followed at long interals.

The four great catastrophes which engulfed this superb continent were not of the same character as the Lemurian cataclysms. We see the same powers at work, but they manifest differently under different stimuli.

The earth is a living being. Its solid mineral crust is only a thin rind compared to its interior concentric spheres of subtler matter. These are the planet's organs of sensation and generation. Reservoirs of primordial forces, the vibrant entrails of the globe respond magnetically to the movements that agitate humanity. They store up, as it were, the electricity generated by human passions, and periodically return it to the surface.

In the Lemurian age, the unchaining of brutal animalism had caused the terrestrial fires to break through the globe's surface, so that the whole Lemurian continent became a boiling solfatara, where millions of volcanoes brought about the destruction of a world swarming with shapeless monsters.

In the Atlantean age, the effect of human passions upon the fiery soul of the earth was more complex, and no less fearful. Black magic, then at its height, acted directly upon the centre of the earth from whence its power was drawn, and so caused other movements to take place in the sphere of elementary fire. This fire, rising from the depths through many tortuous passages, accumulated in the fissures and caverns of the terrestrial crust. Then the Powers who preside over planetary evolution turned this force—so subtle, but capable of such prodigious expansion—in a horizontal direction towards the West, thus causing the earthquakes which periodically shook Atlantis from East to West, in a line parallel with the Equator. These waves of subterranean fire cracked and undermined the surface of the continent from one side to the other, and, with her foundations removed from under her, Atlantis crumbled away by degrees, and finally sank beneath the sea with a great number of her inhabitants. But in proportion as Atlantis was submerged, another land with chains of mountain-peaks arose in the West; for the undulations of the enormous waves of fire from the interior of the sinking continent threw up the volcanic crests of the Cordilleras, the Andes, and the Rocky Mountains—backbone of the future America. Added to this, the discharges of electricity which accompanied these phenomena let loose cyclones and tempests of unparalleled violence. Quantities of water, which had hitherto floated in the air in the form of vapour, descended on the continent in cascades and torrents of rain. The flooding and the sinking went on simultaneously, as though the powers of sky and sea had conspired in the work of destruction. According to tradition, sixty million men perished in the last of these deluges alone.

Thus was the earth swept clear of Atlantis, the arsenal of black magic; and as the Golden-gated City, the palm-covered islands of Routa and Daitya, and the lofty peaks of Poseidonis, disappeared in succession beneath the waves of victorious ocean, the blue and luminous sky, like the Eye of the Eternal, became more and more visible amid the scattered clouds.

In terrestrial evolution nothing is lost, but everything is

transformed. The Atlanteans lived again in Europe, Africa and Asia, both as emigrated tribes and by means of periodic reincarnation ; but in the memories of the new thinking, conquering humanity the story of the submerged continent remained merely as a fabulous dream, a mirage from beyond the seas and the skies, the confused recollection of a lost Eden, a Fall, and a Deluge. The Greek poets, whose plastic imaginings often conceal a profound meaning, spoke of a Colossus seated in the midst of the ocean, beyond the Pillars of Hercules, supporting the cloudy sky with his head. They called this giant Atlas. Did they know that at the dawn of their epoch the Atlantean seers had truly communicated with the Gods who dwelt beyond the clouds ? Or is it that in the depths of the human mind there sleeps ever the dream of a lost paradise and of a heaven to be won ?

CHAPTER V

FIRST DEVELOPMENT OF THE WHITE RACE—ITS SOLAR RELIGION—ITS EXODUS

AFTER this bird's-eye view of the growth and decline of the Atlantean civilisation, it remains for us to see how the Semitic and Aryan races arose from it, like the half-human, half-divine body which rises from the flanks of the Sphinx of Gizeh. For as each new Root-Race enters upon the scene, we behold the miracle of the phoenix reborn from its own ashes. Before the old race finally decays, the nucleus of a new one is formed within it, drawing fresh youth from a higher mode of life.

Let us first imagine the change produced in human mentality by the gradual clearing of the atmosphere. As long as his sky was veiled by heavy clouds, man was condemned to a life of darkness and dream ; but now the flaming torch of the sun moved all day long across the azure spaces, and the night was lit by innumerable stars, a symphony of worlds that moved in harmonious rhythm. The unveiled universe sparkled in its beauty, and all the roads of earth and sea were opened up beneath a boundless sky. Was this not the time for vast desires and great departures ? When all things in the universe are moving, shall not man also move, to learn and to conquer ?

This was the task of the white race, the Semitic and Aryan branch, in whom the masculine qualities of reason, reflection and judgment were to dominate all others.[1] But in order to develop these qualities, long discipline was required, and separation from the other races. It was led by its guides towards the East and North, the final goal of this exodus, which lasted for many thousands of years, being the central regions of Asia. On those high plateaux at the base of the Himalayas, in the pure air, far removed from all other races, the Aryan civilisation was to be definitely established. From here there would pour forth later on the diverse tribes of the new race that was destined to rule the world, often called the Indo-European race : the Aryans of India, the Iranians, Scythians, Sarmatians, Greeks, Celts and Germans,

---

See the admirable study of the white race, compared to the yellow and lack races, in ' L'Inegalite des Races Humaines ' by Gobineau.

together with the primitive Semites of Chaldea. But before attaining this Asiatic stronghold, protected by the earth's highest mountains, the white race found many resting-places and sojourned long in various countries. The first of these was Ireland, which then formed one large island together with England, the North of France and Scandinavia, and here the chosen Atlanteans were put through a special training and education by their guides.[1]

"Humanity," says Rudolf Steiner, "had at that time guides who obtained their wisdom from a superhuman source. They were venerated as Messengers of the Gods—which, in fact, they were. These were the instructors of the Atlantean kings, of whom it was said truly that they "held commerce with the Gods." What took place in the Atlantean temples was inaccessible to the people. They did not comprehend the aims of their guides, whose teachings were expressed in a particular manner.

The language in which the Gods spoke to their Messengers was no earthly language. They appeared to them in "clouds of fire," instructing them as to how they should guide mankind, and the Messengers were able to receive these instructions because they were the most perfect of their race, having already reached a high degree of development in their previous lives. They might be called higher spirits in human form, for the earth was not their true home. These Spirit-Guides, or Messengers of the Gods, ruled men without revealing to them the principles on which they acted ; for, before the fifth Atlantean sub-race, the branch of the first Semites, men could not have understood. *Thought* was not developed in them. The Semitic-Aryan race had to develop a new kind of thought. . . . Up till then the Gods had led mankind through their Messengers, but now men were to learn to know the essence of the Gods, and to look upon themselves as the executors of Providence." [2]

These lines sum up the main trend of the white race, and the difference between it and the Atlantean race. The latter had

---

[1] Nineteenth century science established the unity of the Aryan race on the basis of comparative philology and mythology. It thus fixed the cradle of our civilisations in Central Asia, whence took place their migrations towards the south and west—an origin of which our languages and records show traces. This is an admirable conclusion, but exoteric science goes no further. It lacks the data for informing us of the origin and early development of the white race.

Consequently there has arisen the rather infantile idea that the white race appeared in the world as a primordial fact, a completed whole, and that it was somehow the natural product of Central Asia. Occult tradition, in asserting that the white race, like all the rest, was evolved from the Atlanteans (themselves evolved from the Lemurians), links up our humanity with the organic whole of terrestrial and planetary development, in accordance with the known laws of natural history.

[2] *Unsere Atlantischen Vorfahren*, by Rudolf Steiner.

communicated instinctively with cosmic forces; the mission of the former was to realise the divine through its own efforts. To prepare it for this difficult task, its guides imposed on it a rough life in a cold and rainy climate. The whole civilisation of Atlantis was spurned. The warrior chiefs launched imprecations against the huge cities where many white captives had worked like slaves at the erection of cyclopean buildings, among troops of others, male or female, red, yellow or black. They cursed the tyrants, their vices, their perverted luxury. They cursed carven stone, seeing in it a sign of slavery; while rough stones and masses of rock were looked upon as symbols of liberty and the only altars worthy of the Gods. The people desired only an open-air life, in wooden huts, or on their war-chariots. They made encampments in the pine and beech woods, where the deer and the elk abounded. No more squat temples roofed with metal, where the blood of victims flowed and the golden fetish-statues gleamed; but upright stones beneath the open sky, on vast plains, like those of Karnac in Brittany, or great menhir circles, as at Stonehenge, veritable astronomical quadrants set according to the solar revolutions. Human life was to be regulated by the succession of the seasons and the movements of the stars. Atmospheric phenomena were to become the basis of religious teaching.

We may imagine the guide of one of these tribes standing on a high cliff at the close of a stormy day, when the sky lights up the ocean through torn fragments of cloud; we may imagine the Manu pointing out to his people the rainbow, one end resting on the sea and the other on a wave-washed island, and saying: "Your ancestors inhabited a country that was always shrouded in fog, where the sun was never seen—but they had communion with the Gods. To-day the Gods appear but rarely, but they have given man a sign of friendship. By the rainbow the Gods descend to earth and reascend to their dwellings. Remember that you are sons of the Gods!" There was no longer a direct vision of the divine world, but nature, steeped in divine mystery, served as its vehicle.

Among some of the white races, ancestor-worship was connected with the moon, the globe consecrated to the dead, and many centuries later, their descendants, returning to the same places by a contrary route, evoked the souls of their ancestors through the lunar rays, calling them to their aid against their enemies. But in remote epochs ancestor-worship had a deeper significance, and played a mysterious part in the generation of children. At the winter solstice, during the longest night, which was called the 'mother-night' of the year, and reputed to be that of favourable conceptions, the Manu would say to the men and women gathered around the sacred stone : " Your ancestors are near to the Gods. Live according to the holy laws and rites, and they will come again among you. They will incarnate in your children. Men, be strong, and beget intrepid warriors ! Women, be pure, and bear the heroes of the future race ! "

Very different were his words at the summer solstice, when the people gathered at dawn in the vast circle of giant menhirs, symbols of the months and the seasons, the ancestors and the Gods. When the sun appeared between the two loftiest stones of the sacred enclosure, the Manu said to his people : " Behold the image of the supreme God towards which you must travel, that the earth may be conquered by the pure and the strong, and the living City of the Gods be built. Move ever towards the rising sun ! " [1]

The sunward journey with fire stolen from heaven—is not this typical of the Aryan race, at the dawn as at the noonday of its history, in its first eastward migration as in its later return towards the west ? The rising sun, or earthly future—the setting sun, or heavenly future ; the aim of this race shall ever be Divinity and Truth. Whether led by the light of science, the fire of sacrifice, or the torch of faith, its power shall always lie in freedom of effort and the combined aspiration of heart and mind. If the race should lose either of these qualities, it would sink into fanaticism or anarchy; it would be faithless to its genius and to its mission. For the Aryan has had the courage to seek the Eternal through Freedom.

---

[1] See the account of the migration of the white race to Asia in the Book of *Rama*, in *The Great Initiates* (É. Schuré.)

BOOK III

THE MYSTERY OF INDIA

Krishna: Many births have been left behind
by me and by thee, O Arjuna. I know
them all, but thou knowest not thine.
—BHAGAVAD GĪTĀ.

CHAPTER I

THE VEDIC AND BRAHMANIC WORLD

INDIA is pre-eminently the land of mystery and occultism, because it is the oldest in the world and the most burdened with history. In no other region has more of humanity been piled up on more of nature. Mountains tower behind mountains; animal species swarm one upon another; human races are born and spread abroad like water. This land 'bristling with mountains' (as it was described by Valmiki, India's Homer) has witnessed the evolution of living beings from the saurians and monstrous serpents of Lemuria up to the finest specimens of the Aryan race, the heroes of the *Ramayana*, clear-skinned and lotus-eyed. India has beheld the whole scale of human types, from the descendants of early races fallen into a state bordering on animalism, to the solitary sages of the Himalayas and the perfection of the Buddha, Sakya-Muni; and of all the accumulations during innumerable years, on this fertile soil under the tropical sun, something has been preserved—magnificent buildings, rare animals, extinct types of humanity, souvenirs of immemorial epochs hovering, as it were, in her perfumed breezes, and breathing through her ancient prayers. From antediluvian times she has preserved the wise and majestic elephant, the boa-constrictor, and armies of sportive monkeys; from the Vedic times, the worship of the elements and the cult of ancestors. Despite the Mussulman invasion and the English conquest, the Brahmanic civilisation still reigns triumphant, with its thousands of divinities, its sacred cows, its fakirs, its temples carved out of the mountains, and its pyramidal pagodas rising above the forests and the plains. The most violent contrasts exist side by side; the grossest fetichism and the most elevated philosophy, transcendent mysticism and the emotional cults of primitive religions.

Travellers who have been present at the spring festival of Siva, at Benares, bear witness to this. They have seen, with amazement, a whole people, brahmans and maharajahs, princes and beggars, sages and fakirs, half-naked youths and women of marvellous beauty, solemn infants and tottering grandfathers, pour like a human flood from the palaces and temples that stretch for two leagues along the left bank of the Ganges. They have seen this crowd, robed in costly silks and sordid rags, descend the wide steps in order to wash away their sins in the purifying waters of the sacred river, and greet with ardent cries and avalanches of flowers the rose and amber Indian dawn, which precedes the sunrise.[1] These eye-witnesses have been overwhelmed by a realisation of the Vedic cult still living in the heart of India, together with religious emotions dating from the first days of Aryan humanity. Other travellers have penetrated as far as the source of the Ganges, and have experienced rarer and more subtle sensations. For they have heard the pilgrims chanting their sacred hymns at dawn, to the sound of waters flowing from the eternal snows, by the light of the first glimmerings of sunrise in the pure air of the Himalayan heights.[2]

Whence then has this land, and this people, derived its unique and wonderful character? How comes it that here the distant past dominates the present, while in our Western towns the present disowns the past, and seems to wish to annihilate it in the blind fury of its newly invented machinery?

The reply to these questions lies in the providential mission that has been assigned to India. This mission was to preserve throughout the ages, and to spread among other peoples, the oldest human traditions and the divine knowledge which inspired them. Everything has contributed to this end : geological configuration, the outstanding qualities of the initiate race, the breadth and the height of its first inspiration, and also the diversity of peoples which has made this land something like a swarming human ant-heap.

Sea and mountain have conspired to encircle India with liquid and rocky barriers, making it the land of contemplation and of dream. In the south the Indian Ocean surrounds its almost inaccessible coasts. In the north rises the insurmountable barrier of the Himalayas, the highest mountain-chain of the globe, " roof of the world, throne of the gods," separating it from the rest of Asia and, as it were, seeking to unite it to heaven. It is the Himalayas that make India unique among tropical countries, for upon their sides are found all the seasons, all the flora and all the fauna— the mighty palm and the Alpine fir, the striped tiger of Bengal and the woolly goat of Kashmir. From their icy pinnacles they send three great rivers down into the burning plains, the Indus, the

---

[1] See the striking description of this festival in M. Chevrillon's *Sanctuaries et Paysages d'Asie* (Le Matin à Benares.)

[2] See the remarkable accounts given by Angelo de Gubernatis, poet and student of India, in his *Perigrinazione Indiane.*

Ganges and the Brahmaputra. And finally, it was through the mountain-passes of Pamir that the chosen race of conquerors descended—a human river which, by mixing with the indigenous races, was to create Indian civilisation. The poet Valmiki seems to sum up this Aryan miracle at the beginning of his epic-poem, the *Ramayana*, when he describes the Ganges falling upon the Himalayas from heaven in answer to the prayers of the wise men.

First the Immortals appear in all their glory, and the sky is flooded with brilliant light. Then the river descends, and the atmosphere is filled with white flakes of foam like a lake silvered over with swans. After leaping in cascades from valley to valley, the Ganges reaches the plain. The gods go before it in their shining chariots; the dolphins and heavenly nymphs (*apsaras*), dance upon its waves. Men and beasts follow its majestic advance. Finally it reaches the sea, but Ocean himself cannot stay its onward course. The holy river plunges into the depths of hell, and there its waters purify the suffering souls, enabling them to rise to the region of the Immortals. This is a magnificent symbol of the primordial wisdom falling from heaven and penetrating the depths of the earth, to extract her secret from her.

I.—*The Rishis of the Vedic Age and the Primordial Wisdom.*

After the victorious Manu, called Rama [1] in Hindu tradition and later identified by the Greeks with their Dionysus, had prepared the way for his successors, a mighty flood of Aryans descended from the heights into the Indian plains, by way of the valley of the Indus. Thus the black and yellow races found themselves in the presence of white-skinned conquerors who, with their golden hair and noble brows, seemed like gods. Mounted on his chariot drawn by white horses, the Aryan chief in shining armour, bearing his spear or bow, appeared like the god Indra of the Vedic hymns, who hunted the clouds of heaven with thunder and lightning. He and his comrades easily triumphed over the dark tribes, bringing them into subjection without violence or cruelty, sometimes by the mere force of their presence. They taught them to be artisans, forgers of steel, weavers of wool or flax, and shepherds of great flocks by means of which the people lived. The timid and superstitious native, adoring his fetiches of serpents or dragons, and looking on the sun and the stars as hostile powers, was amazed to hear the Aryan chief declare that he had descended from the

---

[1] See the *Legend of Rama* in *The Great Initiates*, by Edouard Schuré.

sun, and that the god Indra, who handled the thunder and lightnings of heaven, was his protector. Often too, in the wooden house
inhabited by the Patriarch, in the centre of the great enclosed
pastures, the dark-browed servants, with equal amazement, saw
their white mistress revive the fire on the hearthstone with solemn
gestures, murmuring magic formulas and calling the fire " the god
Agni." They felt then that this race possessed magic of a new
kind, and that the fire it had brought with it proceeded from the
mightiest of the gods.

If the Aryan chief, or Patriarch, had been asked whence came
his power and wealth, his fat flocks, his noble wife, his brave sons
and lovely daughters, he would have replied :

" From the Fire-Sacrifice that we make on the hill with the
Brahman."

What did this Fire-Sacrifice mean ? And who was this Brahman ?

A family or a whole tribe gathers before daybreak on the hill-
side, where an altar of turf has been erected. They hymn the
dawn, " the generous Aurora, daughter of heaven, who awakens
all beings," and she appears, while fire is kindled by the friction of
sticks in the dry grass on the altar, and the sun leaps above the
mountain-peaks. A singer criës : " Behold the greatness and
the marvel of this god : yesterday he was dead, to-day he
lives ! "

Agni was in heaven and on earth, in the sun and in the lightning ;
and man resuscitated the dead god by kindling the altar-fire. All
the gods take part in the ceremony, and the ancestors, wearing
bodies of light, are seated around watching over their children.
So did the primitive Aryan celebrate the universal sacrifice—and
it was a joyful sacrifice. The forms and movements of the gods,
that is to say, of invisible cosmic forces, were perceived through a
transparent universe. Day and Night were described as " dancing
around the pillar of the earth." Earth and Heaven were called
" the two valves of the world," and the Aryan believed that through
one of these valves men ascended to Heaven, and through the other
the gods descended to Earth. He believed this because he saw it
and felt it in his intimate communion with the elements, but still
more because the Brahman who evoked the Fire, the Master of the
Sacred Wisdom, declared it to be so.

The Brahman was indeed the inspirer of the patriarchs, chiefs
and kings ; the ruler of this youthful world. " It is he who per-
forms all the rites. He dedicates the young men to the tribe. He
interprets dreams and omens and helps to expiate sins and impuri-
ties. He knows the secret rites by means of which man becomes
the friend and comrade of the sun, and draws its forces into himself,

and those by means of which he acquires power over the clouds and the rain. He knows all the " magic " of daily life, love charms, war charms, nature charms. He cures diseases. He is both doctor and lawyer, and all these powers come from his spiritual knowledge. Men pay homage to him and bring him gifts that they may receive his blessings and escape his maledictions. He has, above all, the knowledge of innumerable secret rites that render sacrifice fruitful."[1]

When the Bharatas had conquered India, the priest of the victorious king said to them : " I sing the praises of Indra, of the worlds terrestrial and divine, I Visvamitra. My magic words protect the Bharatas." Each of these royal priests was said to be " half of the self " of a prince, and at his nomination the prince pronounced words similar to those spoken in the marriage ceremony :—" What thou art, I am ; what I am, thou art ; thou the sky, I the earth, I the melody of the song, thou the words. Let us thus accomplish the journey together."

But if this Brahman had been asked : " Whence comes your knowledge ? "—he would have replied : " From the Rishis."

These Rishis were the prehistoric founders of the caste of the Brahmans. From the earliest Vedic times they had been a separate and sacred people. The Brahmans then divided themselves into seven tribes, and claimed to be the sole possessors of *Brahmân*, that is, of the sacred magic which establishes communication with the spiritual worlds. They had the right to partake of the intoxicating drink, *soma*, the beverage of the gods, of which the drink of the sacrificial ritual was only a symbol. They claimed descent from mysterious beings called " the seven Rishis," who, " at the beginning of things had, under divine guidance, led mankind across the river of the world Rasa." [2] This seems a clear proof that the Rishis of Vedic times had preserved the tradition of the emigrations from Atlantis into Europe and Asia.

Now these Rishis had successors who lived in the forests, near the sacred lakes, in the Himalayan solitudes, or on the banks of the great rivers. Their only shelter was a wooden structure roofed with leaves. Sometimes they had for companions a few disciples ; sometimes they dwelt alone in their cabin with a fire smouldering in the ashes, and perhaps a gazelle for silent and docile sharer in

---

[1] *Die Literatur des Alten Indiens*, by Hermann Oldenberg, 1903.

[2] This significant passage from the Vedas is quoted by Oldenberg in his work mentioned above (p. 17), and takes us back to a lost civilisation and to the submerged continent spoken of by Plato.

their meditations. The Rishis constituted, in fact, the highest order of Brahmans; they were the dispensers of doctrines, laws and rules of life, the custodians of the secret wisdom. Some of them, like Visvamitra and Vasikta, are mentioned in the Vedas as authors of hymns. This immemorial wisdom, dating from an age when writing was unknown, is so far removed from us that it is difficult to imagine of what it can have consisted. It is based on modes of perception and of thought different from those used by the man of to-day, who only perceives through the senses and only thinks analytically. Let us call it spiritual sight, inward illumination, intuitive and synthetic contemplation of man and of the universe. We may attain to some comprehension of these faculties, now atrophied, by considering the state of mind and soul which developed them.

Like all great things, the wisdom of the first Indian sages was the result of an immense longing and a superhuman effort.

At a still earlier period, in the time of Atlantis, primitive man had known a kind of instinctive communion with the hidden forces of nature and the Cosmic Powers. He perceived them directly and without effort in the life of the elements, as through a translucent veil. He did not formulate them; he scarcely distinguished himself from them. He lived with them and in them; he was part of them. What we call the invisible was visible to him. To his vision, as to his consciousness, the material and spiritual worlds were inextricably mingled in a moving mass of phenomena; but he had the sensation of direct communication with the Source of all things. The Aryans, in developing a new order of faculties (reflection, reason and analysis) had preserved traces of this spontaneous sight, and we find many signs of it in the Vedic hymns. But as they forsook pastoral life for the warlike activities necessitated by the invasion of India and by their internal struggles, these primitive faculties diminished, both in the people themselves and in their leaders. All the same, they still cherished blissful memories of another age when their distant forebears had enjoyed inspiring communion with the Cosmic Powers—with those they called the *devas*, the spirits of fire and light, the ensoulers of earth and heaven. Sometimes the knowledge that they themselves had actually lived in this bygone age visited them in blinding flashes of memory, which they explained by saying that their ancestors were drinking divine liquor, the intoxicating *soma*, in the Cup of the Gods.

But, feeling the barrier between them and the divine world grow ever higher, seeing the veil become ever thicker, the Hindu sages were seized with longing for their lost gods. No longer able to see them in the clouds, or the solar rays, or the wide-spreading firmament, they sought to discover them within themselves, in the secret places of the inner world, through the practice of meditation. This supreme effort, this great spiritual adventure, was entered upon in silence and withdrawal, in the profound peace of the Himalayan solitudes.

And the Rishis found their gods. They found them because man and the universe are woven of one tissue, and because the human soul, withdrawing into itself, becomes gradually permeated with the Soul of the Universe. Immobile and with closed eyes, the Rishis sank into the abyss of silence as into an ocean ; but, as they sank, a pure and gentle light seemed to emanate from them and slowly to spread over the whole firmament—a plastic light which was animated by a breath of Intelligence. All kinds of forms moved through it, and in the midst of them appeared in glowing colours the archetypes of all the primitive beings and states of the earth, whose images ever float in the astral light. They saw the Sun emerge from the Saturnian night, and called it " the golden egg, the egg of the world."

By slow degrees these Rishis learnt to plunge into the Beyond, the Source of all things, the Sphere of the Eternal. The super-physical divine light which flooded them with unknown joy they called *Sarasvati*. The Creative Power, whose thoughts are moulded into innumerable forms in the Soul of the World, they called *Brahmân*. This Brahmân (meaning Inspiration, Aspiration, and Prayer) was to the Rishis the inner God, the God of the human soul and of the universal soul, from whom spring all gods and all worlds, and whose manifestation constitutes the Universal Sacrifice.

We find an echo, though only a feeble one, of this state of mind in a hymn whose unknown writer, taught by the Rishis, is seeking to depict the beginning of the world :

> There was then neither death nor immortality
> Neither day, nor night, nor movement, nor whisper.
> The One breathed in His own strength,
> And beyond Him there was nothing.
> Shadows enfolded shadows,
> The Whole was an ocean without light.
> The One, alone in a vast desert,
> Was born by the force of an inward heat.
> First there issued forth Love,
> The first seed of the Spirit,
> Mingling of Being and Non-Being ;
> The sages found it in their hearts. . . .

It follows from all this that the first Rishis of India drew their knowledge from the primal fount of wisdom, that they contemplated the mysteries of creation in broad outlines, not distinguishing details, and that their disciples, the Vedic singers, could only express these truths in confused, and often distorted, forms. But these early sages were none the less the fathers of all later mythologies and philosophies. Their intuitive wisdom is, to the reasoned knowledge that followed, what white light is to the seven colours of the prism. It enfolds them all in its incandescent fire. The prism is nevertheless equally marvellous, and a new creation—for as Goethe, who was both poet and naturalist, and one of the wisest men of modern times, has said : " Colours are the actions and the sufferings of light." One might say that primitive vision was the mother of wisdom, and that wisdom was the mother of the arts and sciences. Only vision rediscovered can bring about their synthesis.

So we see that it was by a supreme effort of will that the Rishis opened the doors of the spiritual worlds. They called the ascetic discipline and exercises in meditation by means of which they attained vision *Yoga*, or the Science of Union ; and the spiritual influx that resulted was to mould the destiny of India. Whether one conceives the ideal as a purely subjective force or as a supreme reality, its influence on history is always proportionate to the aspiration towards it of a chosen few. One thing can prove God, or the gods, and that is the response of cosmic forces to the appeal of the human will. Man's conception of nature and her forces may vary infinitely, but the influx of divinity into the soul that aspires towards it is the sign of its existence.

Let us try to enter a little further into the idea that the Brahmans held of their masters, the Rishis, and their communion with spiritual worlds, however strange this idea may seem to our western mentality. According to the Vedas, some of these sages were powerful enough to reach the divine worlds through their own efforts, but the greater number of them had need of invisible guides. These guides were semi-human, semi-divine beings, the Manus of former world-cycles, or spirits from other realms, who hovered above the aspirants and overshadowed their souls, so that such Rishis possessed a double personality. ' In their ordinary lives they were simple men, but when they were inspired another spirit spoke through their lips. They seemed as though possessed by a god. These were called, in Hindu tradition, *Boddhisatvas ;* which means, inspired by Divine Wisdom. There were, of course, different grades of Boddhisatvas, according to the nature of their inspirer and the degree of their union with him. The Buddha himself, or Gotama Sakya-Muni, a more definitely historical personage than the others, was looked upon by his followers as a higher spirit completely incarnated in a human body. By his own efforts and in the flesh, the Buddha publicly went through the various stages of initiation, leading to the divine state called *Nirvana*. But it is impossible to comprehend the significance of the Buddha, in the development of India and the history of religions, without first taking a rapid glance at Brahmanism, and at the brilliant civilisation which it moulded out of such diverse elements, and such a mixture of races, amid the feverish magnificence of tropical nature.

II.—*The Brahmanic Civilisation. The Three Worlds : Brahma, Vishnu, Siva. The Triumph of the Eternal Feminine : The Wife and the Dancer.*

The nature of a religion is revealed in the civilisation to which it gives birth. In its human expression the moulding thought, the plastic force, of the divine is made manifest. Brahmanic society, whose outlines still exist to-day, though marred and broken by the passage of ages, was founded upon a system of castes. The division of society into various classes is common to all times and peoples. The causes and modes of inequality may change, but the inequality itself persists, like a law of nature, a necessary condition of life and work. India pushed this law to an extreme, and in no other land has the system of water-tight compartments between the social classes been so rigidly enforced. The man or woman who married into an inferior caste was unalterably degraded, according to the Hindu code. When we read in the *Laws of Manu :* " The Brahmans sprang from the head of Brahma ; the warriors from his arms ; the merchants from his belly ; the craftsmen from his feet," we smile at the grotesque metaphor, and do not see in it the ruse of priests who wished to dominate their barbarous kings, and to govern an infant nation. This curious saying is really the theological formula of a profound and ancient wisdom. Translated into modern language, the law enshrined in the Brahmanic adage might be thus expressed :—Nature is aristocratic, and the universe is a hierarchy of forces which are reflected in humanity by a scale of values.

The Brahmans believed in two kinds of atavism for man : a spiritual atavism proceeding from the former existences of his soul, and a physical atavism derived from his ancestors. The Manus of pre-Vedic times had classified human beings according to the stars that represented their chief qualities, dividing men into solar, lunar, saturnine and martian types. Various cults had been founded, and the people grouped themselves around these ideas. Because of the unity of the Aryan race and the purity of its blood, its guides found it unnecessary to concern themselves with physical atavism. But when, after the conquest of India, the Brahmans saw the masses of indigenous tribes, black, yellow and red, becoming gradually intermingled with the white race, they were faced by a much more difficult problem than that of Vedic times, when they had only to guide their own select and homogeneous people. The situation was a serious one. In truth, the whole tragic history of India can be attributed to an excessive diversity of races, and to the inevitable submersion of the superior race by its inferiors, who, in spite of some remarkable qualities, were infected by the germs of weakness and corruption inseparable from the dregs of a retrograde humanity.[1]

The Brahmans checked the evil to the best of their ability by the erection of caste-barriers, which divided the various social functions. The highest caste was that of the Brahmans themselves, the directors of science and religion, who were of the purest Aryan blood. Next to them came the Ksatriyas, the kings and warriors, noble types of the conquering race, though already slightly mingled with other blood ; then the merchants, farmers and superior crafts-men, in whom the conquered races often predominated ; and last of all, the *sudras* (later called *pariahs* by the Portuguese), those who performed all menial labour, the lowest of the native peoples, who were held to have no religion and to be outside the law. This caste was the only one excluded from the Brahmanic religion. The others read the Vedas and took part in the rites. Those who were initiated into the religious mysteries were called *twice-born*.

Brahmanic society thus represented a four-storied pyramid, each caste having its special mentality and social functions. At the bottom the black-skinned pariahs, slaves who were outside the law and had no civil estate. Above them, the wealthy class of yellow-skinned agriculturalists and merchants, who formed the body of the nation. Next, the bronze-complexioned warriors, possessing territory by right of conquest or birth, who commanded armies and distributed justice. At the top, the white-skinned Brahmans, sovereign masters by reason of their superior intelligence, who promulgated the laws and held supreme religious authority. In this way the Aryan race was still governed by a select minority, but as time went on its influence decreased together with its purity.

In spite of the severity of the laws they laid down, the Brahmans were not able to prevent their frequent transgression.

---

[1] This point of view is illuminated in a remarkable fashion in Gobineau's work, *L'Inégalité des Races Humaines.*

Hence there was a gradual intermingling of the lower peoples with the higher, and a steady infiltration of black and yellow blood into the white race. The Brahmanic edifice was admirably constructed, but there was not sufficient moral union between its many compartments. The mixture of races caused it to crack from top to bottom. Envy and scepticism, and the class hatred which preys upon humanity to-day, did not then exist, but violent passions, ambition, sexual indulgence, and the curious animal attraction which the lower races have for the higher whenever they are brought into contact, had their usual effects. The mingling of such different bloods raised the level of the conquered races, but enervated the masculine vigour of the conquerors, while at the same time refining their senses and causing them to develop new artistic qualities. At the bottom of the ladder the *vaisyas* married in large numbers the black women of the *sudras*, and their descendants usually adopted the barbarous cults of their mothers. At the top, the kings indulged in polygamy with women of all colours, and even the Brahmans married into inferior castes. Some of these, jealous of the great influence of the ascetic Brahmans, sought to have them banished, and the latter, in order to hold out against their adversaries, were obliged to take the black kings of the South under their protection, in accordance with a maxim from the *Laws of Manu* : " Thy neighbour is thine enemy, but the neighbour of thy neighbour is thy friend." These black kings of the South, invested with sovereign prestige by the authority of the Brahmans, rose up against the white kings of the North, and menaced the whole structure of Hindu civilisation with their brutal customs and orgiastic religious cults. The epic poem of the *Mahabharata*, with its interminable wars between the solar kings and the lunar kings, is an echo of these ancient wars between races and religions.

There was indeed a vast gulf between the high Brahmanic culture and the motley world of the three lower castes ; and a similar gulf lay between the North and the South of India after the fabulous conquest of the peninsula by Rama, who symbolised the first descent of the Aryans into the Indian plains. In the Himalayan heights there dwelt noble ascetics, at the source of the Ganges and on the banks of sacred lakes, wrapt in prayer and in contemplation of Brahma, the Eternal. On the lower slopes, near the rivers, stood the altars where Agni, the sacred fire, was worshipped. In the pure morning air, the faithful priest would behold the god Brahma hovering above the flames, seated on a lotus-flower and meditating on the creation of the world, while the kings and warriors adored the cosmic powers, Savitri the sun, and Indra chasing the clouds before him. In this worship of celestial light and fire lay the mainspring of their faith and of their joy in life. But in the centre and the south of India, the people had for idol a fierce and cruel god, Siva the Destroyer. They bowed before him in terror, to avert his anger and obtain his favours. He was represented as " hideous, grinning, with black belly and red back, strings of human skulls hanging around his shoulders ; sending forth his messengers who scatter abroad fever, pestilence and death."[1] Often he was worshipped in the form of one of the antediluvian reptiles that still lived in the wild mountain gorges ; and sometimes the northern kings, when tiger-hunting in the forests, mounted on elephants, would come upon whole tribes prostrated before one of these monstrous serpents, coiled in its cavern, and offering to it human victims.[2] Beholding this, the king would sometimes attack the monster and hack it in pieces ; but sometimes, fearing to fall under the dark spell of the " king of the serpents," he would fall back in horror, and in blind panic the whole royal cortège, with its horses and elephants, would rush from the forest.

The abyss which thus opened at moments between these two races and religions, between these two worlds, caused much serious reflection among the Brahmans of the great cities and the ascetic visionaries of the Himalayas. Was not this irruption of lower forces the revenge of the conquered races upon their conquerors ? Was it not the revolt of lower nature against the subduing *devas* who had used it as a stepping-stone ? Must the conquerors be submerged by the conquered ? Must Brahma retire before Siva, and the bright gods of the Vedic heaven be dethroned by the demons of a degenerate people ? Was no bond of union, no reconciliation, possible ?—The chasm seemed impassable, and the evil without remedy.

It was then that there appeared a reformer destined to give India a new soul and to make an indelible impression. He came from the Himalayan hermitages and was called Krishna ;[3] his successors identified him with the new god whose worship he instituted. Some of those scholars who perform prodigies of erudition in order to explain all ancient religions as solar myths, have declared that Krishna was merely a personification of the Sun. But the religion that he brought to the world attests the existence of its founder better than any biography. It was Krishna who gave to the Hindu soul its love of nature, its dreams, its longing for the infinite, infusing into it all the ardent colours of India's crimson and purple evening skies.

---

[1] *Les Littératures de l'Inde*, by Victor Henry.
[2] One of these serpents is described in the *Vishnu-purana* as *Kalayeni*.
[3] See *The Legend of Krishna* in *The Great Initiates*, by Edouard Schuré.

In the Vedic age, Vishnu was merely one of the names of the solar god, personifying the diurnal journey of the sun around the earth in three stages, dawn, noon and sunset. Krishna made it the spiritual Solar Word, the second person of the divinity, the visible manifestation of Brahma in all worlds, and especially in humanity. Krishna was an ascetic, who in the depths of his solitude had experienced, from childhood up, an immense love for life and beauty, not through desire, but through sympathy. He did not condemn life as Buddha was to condemn it, but blessed it as the way of salvation, leading the soul to consciousness and to perfection. He showed man, in perspective, his possible liberation and transfiguration, and declared that whenever the world became corrupt, whenever its need was great, Vishnu would incarnate in a sage or a saint in order to remind man of his high origin. As the higher consciousness of Brahma, Vishnu comes to correct, as it were, the inevitable mistakes of God the Creator, who, being infinitely divided up in His creations, is forced to allow some of them to become alienated from their Divine Source. The monsters of earth and sea are the necessary experiments and errors of Brahma, just as sins and crimes are the unconscious or voluntary errors of man. Krishna thus taught both the love of life in its multiple forms—life which is the descent of the Universal Soul into matter, its *involution* into all beings—and the love of God, which is the human *evolution* of the individualised soul, its return to its Source. He pointed out the means—love, charity, compassion, knowledge and faith—towards complete identification of mind and soul with Atma, the Divine Spirit.

In this way was accomplished the union of the two opposed worlds—of Siva, the terrible god of unchained Nature and unbridled animal passions, with his train of demons ; and Brahma, the god of pure Spirit, floating in the skies on his symbolic lotus, surrounded by the shining circle of gods created by his thought, and seen through the multi-coloured veil of Maya, his divine Spouse. For Siva the Destroyer had now become merely the chaotic and distorted counterpart of the supreme God, the sinister shadow of Brahma the Creator in the lower worlds, whilst his son Vishnu, the divine messenger, flying from heaven to earth and from earth to heaven on the eagle Garouda, became the Saviour and Mediator.

This superb conception was marvellously suited to the mentality of India. The three worlds (Spirit, Soul and Body) represented by the three gods (Brahma, Vishnu and Siva) were exactly applicable to the social structure, which was itself an image of the universe and formed like it an organic whole. To each of the three social classes was given a religion suited to its needs and a function corresponding to its faculties: to the *spiritual intellectuals,* the Brahmans, the religion of Brahma with its divine wisdom, and the function of teaching and education; to the *passional intellectuals,* the kings and warriors, the religion of Vishnu, which inculcated heroism and enthusiasm, and the function of material government and the exercise of justice; to the *instinctives,* the lowest caste, the religion of Siva, which the Brahmans strove to ennoble by making him the god of nature and of the elements, who rules over reincarnation, life and death. Thus the divine trinity which is expressed in the constitution of the universe and of man, was also reflected in the social organism for the maintenance of unity and harmony as far as possible. We may add that the Brahmans showed the lower castes the possibility of mounting a degree higher, through a virtuous life, but only from one incarnation to another.

To this conception of the universe and the social world Krishna added another innovation of great importance and incalculable consequences. This was the glorification of the principle of the Eternal-Feminine and of Woman. In their heroic youth the Aryans had only worshipped the male principle of the universe, Agni, the fire hidden in all things, which in man becomes intellect, will and action. They paid homage to Aurora, the Dawn, because she remained virgin; but nearly all the other gods were masculine. Hence a strong, serious and austere people. But it was necessary to unveil the mystery of the Eternal-Feminine to a riper and more refined civilisation, and Krishna did not hesitate to do so. Is not nature as divine as her creation? Does not God need, in the three worlds, a substance emanated from Himself, His receptive and feminine counterpart, in which to mould His creatures? Are not the gods moulded in etheric substance, souls in the astral light, and living beings in flesh and blood? So the three great gods had now their divine spouses, soon more celebrated and more worshipped than themselves. Brahma had for spouse Maya the subtle, who enveloped him in her radiant veil; Vishnu had Lakshmi, goddess of Love and Beauty, weaver of souls; Siva had Bavani, ardent arouser of carnal desires, whose shadow-side is Kali, goddess of Death. From then onwards, wife and mother were placed upon a pedestal. The *Vishnu-Purana* speaks in dithyrambic style of the mother of Krishna: "No one could look upon Devaki because of the light that surrounded her, and those who contemplated her splendour felt their spirits troubled; the gods, invisible to mortals, continually celebrated her praises while Vishnu was enclosed within her form. They said, 'Thou art the Word, the Creative Energy, mother of wisdom and of courage. Thou hast come down to earth for the salvation of men. Be proud to carry the god who sustains the world.' "

Woman was thus glorified by Krishna as the organ of the Eternal Feminine, the matrix of the divine on earth ; and with her was glorified love. Conceived in the pure Himalayan ether, love descended like a heady perfume into the burning plains, entered the hearts of men and women, and spread itself abroad in poetry and in life, like the lotus-pollen which swans carry on their wings in their amorous sports, and which floats away to fertilise the blue water-lilies along the river-banks. It is this apotheosis of the feminine principle which lends to the Hindu soul its peculiar gentleness, its deep respect for all living things, its almost morbid tenderness—source of weakness and degeneration, but also of an unique and penetrating charm.

At the height of its perfection the Brahmanic world presented one of the most remarkable spectacles that the earth has witnessed. It was a civilisation that did not give the same impression of solidity as the Egyptian, nor had it the beauty of the Greek, or the strength of the Roman ; but its variety of grades formed a structure of imposing magnificence. It was as though the genius who presides over the destinies of our planet had said : " Let us see what sort of world we can make by mixing all the races of the earth into one nation. We shall then see what can be done with each race separately."   In any case, it seems as though the Rishis and Brahmans who built up this civilisation had some such idea in mind ; for it contained men of almost every colour, and included every kind of custom, religion and philosophy, from savagery to ostentatious luxury, from gross fetichism to trans- cendent idealism and mysticism. All these elements, laid one upon another according to a wise hierarchical plan, coalesced into a dazzling, many-coloured fresco, which harmonised perfectly with its natural setting—with the slow majesty of the Ganges as with the lofty Himalayan heights.

At the apex of this world, living apart in solitude, we find the ascetics in their hermitages on the mountain slopes, by limpid pools and rivers, and in the depths of mighty forests. They dwell with their disciples, wrapt in the study of the Vedas, and in prayer and meditation. Held back by a mysterious fear, the wild beasts recoil at the tranquil step of these solitary men, and dare not cross the barriers erected by the magic power of their glance. Antelopes and gazelles, herons and swans and multitudes of smaller birds, flourish under the protection of these anchorites, who live on rice, roots and wild berries. The peace and calmness of their retreats make them like earthly paradises.   In the drama of *Sakuntala*, the king Dushmanta, descending from the skies in

Indra's chariot, beholds the groves of some hermitages on a mountain slope, and cries: " O this peaceful retreat is even sweeter than heaven! I feel as though plunged into a sea of nectar!" One might suppose that these humble sages, living far removed from worldly agitations, deep in the contemplation of Eternity, would have no influence upon their country; yet it is they who secretly govern it. Their prestige is unchallenged; their authority supreme. The Brahmans consult them; the kings obey them, and in old age sometimes join them. In truth, these hermits watch over and guide the whole Brahmanic civilisation. It is dominated by their thoughts, their moral teachings, their religious conceptions. Though austere towards themselves, they are not so towards others. Free from all illusions, but indulgent to human weaknesses, they can estimate the efforts, sorrows and joys of all beings. Their retreats are not entirely closed to outer life, or even to love. Sometimes, in the neighbourhood of an ascetic community and under its authority, the aged wife of a Brahman would found an institution for young girls of noble birth who wished to prepare themselves for marriage by a period of retirement and contemplation. The poet Kalidasa has placed his exquisite idyll *Sakuntala* in one of these retreats. In a word, the ascetics are not entirely inaccessible to the attractions of the senses. They give way to them under exceptional circumstances, but any such happening is always presented to us in Hindu poetry in the form of a legend, and as a providential occurrence having a sublime object. The poets relate that when the gods desire to give human birth to a being endowed with divine virtues, they send one of the heavenly nymphs called *apsaras* to a hermit of particular merit. The nymph overcomes him by her marvellous beauty, and a child is born who is adopted and educated by the anchorites, and who eventually becomes a famous hero or queen. This legend may conceal a secret. It may mean that the Brahmans sometimes permitted a temporary union between an ascetic and a chosen woman in order to provide a worthy incarnation for some soul of high spiritual attainments. In any case it proves that the Brahmans looked upon asceticism itself as a source of integrity and strength in human generation.

It would be difficult to imagine a more violent contrast than that between these hermitages and the great Indian cities of legendary times, such as Ayodyha, Indrapeshta, or Hastinapura. They are described by Vyasa and Valmiki as splendid and vast, encircled by walls and adorned with flags, having broad, well-watered streets, rich bazaars, imposing terraced houses, and public gardens. Among the variegated multitudes of citizens and slaves, there swarm crowds of dancers, singers and comedians.

The reigning kings dwell in magnificent palaces, surrounded by a luxurious court and a large harem; for polygamy had soon displaced the patriarchal customs of the early Aryans. But there is always one special queen, whose eldest son is the lawful heir to the throne. In epic and drama these monarchs are depicted as demi-gods possessed of all the virtues; but, except for Rama, whose great soul shines through all his fantastic exploits, the Indian kings appear a little cold and conventional. Under all the showers of flattering epithets bestowed on them by courtier-poets, they strike us as often weak and puerile. In the excitement of a game of dice, the king Naal forfeits his kingdom and his wife, and then, overcome by despair, abandons the latter in a forest. The king Dushmanta, after having seduced Sakuntala, repulses her and refuses to recognise her. It is true that he is influenced by the maledictions of an angry hermit, but his character seems none the less weakened.

It is woman, when all is said, who triumphs in Hindu poetry; woman to whom all the finest rôles, the deepest feelings, the proudest resolutions, are allotted. Dayamanti, Sita and Sakuntala are equally lovable, but their characters are individual and clearly drawn. They shine beside one another like the diamond, the sapphire and the ruby. What ingenuous and impetuous charm has Dayamanti with her " dazzling skin, her marvellous eyes whose brilliant beauty makes the moon grow pale." Faced with a choice between the immortal Devas who desire her, and the king Naal, she is neither intimidated nor blinded by the glory of the gods. She chooses the man, whose noble brow is shadowed by sorrow and death, because she finds him thus " more beautiful."

The heroic Sita is the perfect type of Hindu wife. When Rama, condemned to exile by his father, wishes to depart alone into the forests, she says : " A father does not obtain reward or punishment through the merits of his son, nor a son through the merits of his father; each earns for himself good or evil by his own actions. But the wife who is devoted to her husband is permitted to share the happiness won by his merits, and I will follow thee in all places, wheresoever thou goest. Parted from thee, noble son of Raghu, I would not wish to dwell even in heaven. Thou art my lord, my master, my road, and my divinity; I will then accompany thee ; this is my final resolution."

As to the ravishing Sakuntala, there is scarcely to be found, in any literature, a maiden more attractive, with her mutinous grace, her naïve coquetry, her insinuating charm. Her trembling modesty exhales a perfume of innocence and sweet voluptuousness. " Large eyes, triumphant brows ; tender plant swaying in the

breath of love," says her royal lover. She is of a burning sensitiveness. Only in her brilliant and languishing eyes can be read
the troubles and ardours that her passionate silences conceal ;
her heart flames like tinder "set on fire," and passion overwhelms
her with a devastating languor. But her dominant trait, which
colours her with tenderest rose in the galaxy of famous lovers,
is her sympathy for all living creatures. Animals and plants
alike are drawn to her. She speaks of the convolvulus that she is
watering as her sister ; she has a little pet fawn whose name means
"protected by the birds." Sakuntala is indeed the Indian Eve
of a tropical paradise, where men, animals, trees and flowers are
united in a loving brotherhood, where all that breathes is sacred
in the name of Brahma—for all living things have a soul that is
a part of His.

Thus the cosmic power invoked by Krishna under the name of
the Eternal-Feminine, comes down to the Brahmanic world
through the heart of woman, and expands into the double flower
of conjugal love and sympathy for living nature.

But not only in the devoted wife, or in the virgin wedded to
the soul of nature, was the ideal of the Eternal-Feminine expressed
in Brahminism. It was given yet another plastic form, subtly
related to the deepest mysteries of religion. Brahminism made
woman an instrument of art, a medium for expressing the divine
through the beauty of her attitudes and gestures—and this was
its most artistic and original achievement. I refer to the *devadasi*,
or sacred dancer, known to us to-day only in the degenerate form
of the *bayadère*. The courtesan has taken the place of the temple
virgin, interpreter of the gods, who in ancient times revealed to
the many the same ideas and sentiments that poetry evoked only
in the few. There is a legend of the god Krishna instructing
the shepherdesses in the sacred dances ; that is, teaching them to
express in rhythmic movement the grandeur of the gods and
heroes. These dances, symbolic in essence, were a harmonious
combination of rhythm and pantomime. They interpreted feeling
rather than passion, thought rather than action. It was not an
imitative art, but an art of the expression and exaltation of an
inner world. In the Brahmanic temples there were colleges for
young girls, who lived in the care of aged women, and were instructed in the art of religious dancing. The strictest chastity
was enforced, and these dancers were never seen except at public
festivals. They danced to the recitation of sacred poems, and their
religious functions absorbed their whole life.

But we should have only an imperfect idea of these *devadasi*,
and of the respect which they inspired in the people, if we ignored
the mystical meaning with which religion endowed them. In the

THE MYSTERY OF INDIA 93

Vedas we read of the celestial nymphs, or *apsaras*, the dancers of
Indra. These were radiant beings who dwelt near to the *devas*,
serving them as messengers to mankind, and sometimes incarnating
in female form. The sacred dancer of the temples played, in
the official religion, much the same part as that played by the
apsara in mythology. She was the mediator between heaven and
earth, between gods and men. In the public festivals she represented, by the beauty of her attitudes, the profoundest religious
symbols ; and by her eloquent mimicry she interpreted the sacred
poems recited to the people by the Hindu bards, or *bharatas*.
Hence the high rank of the temple dancer, and hence her name
of *devadasi*, which means ' servant of the gods.' [1]

Let us picture, on the outskirts of one of these ancient Indian
capitals, the great temple-pagoda with its pyramidal roof, and
the sacred pools surrounding it. The overpowering heat of the
day has given place to the exquisite freshness of night. The
firmament is thickly powdered with stars, and the moon swims
in the sky like a swan in a blue lake. The vast courtyard is lighted
by ' trees of fire,' and on a raised platform the king is seated with
his courtiers. Around him there stretches an immense crowd
of people which includes every class, even the pariahs, and all
are listening in silence to the voice of the rhapsodist, who, from
the terrace in front of the temple, conjures up by his eloquence
the heroic world of ancient times. Suddenly a murmur runs
through the crowd. From the illuminated temple-porch issues
the procession of sacred dancers with their hand-bells and elaborate
head-dresses, their supple limbs swathed in silken draperies, and
on their shoulders golden flames or wings. Their leader wears
the royal diadem, and a cuirass glittering with precious stones.
Then the stringed instruments are heard, the bamboo staves
mark the rhythm, and the dancers begin their sacred evolutions.
They link themselves into a garland, they extend across the
terrace like a necklace of pearls. Keeping step to the music and
to the rhythmic utterance of the rhapsodist, they prostrate themselves before the principal dancer, or group themselves expres-
sively around her, waving their flexible hands and their fingers
sensitive as convolvulus-tendrils. The radiant *devadasis*, with
their dilated eyes, their amber and opal faces, have now veritably
become the messenger of the *devas*, the true *apsaras*. They seem
to carry the souls of heroes in their tender virgin arms, and to
incarnate them in their delicate bodies as in pure and perfumed
chalices.

[1] Sculptured representations of the *devadasi*, in varied and graceful poses,
are to be seen in the friezes of the magnificent temple of Angkôr-Tôm in Cambodia.

We can conceive that even the pariah, losing himself in such a spectacle, might experience some dawning realisation of the profound mysteries of the Vedic wisdom and of a divine world.

Will it be objected that this picture of the *devadasis* is but a fanciful idealisation of the *bayadère*, the voluptuous siren of to-day? Such is not the impression of those who have visited the colossal ruins of Angkôr-Tôm in Cambodia, and who have felt the strange fascination of those amazing sculptures.

The ruins of this architectural marvel of a dead civilisation rise like a fantastic city in the midst of a great forest, whose wild solitude protects them and has half buried them in its luxuriant vegetation. The traveller enters through a gate surmounted by an enormous mask of Brahma, and flanked by two stone elephants which the tropical creepers have vainly tried to strangle for a thousand years. In the centre of the sacred city towers the chief pagoda, a vast cathedral. Here the visitor may wander for hours beneath the vaulted arches of endless cloisters, where colossal statues loom in the semi-darkness. He mounts and descends innumerable stairs, he passes innumerable doors, he loses himself in a labyrinth of irregular heads of *devas*, griffons, or praying saints. He is watched and pursued from every quarter at once by the head of Brahma, repeated to infinity, carved on every side of the capitals of the pillars, gigantic, inescapable. On the walls and friezes the epic of the *Ramayana* is represented in an interminable series of haut-reliefs ; it is as though the legendary hero passed through the temple with his army of monkeys on his way to conquer Ceylon.

In this pandemonium of monsters, men and gods, one figure above all impresses the observant visitor—the figure of a woman, frail, aërial, curiously alive. This is the heavenly nymph, the divine *apsara*, represented by the sacred dancer. She is to be seen everywhere, in various poses, alone or in groups, now upright and pensive, now swaying in undulating movement on bended knee, or with arms languorously curved above her head. Sometimes, at the foot of the wall, she seems to be holding back with a graceful gesture an avalanche of warriors and chariots ; sometimes, on a pediment, a dozen *devadasis* are seen weaving their rhythmic dances, as though to invite the heavy warriors to follow their airy flights. Many of these sculptured dancers are shown emerging from the heart of a water-lily, or holding a lotus in the hand. Blossoms unfolded from the calyx of universal life, they stir the petals of the soul like a silver-tongued bell, and seem to desire to uplift the tumultuous revelry of the universe into the starry dream of Brahma.

And so the sacred dance—this lost art bordering on religious ecstasy, this art in which the thought of a nation was incarnated in living sculpture, this physical and spiritual magic whose deep import neither scholars, philosophers nor historians have fathomed —comes to life once more in the vast ruin of Angkôr-Tôm, under the giant palms and acacias that sway their plumy branches above its silent temples.

CHAPTER II

THE LIFE OF BUDDHA [1]

THE Brahmanic civilisation had flourished for many thousands of years, preserving its equilibrium throughout racial wars, dynastic rivalries, and the innovations of popular religions. This equilibrium was derived from the Vedic wisdom, whose power still endured. Nevertheless, six or seven centuries before our era, the period of decline began. In spite of the strong religious unity which held its diverse sects together, India, divided up into a multitude of kingdoms, was weakened from top to bottom, and ripe for the foreign invasions for which Alexander the Great gave the signal three centuries later. The kings, enfeebled by polygamy, and engaged in civil wars and harem intrigues, gave themselves up more and more to luxury and idleness, while the people rapidly degenerated through intermarrying with inferior races. Fanatical *fakirs*, caricatures of the true ascetics, indulged in hideous mortifications before the temples of Siva, on the pretext of attaining sanctity ; while the sacred virgins who still danced in the temples of Brahma and Vishnu were now rivalled by the priestesses of Kali, whose burning and voluptuous glances, more ardent than their flaring torches, lured the fascinated onlookers into their shadowy temples. The *pariahs* indulged in still viler pleasures, seeking to forget their sufferings and the yoke of slavery ; and from the depths of the nation there arose groans mingled with cries of savage joy, miasmas of vice and clouds of passion, menacing both its secular virtues and its spiritual conquests.

These were, however, preserved by the Brahmans, for with them, at the summit of this world, tradition and immemorial wisdom still kept watch. But even this tradition, this wisdom,

---

[1] In this study I have chiefly made use of the valuable book *Buddha, seine Lehre, seine Gemeinde*, by Hermann Oldenberg. The celebrated German scholar has gathered into this volume, and has arranged in masterly fashion, all the oldest and most authentic documents concerning the life of Gotama, and has given to his historic personality a reality which had often been contested. It goes without saying that, in making use of this remarkable work, I reserve the freedom to describe, from an esoteric point of view, the psychology, the initiation, and the achievement of the Indian reformer.

was growing narrower with age. It had lost its pristine spontaneity, its wide outlook over the Cosmos and the inner realms. Compressed into abstract formulæ, it was becoming fossilised in ritualism and pedantry, and seemed to be overweighted by its great knowledge of the past. Happy the peoples who, intoxicated by the joy of action, drink the waters of Lethe and forget their wanderings around the world! Revivified by new draughts of hope and life, they believe themselves to have been born only yesterday. The Brahmans were bowed down by the burden of humanity's past. Centuries, millennia, *kalpas* or world-periods, weighed heavily upon their shoulders, and their arms drooped with lassitude like the branches of ancient cedars burdened with snow. Just as the Indian Aryans had gradually lost the spirit of adventure and conquest, the Brahmans had lost faith in the future of humanity. Separated from the corrupt and swarming masses, in their Himalayan retreats, they buried themselves in their meditations. In the *Upanishats* there are noble thoughts and astonishingly profound conceptions, but there is also a suggestion of discouragement and indifference. While seeking union with *Atma*, the supreme Spirit, in egoistic contemplation, the Brahmans had forgotten mankind and the outer world.

At this point there arose in the Brahmanic world a man who challenged it to mortal combat. But in challenging it he was, curiously enough, to carry its secret thought to an extreme, and to perpetuate its ideals in an unforgettable figure of perfect renunciation. His doctrine seems to us an exaggeration of Brahmanism, and at the same time its negative side. It is the last venture of the Hindu genius into the ocean of infinity, a venture desperately courageous, though doomed to end in failure. But from this failure there emerged two great ideas, like migratory birds escaping from a shipwreck—rich and fruitful ideas which were to carry the quintessence of the ancient wisdom to the West, whose genius would transform it.

1.—*The Youth of Buddha*

Between the Himalayan buttresses of Nepal and the river Rohini, there lived formerly the prosperous race of the Sakyas (meaning *powerful*). The vast marshy plains, watered by mountain torrents, had been transformed by human labour into a rich and flourishing country, with leafy forests, rice-fields, and pastures which afforded nourishment for fine herds of horses and cattle. Here was born in the sixth century B.C., a child named Siddârtha. His father, Suddhôdana, was one of the numerous kings of the country, a sovereign ruler like the rajahs of to-day. The name of Gotama, given by tradition to the founder of Buddhism, suggests that his father was descended from a family of Vedic singers who bore this name ; and the child, dedicated to Brahma before the household altar where burnt the sacred fire of Agni, was also to be a singer and a charmer of souls—but a singer of a unique kind. Not his to celebrate in song the rosy Aurora with her sparkling diadem, nor the Solar God of the many-coloured bow, nor Love whose arrows are flowers and whose breath intoxicates like strong perfume. He was to intone a mournful, strange and impressive melody, seeking to enfold both men and gods in the starry shroud of Nirvana. The large, serious eyes of this child, glowing beneath a peculiarly prominent brow—for it is thus that tradition has always depicted the Buddha—were filled with sadness and re-membrance, and gazed upon the world with astonishment. His childhood was spent in luxury and ease. Around him smiled his father's magnificent gardens, with bowers of roses, lily-covered pools, tame gazelles and antelopes ; while birds of varied song and plumage abounded in the shadows of the peepuls and mango-trees. But nothing could remove the shadow that veiled his face, nothing could calm the unrest of his heart. He was of those who speak little because they think too much.

Two things rendered him different from others, separating him from his kind as though by an abyss : a boundless pity for the sufferings of all creatures, and an impassioned search for the cause of all things. A dove seized by a hawk, a dog dying from snake-bite, filled him with horror. The roarings of wild beasts in the showmen's cages seemed to him even more dreadful, more sorrowful, than the cries of their victims, and caused him to tremble, not with fear, but with compassion. How could he, the prey to such emotions, rejoice in royal feasts and dances, in elephant combats, in the cavalcades of men and women who passed before his eyes to the sound of drums and cymbals ? Why had Brahma created this world full of such frightful sufferings and senseless joys ? Where were all these beings going ? To what did they aspire ? What were those flights of swans seeking, who departed every spring towards the mountains, and returned to the Ganges with the rainy season ? What lay behind the black hills of Nepal and the snowy domes of the Himalayas piled up towards heaven ? And when, in the stifling summer evenings, a woman's languorous song sounded from the arched galleries of the palace, why did that solitary star flame upon the red horizon of the torrid, feverish plains ? Was it also tortured by unsatisfied love ? Did the selfsame melody ring through that distant world in the silences of space ? Was it visited by the same languor, the same infinite desire? Sometimes, almost as though speaking to himself, the young Gotama put these questions to his friends, his teachers, or his parents. His friends laughed and replied: "What does it matter to us?" The Brahman who taught him said: "Perhaps the wise ascetics may know." His parents sighed: "Brahma does not wish us to ask about these things."

In accordance with custom Gotama married, and his wife bore him a child named Rahula. But even this could not dissipate his griefs, or change the course of his thoughts. He was deeply moved by the love of his young wife and innocent child, but what could the caress of a woman or the smile of a babe do for this soul tortured by the sorrows of the world? He only became conscious, with a greater anguish, of the fate that bound him to universal suffering, and the desire to free himself grew ever more acute.

Tradition has gathered up into one episode the influences that forced Gotama to a decision. It recounts that one day when out walking he saw an aged man, a beggar stricken with plague, and a corpse. The sight of the decrepit and tottering old man, the tortured, dying beggar, and the decomposing corpse, was like a lightning flash that revealed to him the inevitable end of all life, and the deepest cause of human misery. It was then that he resolved to renounce the crown, and to leave for ever his palace and his wife and child, in order to dedicate himself to an ascetic life. This legend condenses into one dramatic scene the experiences and reflections of many years. But the examples it gives are striking; they paint a character, and illumine the motives of a whole life. A Pali document dating from about a hundred years after the death of Buddha represents him as saying to his disciples: "The man of every-day, the foolish man, experiences disgust and horror at the sight of old age. He knows that it will overtake him, but he adds, 'It does not concern me.' In thinking of this, I felt all the courage of youth die away within me." The fact is that in all the teachings of Buddha, and in all Buddhist literature, old age, sickness and death recur ceaselessly as the three typical examples of humanity's inevitable ills.

Gotama was twenty-nine years of age when he took the definite step of leaving his father's palace and breaking away from his past life, in order to seek deliverance in solitude and truth in meditation. Tradition tells us in simple and touching words of his silent farewells to his wife and child. "Before leaving, he thought of his new-born son. 'I must see my child.' He went to his wife's chamber and found her sleeping. stretched upon a flower-strewn couch, her hand resting on the infant's head. Gotama thought, 'If I remove my wife's hand, to lift up the child, I shall awaken her. When I am Buddha I will come again to see my son.' Outside, his horse Khantaka awaited him, and the king's son rode away unseen. He fled far from his wife and child, that he might find peace for his own soul, for the world, and for the gods, and behind him there moved, shadow-like, Mâra the Tempter, lying in wait for the hour when a thought of desire or of injustice should arise in this soul fighting for salvation, a thought that would give him power over this detested enemy." [1]

II.—*Solitude and Illumination*

The royal heir to the Sakyas had now become a wanderer upon the high-roads, yellow-robed, and with shaven head, a beggar through the villages, wooden bowl in hand. He went first to the highest Brahmans, requesting them to show him the way to truth; but their abstract and complicated statements concerning the origin of the world and the doctrine of identity with God did not satisfy him. These guardians of the ancient tradition of the Rishis were, however, able to teach him certain methods of breathing and meditation necessary for the attainment of perfect concentration, and these he used later in his spiritual exercises. He then spent several years with five Jaïn ascetics, [2] who took him to their school in the Maghada region, on the banks of a river where there was a beautiful bathing-place. But after a lengthy submission to their rigid discipline, he realised that it led to nothing, and thereupon informed them that in future he would indulge in no more useless mortifications, but was resolved to seek the truth through his own strength and in solitary meditation. The fanatic visionaries, proud of their haggard faces and emaciated bodies, rose in disdain on hearing this, and left him alone on the river-bank.

Then Gotama doubtless experienced that ecstasy of solitude in the morning freshness of virgin nature, described in a Buddhist poem : " When my eye perceives no one, either before or behind me, it is sweet to be alone in the forest. There life is joyous for the solitary monk who aspires to perfection. Alone, without companions, in the kindly forest, when shall I have attained the end ? When shall I be free from sin ? " And the evening found him in the same spot, seated cross-legged beneath the tree of meditation, with its hundred thousand rustling leaves. " On the

---

[1] Summary of the legend given by Oldenberg.

[2] The Jaïns (whose name means *conquerors*) were a sect of fanatical ascetics. They existed in the South of India long before Buddhism, with which they had much in common.

bank of the river, bordered with flowers, garlanded with forests, the monk sits joyfully, wrapped in meditation ; there is no greater joy for him." A shepherd, fascinated by the serious air and benevolent atmosphere of the young ascetic, brought him milk and bananas each day. A gazelle, attracted by his gentleness, came and ate grains of rice from his hand. He was almost happy.

But his thoughts plunged desperately into the infinite spiral of the inner world. By day, he meditated rigorously and intensely upon himself and others, upon the origin of evil and the supreme object of life. He sought to find a clue to the fatality of human destinies by means of keen and pitiless reasoning. But what doubts, what chasms, what fathomless gulfs ! By night he let himself drift out upon the ocean of dream, and his sleep became more and more transparent. It was as though a series of diaphanous veils were withdrawn, one by one, revealing worlds beyond worlds. First, his own life was unrolled backwards, in successive images. Then he saw and recognised himself in another form, with other passions, as though in another existence. And behind the veils unknown forms appeared, strange and enigmatic, and seemed to call him. . . . " O limitless kingdom of sleep and dreams," thought Gotama, " are you the under-side of the world, containing all the hidden sources of things ? Are you the reverse of the embroidered fabric, behind which unknown powers guide the threads out of which are woven all beings and objects that form the ever-moving picture of this vast universe ? "—He resumed his meditations without being able to link together the currents of this multiform chaos. Tradition says that he practised his exercises in concentration for seven years before illumination came to him. It came at last in the form of a series of ecstasies during sleep, and we must follow carefully the psychic phenomena which legend has condensed into four ecstatic nights ; for from their special character and interpretation has sprung the doctrine of the Buddha and the whole of Buddhism.

During the first night, Gotama entered the region called in India *Kama-loka*, the place of desire. This is the *Amenti* of Egypt, the *Hades* of the Greeks, the *Purgatory* of Christians. It is the sphere, or the psychic state, called astral by Western occultists ; the *sphere of penetrability*, a dark and nebulous chaos. Here he was first attacked by all sorts of animal forms, serpents, deer, and others ; and as his mind became clear he realised that these were his own passions, passions from former lives, which took shape in his soul and assailed him. When he advanced upon them they were dissipated by the power of his will. Then he saw his wife, whom he had loved and left. He saw her holding his child towards him, her breasts bare, her eyes filled with tears of longing and despair. Was it the spirit of his still living wife, who thus appealed to him in sleep? Overwhelmed by love and pity, he would have embraced her, but she fled with a heart-rending cry that echoed through his soul. Next he was surrounded by whirling clouds of dead souls, still torn by the passions of earth—flying shadows that pursued their prey, flung themselves upon it without being able to grasp it, and sank breathless into unfathomable depths. He saw criminals, haunted by the pain they had inflicted, themselves tormented until the horror of the deed had killed the culpable will, until the tears of the murderer had washed away the blood of the victim. This desolate place was indeed a hell, for in it souls were tossed from fires of unquenchable desire to icy darknesses of anguish. Sakya-Muni thought he beheld the prince of this kingdom, whom the poets depict as Kama, god of desire, only instead of purple robe, crown of flowers, and eyes smiling behind a bent bow, he was wrapped in a shroud, with ashes on his head and an empty skull in his hand. Kama had become Mâra, god of death.

When Sakya-Muni awoke after his first night of initiation, his body was bathed in a cold sweat. His dear companion, the tame gazelle, had fled. Was she afraid of the shadows through which her master had been passing? Had she sensed the presence of the King of Death? Gotama remained beneath the tree of meditation with its hundred thousand rustling leaves, too exhausted to move, until the watchful shepherd came to revive him with a cocoanut shell filled with foaming milk.

During the second night the solitary dreamer entered the world of happy souls. Before his closed eyes there passed a vision of enchanted countries, aërial islands, magical gardens, where the flowers and trees, the scented air, the birds, the sky, the stars, the gauzy clouds, seemed to caress the soul and speak a language of love, moulding themselves into significant forms to express human thoughts or divine symbols. He saw radiant beings wandering about in couples, absorbed in one another, or lying in groups at the feet of a Master; and the bliss that streamed from their looks, their voices, their attitudes, seemed as though rained down from some higher world that hovered above them, a world to which they now and then stretched out their arms, and which seemed to unite them all in one celestial harmony. But suddenly Gotama saw some of these beings turn pale and shudder, and he then perceived that each one was attached to the lower world by an almost invisible thread, so that a whole network of threads passed downwards through a purple cloud which hung above the abyss. And as this purple cloud rose upwards, it thickened, while the aërial paradise grew paler. Then Gotama divined the meaning of his vision. He understood that those subtle threads were indestructible bonds, the remains of human passions, inextinguishable desires, which drew these happy souls back to earth and forced them sooner or later into new incarnations. Alas, what a perspective of new farewells after the heavenly reunion, of new dispersals, new labyrinths of trial and suffering —and perhaps, after all, eternal separation !

When he awoke after his second night, a flight of swans was crossing the cloudy sky, and he felt still sadder after his paradisal dream than after his visit to the infernal regions. For he thought of the future destinies of all these souls, and of their endless wanderings.

On the third night he rose by a supreme effort to the world of the gods. Would he now at last find the peace he longed for ? It was a vision of unspeakable glory, a panorama of indescribable sublimity. He saw first the luminous archetypes which light up the threshold of the divine world—circles, triangles, flaming stars, patterns for the material universe. Then there appeared to him the cosmic powers, the gods, who have no fixed shape, but who work in multiformity in all the worlds. He saw wheels of fire, whirlwinds of light and darkness, stars that were transformed into winged lions, gigantic eagles, or radiant heads rising from vast oceans of flames. From these, appearing and disappearing, changing and multiplying with the rapidity of lightning, there seemed to flow luminous currents which flooded through the whole universe, encircling the planets and giving shape and form to all beings. But as the seer plunged ecstatically into all this ardent life, he heard suddenly the sorrowful cry of humanity rising from the depths, an ever-swelling chorus of desperate entreaty. Then he discovered a thing that seemed terrible to him. This lower world, this world of struggle and pain, had been created by the gods ! Further, they had grown, they had attained self-consciousness, by means of their universe ; and now, floating above it, but inseparable from its essence, they drew life from the reflux of its forces ! Yes, the immortal gods were clothed in the fire and light that had issued from their hearts ; but for man this fire had become passion, this light, anguish. They fed upon the flame of the human love that they had awakened ; they breathed the perfume of its adorations, the smoke of its torments. They drank these seas of souls filled with sorrow and desire, as the tempest drinks the foam of ocean. They, too, were guilty ! And as the dreamer's vision embraced wider, vaster perspectives of space and time, as his spirit fled from age to age, he seemed to see these gods overwhelmed in the final collapse of their worlds, sunken into cosmic sleep, forced to die and to be reborn, they also, from eternity to eternity, while ever creating new worlds doomed to suffering.

The whole universe now seemed to Gotama like a frightful wheel to which are bound all living beings, together with men and gods. There seemed no way of escape from the inevitable law which caused the wheel to turn. From life to life, from incarnation to incarnation, all beings vainly recommence the same adventure, and are pitilessly beaten down by sorrow and death. Behind them extends the immeasurable past, before them the immeasurable future, throughout an infinite series of existences. Innumerable world-periods roll by through myriads of years. Earths, heavens and hells are born and disappear, arise and are swept away, throughout eternity. How can this wheel be escaped from? How can the torture of living be ended?

From this vision the dreamer awoke dizzy with horror. All night long a north wind had been blowing upon the tree of knowledge with its hundred thousand rustling leaves. The day dawned palely, and a cold rain was falling. The gazelle had returned, and was gently licking Gotama's icy feet. He touched her; she, too, was frozen. And then he took her in his arms, to warm her against his heart, and for a time sought refuge from the sorrows of the world in caressing a little gazelle.

Gotama was not in the habit of praying. He expected nothing from the gods, but everything from himself and his meditations. He did not accuse the gods, or feel any resentment; he enfolded them in his great compassion. Were they not also caught up in the fatal illusion of universal desire, tortured by the uncontrollable thirst for being and living? How should they, who could not save themselves, be able to save men? Nevertheless, before his fourth night, Sakya-Muni, overwhelmed with anguish, prayed to the Unnameable, the Unmanifest, to Him Whom no eye may behold, to reveal to him the secret of happiness and of eternal rest.

On falling asleep, he saw again the terrible wheel of existence, like a dark circle peopled by human myriads. It turned slowly, indefatigably. Here and there, some few valiant strugglers emerged from the circle of darkness into the surrounding halo of light. These were the wise men, the ascetics, the Boddhisatvas of former ages. But none of them had attained to genuine repose, to true salvation, for all had fallen back into the shadow, all had been reclaimed by the fatal wheel. Then Sakya-Muni experienced the greatest of his agonies, a breaking-up of his whole being and of the whole world of appearances; but this disruption was followed by an ineffable rapture. He seemed to be plunged in a deep sea of silence and peace; no more form, no more light, no more eddying of the forces of life. His soul was absorbed into the sleeping soul of the world, unstirred by any breath; his consciousness was dissolved in an immensity of bliss. He had attained Nirvana.

If he had had the will to go further, and the strength to raise himself above this cosmic sleep, he would have heard, seen and felt many more things. He would have heard the primordial Sound, the divine speech which gives birth to light; he would have heard the Music of the Spheres to which the stars and planets dance. Borne on the waves of this harmony, he would have beheld the splendour of the spiritual Sun, the Creative Word. There, the supreme desire of love is identical with the burning joy of sacrifice. There, one is above all while passing through all, for one sees the river of time issue from eternity and return to it. There one is separated from nothing, but united to all things in the plenitude of being; one rises above all sorrows by helping to transform them into joys. All sufferings dissolve into a single bliss, as the colours of the prism into the sunbeam. Repose is attained through transcendent action, and supreme personality through the absolute gift of self. Life is no longer condemned, because the divine essence has been tasted at its source. Completely liberated, and henceforward invulnerable, one re-enters it in order to re-create it in greater beauty. From this sphere of resurrection, foreshadowed in the wisdom of Egypt, and in the Eleusinian mysteries, the Christ was to descend.

But it was not Gotama's destiny to teach the world the word of Creative Love. Nevertheless, his rôle was a great one, for he was to reveal the religion of compassion, and the law which links together human incarnations. His initiation ceased at the *Mystic Death*, without attaining to the *Resurrection*. Nirvana, which has often been held to be the supreme state of divinity, is only the threshold—a threshold which Gotama had not crossed.[1]

After the fourth night of illumination, tradition tells us that Gotama was filled with great joy; a new strength flooded through

---

[1] I have tried here to place *Nirvana* in its right order in the psychic phenomena of initiation. This is essential to an understanding of the Buddha, of his doctrine, and of his rôle in the world. The worth of any initiate, reformer or prophet, depends in the first place on a direct and intensive vision of truth. His doctrine is never anything other than a rational explanation of this phenomenon of initiation, which always takes the form of spiritual revelation or inspiration. *Nirvana* appears to be the last stage but one of the major initiations, divined by Persia, Egypt and Greece, accomplished by the Christ. What Buddhism calls extinction, or the end of illusion, is only an intermediate psychic state, the toneless, formless, neuter phase which precedes the outpouring of supreme truth. But it is a great thing, a great achievement, to have completely realised in life all the phases of initiation, as did the Buddha; and as the Christ was also to realise them, while crowning them with the Resurrection.

his veins and inspired him with courage. He felt that, having attained Nirvana, he was for ever delivered from all evil; that, having bathed in death as in the waters of Styx, he was rendered invincible. From head to foot, from the marrow of his bones to the height of his soul, he now had become the *Buddha*, the *Awakened One*. Having attained truth, he desired to save the world; but he first spent several days in reflecting on his experiences. He saw how his visions were logically linked up one to another, and formulated his doctrines by contemplating in spirit the connected series of causes and effects which lead to suffering. "From not-knowing come forms (*sankara*), forms of thought which give form to things. From forms consciousness is born, and thus, by a long series of intermediary processes, from the desires of the senses attachment to existence is born; from attachment becoming is born; from becoming, birth; from birth, old age and death, sorrow and despair, pain and grief. But if the first cause, not-knowing, is suppressed, all the chain of effects is destroyed, and at the same time evil is conquered." In fine, desire must be killed in order to suppress life, and the evil thus cut down at its root. That all men should enter into Nirvana was the dream of Buddha, and, knowing now what he had to say to the Brahmans and the people, he left his retreat and bent his steps to Benares, in order to preach his gospel there.

III.—*Temptation*

Like all prophets, Buddha had still one trial to go through before beginning his task. There has never been a reformer who has not passed through the temptation to doubt himself, before openly attacking the reigning powers. Obstacles rise up before him like a mountain, and the labour which will be spread over many years takes on the semblance of a rock that has to be rolled uphill. Legend tells us that Mâra the Tempter whispered to him: " Enter into Nirvana, perfected man; the time of Nirvana is come for you." Buddha replied: " I shall not enter into Nirvana until holiness is spread abroad among the people, and preached to all men." A Brahman then approached him and said disdainfully: " A layman cannot be a Brahman." Buddha replied: " The true Brahman is he who has banished all wickedness, spitefulness and impurity from himself." When men could not prevail against the Blessed One, the elements joined in. Torrential rain, cold, tempest and darkness combined against him. This conspiracy of the elements represents the last furious assault of the passions that he had expelled, and that now fell upon him together with the outer powers from which they emanated. In order to explain this occult happening, legend makes use of a symbol, as follows : " At this moment Mukalinda, the king of the serpents, comes forth from his hiding-place and winds himself seven times around the body of the Buddha, to protect him from the storm. After seven days, when Mukalinda saw that the sky was clear and cloud-less once more, he uncoiled his rings, took the form of a young man, and approached the Buddha with hands clasped in adoration. Then the Blessed One said : " Happy the solitude of him who has seen and recognised the truth.' " The serpent Mukalinda here represents 'the astral body[1] of man, the organ of feeling, which interpenetrates his physical body and creates around him a radiant aura in which his passions are reflected in many colours. During sleep the astral body escapes from the physical with the conscious self, in the form of a spiral. It then resembles a serpent. In the astral body all human passions dwell and vibrate, and through it all influences, good or bad, act upon the human being. By ruling and organising it, the initiate, or saint, can transform it into an invulner-able cuirass against all attacks from without. This is the meaning of the serpent Mukalinda coiling himself around the body of the Buddha, and protecting him from the tempest of passions. But there is another meaning also. At a certain stage of initiation, the aspirant sees an astral image of the lower, animal part of his nature, which has been evolved through previous incarnations, and he has to look upon this and kill it by the power of thought. Other-wise it is impossible for him to enter into the astral world, much less into the spiritual and divine worlds. This apparition is called in occult tradition " The Guardian of the Threshold." Much later, after long trials and brilliant victories, the initiate meets his divine prototype, the image of his higher self, in an ideal form ; and that is why the serpent Mukalinda is changed into a beautiful youth as soon as the onslaught of the lower world has been repelled.

IV.—The Buddhist Community and its Teaching. The Death of Buddha.

Buddha began to preach at Benares. He first converted five monks who became his fervent disciples, and these he sent away later to preach his doctrine in distant parts, saying to them : " You are delivered from all bonds. Go out into the world for the salvation of the people, for the joy of men and gods." Soon

---

[1] Paracelsus gave it this name—which has been adopted by Western occultism—because it has a magnetic relationship with the stars of our solar system.

afterwards, a thousand Brahmans, who practised the sayings of the Vedas and the fire-sacrifice, and performed their ablutions in the river Neranjara, declared themselves on his side. Crowds soon followed. Pupils left their masters for him. Kings and queens arrived mounted on elephants, and offered him homage and friend-ship. The courtesan Ambapâli presented him with a forest of mango-trees. The young king Bimbisâra was converted, and be-came a mendicant monk, and his chief protector. For forty years the Buddha taught, without the Brahmans putting the slightest hindrance in his way. His life was divided up each year into a period of wandering and a period of repose—nine months of travel, three months of rest. "When after the burning heat of June, the clouds are piled up as in towers, and the breath of the monsoon announces coming rain, the Hindu retires for weeks into his hut or his palace. Communications are interrupted by floods and swollen rivers. 'The birds,' says an old Buddhist book, 'build their nests in the tops of the trees.' So lived the monks for three months. During the nine months of wandering, Buddha found shelter in gardens and parks, in palaces and in merchants' houses. For nourishment, mangoes and bananas were never lack-ing ; but this did not prevent these contemners of the goods of this world from observing their vow of poverty and leading their mendicant life. Every morning they made their round of the vil-lage, led by the Master. Silently, with lowered eyes, and wooden bowls in hand, they asked for alms. They blessed those who gave and those who gave not. In the afternoon, deep in the quiet forest or alone in his cell, the Blessed One meditated in Sacred silence."[1]

In this way the Buddhist sect increased. In many places groups of monks were formed under the direction of the Master, and later became rich monasteries. Around these there grew up lay com-munities which, without adopting the monastic life, saw in it their ideal, and took the monks for teachers. The writings which give us these facts in cold, reasoned sentences, entirely fail to convey the eloquence of the Buddha, the charm of his person, the magnet-ism of his powerful will, clothed in imperturbable sweetness and perfect serenity ; neither do they render the strange fascination that he knew how to throw into his mysterious evocations of Nir-vana. He would first desscribe the life of the senses as a stormy sea, with its waves, its unfathomable depths, its monsters—a sea on which are tossed to and fro the frail barques that are called human souls. Then he would gradually lead his hearers to a calmer region, where the waves are stilled. On the smooth and motionless surface is outlined a circular current, which sinks downwards in

---

[1] Oldenberg's *Life of Buddha*.

the shape of a funnel, and at its deepest point there shines a brilliant star. Happy are those who enter this circle and descend to the depths, for they find themselves in another world, far from sea and storm. What lies beyond the gulf, beyond the brilliant star? The Master affirms that it is the supreme beatitude, and adds : " I come from there. That which has not been for myriads of years has now happened. I bring it to you."

Tradition has preserved the sermon at Benares, which is Buddha's Sermon on the Mount. In it we may perhaps find a distant echo of his living speech. "You call me friend, but you do not give me my true name. I am the Delivered One, the Blessed One, the Buddha. Open your ears. Deliverance from death has been found. I instruct you. I teach you the doctrine If you live according to the doctrine, you will soon find what those young men seek who leave their homes to become wanderers ; you will attain the perfection of holiness. You will recognise the truth in this life, and see it face to face. Not mortification, but renunciation of the pleasures of the senses. The Middle Way leads to knowledge, to illumination, to Nirvana. The Eight-fold Path is called : Right Doctrine, Right Purpose, Right Discourse, Right Action, Right Living, Right Aspiration, Right Thought, Right Meditation. This, O monks, is the sacred truth concerning the origin of suffering : it is the lust for life, from rebirth to rebirth, the lust for pleasure, for becoming, for power. This, O monks, is the sacred truth concerning the cessation of suffering : the suppression of lust by the destruction of desire—putting it outside one's self, freeing one's self from it, leaving no place for it. This, O monks, is the sacred truth concerning the cessation of suffering."

Sakya-Muni, being now in possession of the four essential truths—namely, suffering, the origin of suffering, the cessation of suffering, and the way of cessation—is able to declare that in the worlds of Brahma and of Mâra, among all beings, ascetics and Brahmans, gods and men, he has attained to perfect felicity, and to the noble rank of Buddha. His whole career, his teaching, and all Buddhist literature, sacred and profane, form but a perpetual and varied commentary on the sermon at Benares. It is a doctrine of a rigorously moral nature, characterised by an imperious gentleness and a devout hopelessness. It preaches a fanatical repose, and might be called a pacifist conspiracy for hastening the end of the world. It has neither metaphysic, nor cosmogony, nor mythology, nor prayer, nor worship ; nothing but moral meditation. Solely preoccupied with putting an end to suffering and attaining Nirvana, Buddha distrusts all else. He distrusts the gods, because these unfortunate beings have created the world. He distrusts earthly life because it is the matrix of reincarnation. He distrusts the

Beyond because it still has life, and consequently suffering. He distrusts the soul because of its unassuageable thirst for immortality. The next life is, in his eyes, another mode of seduction, a spiritual indulgence, and though he knows, from his own experiences when in ecstasy, that this life exists, he refuses to speak of it. It would be too dangerous. His disciples ply him with questions on this point, but he is inflexible. "Does the soul live on after death?" they cry in chorus. No reply. "Must the soul then die also?" No reply. When Ananda, his favourite pupil, is alone with him, he demands the reason for this silence. Buddha answers: "It would be harmful to reply in one sense, or in another;" and guards his secret. A monk who is shrewder and more of a logician than the others one day brings forward an acute and courageous argument. "O Blessed One," he says, "thou sayest that the soul is but a compound of vile and ephemeral sensations. How then can the self, which passes from one incarnation to another, be influenced by the not-self?" Without doubt the Buddha would have found it difficult to reply to this question, worthy of Socrates or Plato. He contents himself by saying: "O monk, at this moment thou art swayed by concupiscence."

If Buddha distrusted the gods and the soul, he distrusts women still more. In this, as in all else, he is the antithesis of Krishna, the apostle of the Eternal-Feminine. He knows that love is the strongest of life's allurements, and that woman, like a coffer of philters and perfumes, contains the quintessence of all seductions within herself. He knows that Brahma only decided to create the gods and the world after he had drawn forth from himself the Eternal-Feminine, the many-coloured veil of Maya containing the images of all living things. He suspects in woman not only the fever of the senses which she can excite with a look or a smile, but also her arsenal of lies and subterfuges, which are the warp and the woof used by nature to weave the web of life. "The essence of woman," he says, "is deeply hidden like the movements of a fish in the water." "How are we to act towards woman?" asked Ananda. "Avoid her." "But if we see her, nevertheless?" "Do not speak to her." "And if we must speak to her nevertheless, what shall we do?" "In that case, guard yourselves!" After long hesitation, however, Buddha allowed the founding of convents for women, but he never admitted then into intimacy, and seldom into his presence. We find in his life-story neither Mary Magdalene nor Mary of Bethany.[1] In justice and honour to Indian women, it

---

[1] It may be noted here that there are different opinions concerning the Buddha's attitude towards women, and that the Pali scriptures—in spite of having been rigorously edited by monks—contain a number of references to women who obviously looked upon Gotama as their guide, benefactor and beloved friend.

must be added that the charitable institutions of the Buddhist faith were very largely due to them.

How are we to explain the prodigious success of this religion, this doctrine shorn of the joys of both earth and heaven? It was a doctrine of implacable moral law, as excessive in its mystical nihilism as in its negative positivism; it suppressed the castes and the traditional faith in the authority of the Vedas; it abolished the impressive rites of Brahmanism, and substituted hundreds of monasteries and an army of mendicant monks overrunning India with their wooden begging-bowls. Its success can, however, be explained by the premature degeneracy of India, and by the corruption of the Aryan race, mingled with inferior elements and enfeebled by idleness. It can be explained by the sadness of a people growing old between the lassitude of tyranny and the lassitude of slavery; a people without historical perspective or national unity, having lost the desire for action and having never experienced the sense of individuality save in the Vedic times when the white race ruled in all its purity and strength.[1] Further, it must be added that the temporary triumph of Buddhism in India is due less to its philosophy than to its moral teaching, to that serious labour upon the inner life which it inculcated in its disciples. " Step by step, bit by bit, hour by hour, the sage must purify himself as the goldsmith purifies gold."* The Self, to which Buddhist metaphysics denies reality, here becomes the principal agent. To find the Self becomes the object of all seeking. To have the Self for friend is the truest and highest form of friendship. For the Self is the protection of the Self. It must be curbed as the merchant curbs his prancing horse. From this austere discipline there emerges at last a feeling of liberty which

---

Vāsitthī, Sundarī and Patākārā are only three of those mentioned in the *Therī-gāthā* (*Psalms of the Sisters*), while in the *Vinaya* the laywoman Visākhā is shown conversing with him. In another place we find Gotama saying to the king of Kosala, who is disappointed at having heard of the birth of a daughter, that this may be a happier event for him than a son's birth—a most unusual suggestion to have been made in early times in India. The reported conversation with Ananda is taken as a semi-humorous episode by Dr. Annie Besant (in *Four Great Religions*, p. 107-8). " It is not difficult," she says, " to picture the scene between the anxious disciple and the gentle, slightly amused Master. . . . ' But if they should speak to us, Lord, what are we to do?' ' Keep wide awake, Ananda, keep wide awake! ' "—See also *The Light of Asia* (Sir Edwin Arnold) for other references to the Buddha's intercourse with women, and his unfailingly gentle and friendly attitude towards them. (Tr.)

[1] We know that Buddhism only endured for about four centuries in India. Except in Ceylon, it practically disappeared in a revival of Brahmanism, which was able to vanquish it without persecution, and to absorb its main elements while renewing its own vitality. We know also that if Buddhism was propagated in Thibet, Mongolia and China, this was only accomplished by re-admitting many of the metaphysical and mythological elements that Buddha had rejected, and by considerably modifying its teachings.

is expressed with all the charm of a St. Francis of Assisi : " We must have need only of what we ourselves can carry, even as the bird has no need of treasure, and carries only his wings which bear him whithersoever he wills." Indeed, through his gentleness of spirit, Buddha was truly the creator of a religion of pity and the inspirer of a new poetry. This is shown in the parables attributed to him, and in the later legends of Buddhism. What a subtle and suggestive metaphor, for instance, is used to express the different degrees of spiritual evolution : " As in a pool of white and blue lotus-lilies there are many under the water and many above the water, so there are many diverse souls, some pure, others impure. The sage is he who rises above the water and lets his wisdom rain down upon other souls, even as the unfolded lotus scatters its dewdrops upon the flowers that float upon the surface of the river."

At the age of eighty years, when the Buddha was in one of his summer retreats, he fell ill, and knew that death was near. But he thought of his disciples. " It is not fitting," he said, " that I should enter into Nirvana without having spoken to those who have cared for me. I must conquer this illness, and retain the life in my body." And the illness of the Blessed One departed, and he went and seated himself in the shade of the house that had been prepared for him. His favourite disciple, Ananda, ran to him and told him of his fear, adding : " I knew that the Blessed One would not enter into Nirvana without having made his will known to the community of the disciples." " What does the community desire ? " said Buddha. " I have preached the doctrine. I do not wish to rule over the community, Ananda. Let the truth be your beacon-light. He who now and after my death is his own torch and his own refuge, he who seeks no refuge other than the truth, and walks in the straight path, he is my disciple."

And Buddha rose, joined the other disciples, and took the road with them, desiring to walk and to teach up till the end. He sojourned for a while at Vesala, but at Kosinara his strength abandoned him. They stretched him upon a mat beneath two tall trees, and there he lay like a weary lion. The disciple Ananda, whom he loved, unable to bear the sight, went into the house and wept. Buddha guessed his sorrow, and sent for him, and said : " Do not complain, Ananda. Have I not told thee that one has to leave all that one loves ? How would it be possible for that which is born and made ephemeral to escape destruction ? But thou, Ananda, hast long honoured the Perfected One ; thou hast been full of love towards him, full of kindness and joy, without falsehood, without cessation, in thoughts, words and deeds. Thou hast done well, Ananda. Now make an effort, and thou shalt soon be free from sin." Shortly before he expired, the Buddha said : " Perhaps you will have this thought, Ananda : the truth has lost its master, we no longer have a master. You must not think so. The Doctrine and the Order that I have given you will be your master when I am gone." His last words were : " Courage, my disciples. I say to you, all that lives shall perish. Strive without ceasing."[1]

Night fell ; and the face and body of the Sublime One shone as though they were becoming transparent. This mysterious shining continued until his last breath, and then was suddenly extinguished. At the same moment, a rain of flowers fell from the trees upon the Buddha who had entered into Nirvana.

The women of Kosinara now came and begged to be allowed to see the Blessed One. Their wish was granted by Ananda, despite the protests of the other disciples, and they knelt beside the body and wept over the Master who, in life, had banished them from his presence.

These details, handed down by tradition concerning the death of the Buddha, perhaps reveal more clearly what took place in the depths of his consciousness, and in that of his disciples, than do their actual last words. The void of Nirvana became marvellous to them, swept as by a wave from the Invisible. The cosmic powers which Sakya-Muni had avoided or fought against as dangerous temptations of Desire, the forces that he had jealously banished from his doctrine and his community, the flowers of Hope and Light, the Eternal-Feminine, the unwearying weavers of earthly and heavenly life, haunted him in his last hour. Subtle, insinuating, irresistible, they came and lightly touched the soul of the redoubtable ascetic, telling him that he had neither suppressed nor vanquished them.

V.—Conclusions.

It is easy to criticise Buddhism from the philosophical point of view. A religion without God, a morality without metaphysics, it builds no bridge between the finite and the infinite, between time and eternity, between man and the universe. To find such a bridge is man's supremest need, and the whole *raison d'être* of religion and philosophy. According to Buddha, the world proceeds from a blind and mischievous desire for life. How then can the harmony of the Cosmos be explained, and the inextinguishable desire for perfection innate in the human spirit ?

---

[1] This is noble and stoical, but how much nobler are the words of the Christ : " Behold I am with you always, even unto the end of the world."

That is the metaphysical contradiction. Again, Buddha teaches that from day to day, from year to year, from incarnation to incarnation, the human ' self ' strives for perfection through the conquest of passion, but he allows it no transcendent reality, no immortal value. How then can this perpetual striving be explained ? That is the psychological contradiction. Finally, Buddha offers to humanity, for sole aim and ideal, Nirvana—a purely negative conception, the cessation of evil through the cessation of consciousness. Is this *saltus mortalis*, this leap into the void of nothingness, worth the immensity of the effort required ? That is the moral contradiction. These three contradictions, which fit logically into one another, are sufficient indication of the weakness of Buddhism as a cosmic system.

It is none the less true that Buddhism has had a strong influence upon the west. In every epoch when philosophy and religion are passing through a crisis—in the Alexandrine period, in that of the Renaissance, and in our own—Europe has heard faint echoes of Buddhist thought. What gives it this power—its moral doctrine and its conclusions ? Not at all—but rather the fact that Buddha was the first to divulge openly the doctrine of which the Brahmans had only spoken in whispers, and which they had kept hidden in the secrecy of their temples. This doctrine is the true mystery of India, the arcanum of her ancient wisdom. I refer to the doctrine of the plurality of existences, and the mystery of reincarnation.

In a very ancient Upanishat we read that a Brahman said to one of his colleagues, in an assembly : " Where does man go after death ? " " Give me thy hand," was the reply. " We alone must know that. Not a word to the others." And they then spoke of reincarnation. This passage proves that at one time the doctrine was considered esoteric by the Brahmans, and with good reason. If there is no truth which penetrates more deeply into the secrets of nature and the processes of universal evolution, there is also none which is more susceptible to vulgar abuse. To illustrate the peculiar fascination which this mystery has exercised in all ages upon eager and thoughtful minds, I will here relate an old Hindu legend.

In very ancient times, says this legend, a heavenly nymph, an *apsara*, wishing to seduce an ascetic who had shown himself proof against all the temptations of earth and heaven, had recourse to an ingenious stratagem. This ascetic lived in a dense virgin forest, on the banks of a pool covered with many kinds of aquatic plants. When apparitions, celestial or infernal, floated above the pool to tempt the solitary man, he lowered his eyes so that he might see only their reflections in the water. These reversed and distorted images of nymphs or demons calmed his senses, and restored the harmony of his troubled spirit, for they showed him what would be the consequences of a descent into the mire of matter.

The cunning *apsara* therefore thought she would conceal herself in a flower. From the depths of the pool she caused a marvellous lotus to arise; but it was not a lotus like others. These, as one knows, close their petals under the water at night, and only emerge when caressed by the sun. But this lotus was invisible by day. At night, when the rosy light of the moon shone upon the pool through the tangled branches of the trees, the glassy surface of the water might have been seen to tremble, and from the darkness below there arose a giant lotus of dazzling whiteness, having a thousand leaves, and as large as a basket of roses. From its golden calyx, shimmering in the moonbeams, there emerged the divine *apsara*, pearly and luminous. Above her head she held a star-embroidered scarf, torn from Indra's sky; and the ascetic, who had resisted all the other *apsaras* descended directly from heaven, succumbed to the charms of this one who, born of a flower, seemed to have risen from the depths, and to be a daughter of both heaven and earth. Thus, even as the heavenly nymph springs from the opening lotus-petals, so, in the doctrine of reincarnation, does the human soul spring from thousand-petalled nature, as the last and most perfect expression of divine thought.

The Brahmans also said to their disciples : Even as the universe is the product of divine thought which ceaselessly organises and vitalises it, so is the human body the product of the soul which develops it by means of planetary evolution, and uses it as an instrument for work and for progress. The animal species have only a collective soul, but man has an individual soul, a consciousness, a self, a personal destiny, which is a guarantee that he shall endure. After death the soul, freed from its ephemeral sheath, lives another, wider life in spiritual realms. It returns to its own country, and sees the world from the side of light and of the gods, after having worked upon it from the side of shadow and of men. But there are few sufficiently advanced to remain indefinitely in this state which all religions call ' heaven.' After a space of time, long or short in proportion to its earthly efforts, the soul feels the need for new trials in order to travel a stage further. Hence, a new incarnation, whose conditions are determined by the qualities acquired in the previous life. This is the law of Karma, or the causal connection of lives—the consequence and the sanction of freedom, the logic and the justice of happiness and unhappiness, the reason for inequality of conditions, the organiser of individual destinies, the rhythm of the soul seeking to return to its divine source across infinity. This is the organic conception of immortality, in harmony with the laws of the Cosmos.

Then came the Buddha, a soul of finest sensitiveness, tormented by the search for the final Cause. At birth he seemed already weighed down by the burden of innumerable lives, and consumed with longing for the supreme peace. The weariness of the Brahmans, in a world that had grown stagnant, was augmented in his case by a new emotion—an immense pity for all men and a desire to tear them from the grip of suffering. Moved by sublime generosity, he desired the salvation of all beings. But his wisdom did not equal the grandeur of his spirit, and his courage was not as great as his vision. An incomplete initiation caused him to see the world through a veil of darkness, and to recognise in it only pain and evil. Neither God, nor the universe, nor the soul, nor love, nor beauty, found favour in his eyes. He dreamed of overwhelming for ever these creators of illusion and suffering, in the vastness of his Nirvana. Despite the excessive severity of his moral discipline, and although the pity that he preached established a bond of universal brotherhood among men, his work was partially negative and destructive. This is proved by the history of Buddhism. Socially and artistically it has had no fruitful results. Where it is wholly accepted, it engenders passivity, indifference and discouragement. The Buddhist peoples have remained in a state of stagnation ; those who have displayed a surprising activity, like the Japanese, have done so through instincts and principles contrary to Buddhism The Buddha had, however, great merit and a great part to play, for he divulged the doctrine of reincarnation which, before him, had been the secret of the Brahmans. Through him it became widespread in India, and entered the universal consciousness. Although officially rejected, or at least veiled, by most religions, it has never ceased to play a lively part in the history of the human spirit. Only, what had been for the Buddha a reason for renunciation and death, became for more vigorous souls a reason for affirmation and life.

What a different guise, indeed, and what different colouring, this idea of the plurality of lives was to take on among the Aryans and Semites who later adopted it ! Whether on the banks of the Nile, at Eleusis or at Alexandria, whether among the followers of Hermes, Empedocles, Pythagoras or Plato, it was to assume a character truly heroic ; no longer the fatal wheel of Buddhism, but a proud ascension towards the light !

India holds the keys of the past, but not the keys of the future. She is the Epimetheus of the races, not their Prometheus. She has sunk into a dreamful sleep. The Aryan initiate, on the contrary, introduces into the doctrine of the plurality of existences the need for action and infinite progress which burns in his heart like the unquenchable fire of Agni. He knows that man possesses only

THE MYSTERY OF INDIA 117

the earth that he has watered with his blood and sweat ; that he attains only the heaven towards which he has aspired with his whole soul. He knows that the universe is formidable and tragic, but that victory lies with the faithful and the brave. The struggle itself is to him a pleasure ; the pain is a goad which he accepts as the price of the sublime joys of love, beauty and contemplation. He believes in the future of earth, as in the future of heaven, and he feels no fear of successive existences, because of their variety. He knows that the blue vault above conceals numberless combats, but also numberless unknown delights ; and his cosmic voyagings hold the promise of marvels greater than those of earthly travel. Finally he believes, with the Christ, in a supreme victory over evil and death, and in a transfiguration of the earth and of humanity at the end of time, through the complete manifestation of Spirit in Matter. Ancient Buddhism and contemporary pessimism affirm that all desire, all form, all life, all consciousness, are evil, and that the only refuge lies in total loss of consciousness. Their bliss is purely negative. The Aryan looks upon weariness of life as a sort of cowardice. He believes in an active bliss through the expansion of desire, and in the supreme fruitfulness of love and sacrifice. To him, ephemeral forms are messengers of divinity. He believes, thus, in the possibility of acting and creating in time while remaining conscious of eternity. Having proved and lived this possibility, his soul is like a vessel that always rides above the storm ; this is the only repose, the only divine calm, to which he aspires. To conclude, in the concept of the Aryan, the disappearance of the visible universe, called by the Indian the Sleep of Brahma, would be merely an indescribable dream, a silence of the Word withdrawn into itself in order to hear the intimate harmonies of its myriad souls, and to prepare for a new creation.

But let us not be unjust to India or to the Buddha, since they have bequeathed to us the treasure of the world's most ancient wisdom. Let us, on the contrary, render them the grateful homage that we owe to our most distant ancestors and to the first religious mysteries of our race.

When the Hindu woman mounted the funeral pyre of her husband, and the murderous flames encircled her, she would throw her necklace of pearls to her children as a last farewell. So has India in agony, seated on the tomb of her Aryan heroes, thrown to the younger West the religion of compassion and the fertile doctrine of reincarnation.

BOOK IV

MANIFESTATIONS OF THE SOLAR WORD

I

ZOROASTER

Glory to Ormuzd ! . . .
Homage to my own soul!

MANIFESTATIONS OF THE SOLAR WORD

THE Brahmanic religion and civilisation represent the first halting-place of post-Atlantean humanity, and can be summed up as follows: *the conquest of the divine world through the primordial wisdom.* The great civilisations that followed—of Persia, Chaldea, Egypt, Greece and Rome, Judo-Christianity, and finally the Celtic-Germanic world, which is still in course of evolution, and of which we form a part—illustrate the forward movement of the white race. Into all these different religions, nations and civilisations the dominating Aryan element enters, and they are linked together, as by a magnetic chain, through one idea which instinctively guides and animates them all. This idea is: *to conquer the earth by applying the Divine Revelation to life.* Such an application is not possible without a progressive weakening of the instrument through which the Divine Revelation had been made manifest, i.e., spontaneous communion with the cosmic powers called gods, and vision in the astral and spiritual worlds (which form the inner world of man and of the universe). These revealing and creative faculties had already atrophied in India, since the time when speculative philosophy began to take the place of primitive intuition, and they were to be still further obscured and obliterated in the Aryan and Semitic races of Central Asia and Europe, in proportion as the rightful faculties of the Aryan race were developed. These faculties—exact observation, analysis and reason, leading to the sense of individual liberty and independence—were indispensable to the understanding and domination of the external world. *Nevertheless the transcendent qualities of the soul are not extinguished in humanity. They are preserved by a select few who discipline and develop them in secret, hidden from all outer corruptions and profanations. This is the reason for initiation.* These few, who are self-selected and self-tested, retain the divine inspiration, but in a different form. Instead of being spread out over the whole universe and losing itself in infinity, as with the Hindus, it tends to be condensed and concentrated upon one single point, which we shall call the *Solar Word.*

The Solar Word is the Logos, giver of life to our planetary system. In glorifying the sun, the early Rishis and Vedic singers were not worshipping the physical sun only. They sensed behind it the *Spirit* that animates the royal sphere. Our solar system and the earth, its densest portion—where Spirit and Matter are at their greatest tension and give rise to the most ardent forms of life—were created by the hierarchy of cosmic powers, inspired by the infinite and incomprehensible God, so admirably described in the Book of Genesis by the term *Elohim*, signifying God-of-Gods. Nevertheless, from the very beginning, from the Saturnian period of planetary life, the Logos who specially presides over our solar system tended to manifest himself in a sovereign organism which should be, as it were, His *Word*, His *Focus*. This Spirit, this God, is the King of all the solar Genii, superior to the Archangels, Dominions, Seraphim and Thrones; at once their Inspirer and the Divine Flower of their common creation, brought to birth by them, increasing with them, and surpassing them, destined to become the human Word of the Creator, as the stars are His universal Word. Such is the Solar Word, the Cosmic Christ, the centre and pivot of earthly evolution.

This sublime Spirit—Who must not be confused with the physical sun, of which He is the spiritual quintessence—could not reveal Himself immediately or all at once to feeble humanity. He could only approach man by successive stages, for the stray beams and reflections must first be experienced before the full blinding light could be borne. The earliest races and religions dimly divined Him beyond the other gods, as the sun is seen through clouds, or a human face through ever more transparent veils. The Christ shines upon India from afar ; He flames for Zoroaster in the aureole of Ormuzd ; He burns for Hermes in the Sun of Osiris ; He speaks to Moses in the Burning Bush, and flashes, like a white meteor, through the red lightnings of Sinai. He incarnates finally in the Master Jesus, in human gentleness and divine splendour. He assumes human flesh in order to become for all mankind a Sun of Love and Resurrection.

So, step by step, the reflection becomes a beam, the beam becomes a star, the star becomes a blazing sun. The star of the wise men, which threw its rays from Central Asia to Egypt, and returned to shine above the cradle at Bethlehem, lights up three main points amid the dark multitudes of peoples who were crowded together for five thousand years between the Caspian Sea, the Persian Gulf, and the Mediterranean.

These three points were the revelation to Zoroaster in ancient Iran ; the coming together of the Babylonian magi and the prophet Daniel ; and the sublime vision of the Sun of Osiris in the crypt of Egypt—a vision which foretold the end of the absolute monarchies of the East, and the expansion of the ancient mysteries through the advent of the Christ.

These were three manifestations of the Solar Word, as well as three enormous steps in the conquest of the earth ; for they allow us to perceive on the one hand, the gradual descent of the Cosmic Christ into humanity, and, on the other, the progress of three powerful civilisations—the Persian, the Chaldean, and the Egyptian—in whom the Aryan trend towards the West continued to be shown.

ZOROASTER

Let us pass from India to Central Asia and take a bird's-eye view of the country. From far distances the mountain-ranges of Pamir and Hindu Kush are unrolled to our feet, the " roof of the world," the Gordian knot of the continent, snow-white crests and grey-green valleys. To the east and north of this mass of mountains, Persia and Afghanistan form a high plateau. Their vast expanses are austerely outlined, with a savage grandeur. Rocky valleys, green oases, and arid deserts are enclosed by these highest peaks of the world. One of the modern travellers who has most intimately felt the spirit of Persia, the Comte de Gobineau, describes the country as follows : " Nature has built up Central Asia in the form of an immense staircase, on whose summit rests, high above all other regions of the globe, the ancient cradle of our race. Between the Mediterranean, the Persian Gulf, and the Black Sea, the earth rises step by step. The provinces are supported by enormous piled-up strata, the Taurus mountains, and the heights of Luristan, while the Caucasus and Elburz mountains, and the ranges of Ispahan, form a tier still more colossal. This enormous platform, whose majestic plains spread out as far as the heights of Sulaman and Hindu Kush, is bordered on one side by Turkestan, with China beyond, and on the other by the river Indus, the frontier of a still vaster country. The dominating note of the landscape, the feeling above all others aroused by it, is one of immensity and mystery."[1]

But it also abounds in violent contrasts, which suggest the idea of struggle and resistance. After the tempestuous storms of spring, the weather from May to September is dry, and the atmosphere of a marvellous purity. The contours of the mountains, and the smallest details of the countryside, are outlined with limpid clearness in colours as pure and fresh as those of the rainbow. The summer is warm and peaceful ; the winter fierce and terrible. In the fertile valleys, oranges and pomegranates flourish, and palmtrees overshadow the springs where the gazelles come to drink ;

---

[1] *Trois Ans en Asie*, Gobineau.

while on the mountain-sides deep snow is piled, and bears and vultures haunt the great forests of oaks and cedars ; and the plains are swept by whirlwinds of dust that flee before the northern blasts.

Such was the land adopted by the early Aryans, a land where no water gushes from the arid soil save under the blows of the pick-axe, a land that yields its fruits only through strenuous ploughing and irrigation, a land where life is an eternal fight with Nature. This was the land of Zoroaster.

CHAPTER I

THE YOUTH OF ZOROASTER

SOME say that he was born in Baktria ; others say not far from Teheran. I again borrow from Gobineau a description of these majestic regions : " To the north stretched a range of mountains whose snowy, glistening summits rose to enormous heights. This was the Elburz range which unites the chains of Hindu Kush to those of Georgia, the Caucasus of India to the Caucasus of Prometheus ; and above this range, dominating it like a giant, the immense pointed dome of Mount Demavend sprang heavenwards, white from head to foot. . . . There are no details to arrest one's thought ; it is an infinitude, like the sea, a horizon of marvellous colour, a sky whose dazzling transparency neither poet nor painter could render, an undulating plain which gradually unrolls to the feet of the Elburz Mountains, and unites itself with their grandeur. From time to time spirals of dust arise, circling and mounting towards the sky, which their whirling summits appear to touch ; they rush to and fro at random, and then sink back to earth. It is a picture never to be forgotten."

At the time when the first Zoroaster was born, four or five thousand years before our era,[1] ancient Iran and Persia were inhabited by nomad tribes descended from the pure white race. Only a few of them knew the arts of ploughing and husbandry, the wheat-ear rising straight as a javelin from the earth, the golden harvests undulating like a woman's breast, the blessed sheaf, rich trophy of the harvester. The others lived a pastoral life with their herds ; but all worshipped the sun, and made the sacrifice of fire on altars of turf. They were divided up into small tribes, having lost their ancient pontiff-kings. But for many centuries

---

[1] Pliny says that Zoroaster lived a thousand years before Moses. Hermippus, who translated his writings into Greek, puts him back to four thousand years before the fall of Troy, Eudoxus to six thousand years before the death of Plato. Modern scholars declare that it is impossible to fix the date of the great Iranian prophet, author of the Zend-Avesta, but place him in any case about 2500 B.C. The date given by Pliny corresponds very closely to the approximate date suggested by modern Orientalists. But Hermippus, who was especially concerned with this subject, must have been in possession of Persian documents or traditions that are now lost. There is nothing improbable in the date of 5000 B.C., considering the prehistoric antiquity of the Aryan race.

the Turanians, from the northern plains and the Mongolian mountains, had been invading the territory of the pure Aryans. These Turanians, an inexhaustible breed, were descended from the most sturdy of the Atlanteans, thick-set, yellow-skinned men, with small, cunning eyes. They were skilled in the forging of weapons, clever horsemen, ever raiding and pillaging, and they, too, worshipped fire—not the heavenly light which illumines and unites the souls of men, but the earthly fire, defiled by impure elements, the father of dark enchantments, the fire which arouses cruel desires and bestows wealth and power. It might be said that they were in league with the demons of darkness. The whole history of the early Aryans is the history of their contests with the Turanians, whose first onslaughts caused the Aryan tribes to scatter. They fled before the yellow men mounted on black horses as before an army of devils. The most refractory took refuge in the mountains ; the others submitted to the yoke of the conquerors, and adopted their corrupt religion.

About this time there was born, in one of the tribes inhabiting the Elburz Mountains—then called Alborj—a young man of the name of Arjasp, a descendant of an ancient, royal family. His youth was spent with the tribe, hunting the buffalo and fighting the Turanians, but sometimes in the evening, in his tent, this son of an exiled king would dream of restoring the ancient throne of Yima the Powerful.[1] It was, however, only a vague dream, for he had neither men, horses nor arms. But once, some visionary madman, some ragged saint of a type that Asia has always known, had predicted that he would be a king without sceptre and without throne, a king crowned by the sun—and that was all.

One fine morning, when on a solitary expedition, Arjasp came upon a green and fertile valley surrounded by high mountain-peaks. There were cultivated fields, and in the distance an archway made of tree-trunks towered above a group of huts enclosed by a palisade. A river flowed through a carpet of tall grasses and wild-flowers. Following its course, Arjasp reached a wood of scented pine-trees, within which there lay, beneath a rock, a pool of spring water as blue as the sky above. A woman robed in white linen was kneeling by the spring and drawing water in a copper vase. Rising, she placed the vase upon her head. She was of the proud type of the Aryan mountain tribes. Her black hair was bound with a golden circlet. Under her arched brows, which met above an aquiline nose, shone eyes of an opaque

---

[1] The Indian Rama, who appears at the beginning of the Zend-Avesta under the name of Yima, and again in Persian legend as Djemchid (or Jamshýd).

blackness—eyes of impenetrable sadness, whence flashed at times a glance like blue lightning issuing from a dark cloud.

" To whom does this valley belong ? " asked the bewildered huntsman.

" Here," said the woman, " reigns the patriarch Vahumano, Guardian of the Fire and Servant of the Highest."

" And what is thy name, noble lady ? "

" I have been given the name of this spring, which is called Ardouizur, meaning ' source of light.' But be careful, stranger ! The Master has said, ' Whosoever shall drink of this water shall burn with an unassuageable thirst, and only a god can quench it.' "

For a moment the young woman's glance, vibrant as a golden arrow, rested upon the stranger. Then she turned and disappeared among the scented pines.

Hundreds of flowers, white, red, yellow and blue, bowed their starry faces above the pool. Arjasp also bent over it. He was thirsty, and took long draughts of the crystalline water out of the palm of his hand. Then he went on his way, and troubled himself no more about the adventure, though he sometimes remembered the smiling valley encircled by lofty peaks, the blue water under the perfumed pine-trees, and the black eyes of Ardouizur which flashed forth blue lightning and golden arrows.

Years passed by. Zohak, King of the Turanians, triumphed over the Aryans, and built a stone fortress at Baktria (now Balkh) on a buttress of the Hindu Kush range, to overlook the nomad tribes. Thither the king summoned all the Aryans, desiring them to recognise him as their ruler. Arjasp came with his tribe, not to submit, but to see the enemy face to face. King Zohak, wearing the skin of a lynx, was seated upon a golden throne on a hillock covered with blood-stained buffalo-hides. Around him in a wide circle stood his chiefs armed with long spears. On the one side, a little group of Aryans ; on the other, hundreds of Turanians. Behind the king, a kind of temple had been carved out of the mountain-side, like a grotto. Two enormous dragons, roughly hewn out of the porphyry rock, guarded the entrance ; and inside, a red fire burnt on a basalt altar. This fire was fed with human bones, and with the blood of bulls and scorpions, and from time to time two huge coiled serpents could be seen warming themselves at the flame. They had the feet of dragons, and fleshy hoods with movable crests, and were the last survivors of the antediluvian pterodactyls. These monsters obeyed the wands of the priests, for this was a temple of Ahriman, the lord of demons, and the god of the Turanians.

Arjasp had scarcely arrived, with the men of his tribe, when some warriors brought a captive before King Zohak—a magnificent

woman, clothed only in some fragments of torn linen. The golden
band around her head proclaimed her to be of noble race. Her arms
were bound behind her, and her white skin was stained with blood.
Around her neck was a plaited rope of horse-hair, by which she
was led, as black as her own loosened tresses that fell over her back
and breasts. With horror Arjasp recognised the woman of the
spring, Ardouizur—but alas, how changed! She was pale with
anguish, and no fiery darts issued from her sorrowful eyes. Her
head was lowered ; death was in her soul.

The king said : " This woman is the proudest of the captives
among the rebel Aryans from Mount Alborj. I offer her to him
who is capable of winning her. He must vow himself to the god
Ahriman, throwing of his own blood upon the fire, and drinking
of the blood of a bull. He must then take the oath to me, through
life, through death, placing his head under my foot. Whoso
doeth this shall take Ardouizur and make her his slave. If no one
offers, she shall become food for the two serpents of Ahriman."

Arjasp saw a long shudder pass over the beautiful body of
Ardouizur. A Turanian chief, yellow-skinned and narrow-eyed,
stepped forward. He offered the blood-sacrifice to the fire and the
serpents ; he placed his head under Zohak's foot and took the oath.
The captive drooped like a wounded eagle, and when the brutal
Turanian laid his hand upon her, she looked at Arjasp. A blue
dart flashed from her eyes, a cry escaped her lips : " Save me ! "
Arjasp flung himself with bared sword upon the chief, but the men
who guarded the prisoner seized him, and were going to transfix
him with their spears, when the king cried ; " Stop ! Do not touch
the man ! " Then turning to the young Aryan, he said : " Arjasp,
I will allow you to live, and I will give you this woman, if you will
take the oath to me and submit to our god."

At these words, Arjasp lowered his head, turned, and re-entered
the ranks of his men. The Turanian chief seized his prey. Again
Ardouizur cried out, and this time Arjasp would have surely met his
death, had not his companions prevented him by seizing him round
the throat and almost suffocating him. The daylight faded, the
sun turned black, and Arjasp could see nothing but a river of blood,
the blood of the whole Turanian race, which he longed to spill as
ransom for the divine Ardouizur, wounded and dragged through the
mud. He fell to the ground and lost consciousness.

When he revived, in the tent to which his men had carried him,
he saw, far off, a woman tied to the saddle of a horse. A man leapt
upon the animal and seized the woman in his arms, and a whole
troop of Turanians with long spears, mounted on black horses,
hurled themselves after him. Soon riders, horses, flying manes and
kicking hoofs had disappeared in a cloud of dust.

Then Arjasp remembered the words that Ardouizur had spoken beside the spring, under the perfumed pine-trees : " Whosoever shall drink of this water shall burn with an unassuageable thirst, and only a God can quench it." He now burnt with thirst, in his blood, in his very bones, thirst for justice and revenge, thirst for light and truth, thirst for the power to deliver Ardouizur and the soul of her race !

CHAPTER II

THE VOICE IN THE MOUNTAIN AND THE SOLAR WORD

GALLOPING at full speed over hills and plains, Arjasp made his way back to the Alborj Mountains. He found the rocky path leading to the valley of flowers, surrounded by its snow-crowned peaks. Approaching the wooden huts, he saw men furrowing the soil with a plough drawn by steaming horses, and the earth, thrown up in long lines, seemed to steam also with pleasure under the sharp plough and the heavy hoofs. In an open field a sword lay upon a stone altar, and beside it a sheaf of flowers in the form of a cross. These things reassured him. He found the patriach, Vahumano, seated in his tent dispensing justice to the tribe. His eyes were like the sun that rises above the snow-peaks ; his greenish-white beard was like the lichens that cover the ancient cedars of the Alborj Mountains.

" What do you require of me ? " he asked. " You know of the rape of Ardouizur by King Zohak ? "

" I saw her in torment at Baktra. She has become the prey of a Turanian. It is said that you are a wise man, and the last descendant of the priests of the Sun. You are of those who have knowledge of the high Gods. I come to seek light and truth from you for myself, and for my people justice and deliverance."

" Have you the patience that outlasts the years ? Are you ready to give up everything for your task ? For you are only at the beginning of the test, and the suffering will endure throughout your life."

" Take my body, take my soul," said Arjasp, " if you can give me the light that satisfies, and the sword that delivers. Yes, I am ready for all things, if, with this light and this sword, I can save the Aryans and free Ardouizer from her tormentor."

" Then I can help you," said Vahumano. " Come and live here for a time. Disappear from among your own people ; when they see you again you will be another. From this day forward your name shall be no more Arjasp but Zarathustra,[1] which means ' star of gold ' or ' splendour of the sun,' and you shall become the

---

[1] Zarathustra is the Zend name, and Zoroaster the later Greek form. The Parsis give the great Aryan prophet the name of Zurthost.

apostle of Ahura-Mazda, who is the aureole of the Omniscient, the Living Spirit of the Universe."

So did Zoroaster become the disciple of Vahumano.[1]

The patriarch and priest of the Sun, holder of a tradition which could be traced back to Atlantis, taught his pupil all that he knew of the divine wisdom and the present state of the world.

"The chosen race of Aryans," said Vahumano, "has fallen under the yoke of the Turanians, except for a few mountain tribes; but these few shall save the whole race. The Turanians worship Ahriman, and are in subjection to him."

"Who then is Ahriman?"

"There are spirits beyond number between heaven and earth," said the patriarch. "Their forms are innumerable, and, like the boundless heaven, so has unfathomable hell its various degrees. There is a powerful archangel named Adar-Assour, or Lucifer, who plunged into the abyss in order to carry the devouring fire of his torch to all living creatures. He is the greatest example of pride and desire, seeking God in himself and in the depths of the abyss. But even in his fall he retains a memory of divinity, and may some day wear again his crown, his heavenly star. Lucifer is the archangel of light. Ahriman[2] is not Lucifer, but his shadow, his reverse side, leader of the hordes of darkness. Frenziedly attached to the earth, he denies heaven, and knows only the forces of destruction. It is he who has degraded the fire-altars and revived the serpent-worship, he who propagates envy and hatred, vice and oppression, and all furious passions. He rules over the Turanians; he incites their evil genius. It is he who must be fought and overthrown—to save the race of the pure and the strong."

"But how can I fight the invisible one who weaves his plots in darkness?"

"By turning your face towards the sun that rises behind Mount Hara-Berezaïti. Climb through the cedar forest until you reach the eagle's nest that hangs above the precipice. There you will see the sun rise every morning above the rocky peaks. By day, pray to the Lord of the Sun to manifest himself to you; by night, await him, and attune your soul to the stars like a lyre. You will have to wait long, for Ahriman will seek to bar the way. But one night, in the peace of your soul, another Sun will rise, more brilliant

---

[1] Certain Jewish Kabalists, some Gnostics, and the Rosicrucians of the Middle Ages have identified Vahumano, the initiator of Zoroaster, with Melchisedek, the initiator of Abraham.

[2] In Zend, *Angra-Mainyu*. In this account I have adopted, for the most part, the traditional Greco-Latin names, because they are more familiar to our ears and more evocative of memories. The conception of Mephistopheles in Goethe's *Faust* corresponds exactly to that of Ahriman, with modern irony and scepticism added.

than that which flames above the crest of Mount Berezaïti—the Sun of Ahura-Mazda. You will hear his voice and he will reveal to you the law of the Aryans."

When the time came for Zoroaster to retire into his solitude, he said to his master : " But when shall I find again the captive whom the Turanian carried off to his tent, and who bled beneath his blows ? How is she to be torn from his clutches ? How am I to escape from the memory of that lovely form bound with ropes and covered with blood-stains, and of that voice that ever calls to me ? Alas, shall I never see again that Aryan maiden who drew water of light beneath the pine-trees, and whose eyes have left their golden arrows in my heart ? When shall I see Ardouizur ? "

Vahumano was silent for a moment. His eyes became dull and fixed ; a great sadness seemed to overshadow him, as the mountain-peaks are darkened when the sun has set. Then he stretched out his right arm with a noble gesture, and replied : " I do not know, my son. Ahura-Mazda will tell you . . . Go to the mountain ! "

Zoroaster spent ten years at the far end of the cedar forest, in a cave overlooking a deep valley. He was clothed in sheepskins and lived on buffalo-milk and bread which Vahumano's herdsmen brought him from time to time. The cries of the eagle, whose nest was among the rocks just above the cave, always warned him of the sun's rising, for when the golden orb began to disperse the valley-mists, the great bird would fly to and fro before the entrance to the cave, as though to see whether he slept, and would then make several circles in the air above the ravine and depart towards the plain.

Years passed, say the Persian records, before Zoroaster heard the voice of Ormuzd, and saw his glory. Ahriman first assailed him with his furious legions, and the days went by in sadness and desolation. After the meditations, prayers and spiritual exercises of the day, he would think of the future destiny of the oppressed and corrupted Aryans, and of the cruel fate of Ardouizur. What would become of that beautiful daughter of the white race in the hands of the bestial Turanian ? Had she drowned her anguish in some deep river, or had she submitted to her ignoble lot ? Suicide or degradation—there was no other alternative. Both were terrible ; and Zoroaster was haunted by the unforgotten sight of that beautiful bruised form with the horse-hair rope around its neck. It was a vision that continually flashed through his meditations like a flaming torch.

The nights were worse than the days, for his dreams surpassed in horror his waking visions. All the demons of Ahriman surrounded him in hideous and terrifying animal forms. Armies of jackals, bats, or winged serpents, seemed to invade the cavern, and their howlings, rustlings and hissings filled him with doubt of himself and fear of his mission. But by day he thought of the many thousands of nomad Aryans who were oppressed by the Turanians, and who rebelled in secret ; of the degraded altars, the blasphemies, the evil rites and invocations, the women carried off into slavery like Ardouizur ; and then indignation gave him courage.

Sometimes he climbed before dawn to the highest point of the cedar-covered mountain. He heard the wind sighing in the great trees that stretched like living harps towards heaven ; he looked out over the ravine, the escarpment of green slopes, the ranges of snow-clad peaks, and far off, veiled in rosy mist, the plain of Iran. If the earth, he thought, had had the strength to raise with such glory a thousand peaks towards the sky, why should not I have the strength to raise my people ? And when the blazing disk of the sun sprang above the snowy summits, dispersing as with a sword-thrust the vapours in the deep valley, his faith in Ormuzd was renewed. Every morning he prayed, as Vahumano had taught him : " Appear, O radiant sun with thy streaming hair ; rise above Hara-Berezaiti and enlighten the world ! "

Nevertheless, Ormuzd came not, and Zoroaster's nightly dreams grew more and more terrible. Ever more frightful monsters assailed him, and behind their surging masses a shade would appear, with face and figure veiled in long black garments. It would stand motionless and observe the sleeper. Was it the ghost of a woman ? It could not be Ardouizur, for the maiden of the blue spring would not have worn so sinister an air. It would appear and disappear, always motionless, always veiled, its gaze fixed upon Zoroaster. For a month it came every night, with the changing crowds of demons. At last it seemed to take courage, and to come nearer. Behind its dusky veils gleamed a pearl-white body of surpassing beauty. Was it a temptress sent by Ahriman ? Was it one of the spectres who lure men to strange loves among the marble tombs, beneath the cypresses of grave-yards ? But no, the veiled shade had too much sadness, too much majesty, for that. One night, however, it bent over him, and from its lips, through the black veil, came a scorching breath that spread through his veins like a river of fire.

Zoroaster awoke in a sweat of agony, on his bed of dried leaves, under his buffalo-skin. He could hear nothing but the wind howling and whirling in the gorge, in desperate response to the wild, harsh voice of the mountain torrent.

But little by little, month by month, the Shadow-Woman seemed to become clearer. From black she became grey, then almost white. She seemed to bring with her flowers and rays of light, and her rosy aura chased away the demons, so that at last she came alone. One day she appeared almost transparent in the gleam of approaching dawn, and held out her arms to Zoroaster in an ineffable gesture of farewell. She remained thus for some time, still silent, still veiled. Then she pointed to the rising sun, turned towards it, and seemed to be gradually absorbed into its rays.

Zoroaster awoke, and walked to the extreme edge of the cave. It was broad daylight; the sun was high in the heavens. And though he had not seen the face of the Shadow-Woman, he was now convinced that this phantom was the soul of Ardouizur, and that he would never see her again in this world.

He stood there motionless for a long time. A sharp pain stabbed his heart; a flood of silent tears fell from his eyes, and froze upon his face as they fell. Then he climbed to the summit of the mountain. Long icicles hung in the branches of the ancient cedars, and were slowly melting in the spring sunshine. The sparkling, crystalline snow upon the heights of Alborj seemed everywhere to be weeping icy tears.

The three days and nights that followed were Zoroaster's worst time of desolation. He experienced Death—not his own death, but that of all beings; he dwelt with Death, and Death dwelt in him. He no longer hoped. He did not even call upon Ormuzd, but found rest only in the unconsciousness of complete exhaustion.

But the third night, when lying in this condition, he heard a great voice like the rolling of thunder, which died away in melodious murmurings. Then a hurricane of light seemed to hurl itself upon him with such violence that he thought his soul must be driven from his body. He felt that the unnameable Cosmic Power that had haunted him since childhood, that had plucked him from his valley and led him to the mountain-top, was going to be made manifest to him by means of the language in which the gods speak to men. And the Lord of Spirits, the King of Kings, Ormuzd, the Solar Word, then appeared to him in human form. Clothed in beauty, strength and light, He shone upon His fiery throne, which was supported on either side by a winged bull and lion, while the wings of an enormous eagle were spread beneath it. Around Him in three glorious semi-circles stood seven Cherubim with golden wings, seven Elohim with azure wings, and seven Archangels with violet wings.[1] From moment to moment a blaze of light issued from Ormuzd, penetrating all

---

[1] In the Zend-Avesta the Cherubim are called *Amschapands*, the Elohim *Yzeds*, and the Archangels *Feroher*.

three spheres, and the Cherubim, Elohim and Archangels shone like the God Himself with the dazzling whiteness of snow, and thus reassumed their former colours. Bathed thus in the glory of Ormuzd, they manifested His unity ; glowing in gold, azure and violet, they became His prism. And Zoroaster heard a melodious voice, vast as the universe, which said : " I am Ahura-Mazda, who created thee ; I have chosen thee. Hear now my voice, O Zarathustra, best of men. I will speak with thee by day and by night, and reveal to thee the living word."[1]

Then there was a blinding flash in which Ormuzd and the attendant Archangels, Elohim and Cherubim seemed to grow colossal, till they filled the whole valley and hid from sight the jagged peaks of Alborj. The light paled, and spread itself over the whole firmament. For some seconds, the constellations glittered through the wings of the Cherubim ; then the vision faded, and was lost in space. But the echo of the voice of Ahura-Mazda rang through the mountains like distant thunder, and died away in palpitating vibrations.

Zoroaster had fallen with his face to the ground. When he awoke he was so overcome that he retired into the darkest corner of the cavern. Presently the eagle that nested in the rocks above rose from the gulf where it had vainly been seeking its prey, and alighted familiarly a few yards away from him. It was as though the royal bird of Ormuzd at last recognised His prophet. It smoothed its wet, tawny feathers with its beak, and as the sun emerged from behind a cloud, spread out its wings to dry them, and gazed steadfastly at the orb of day.

From now onwards Zoroaster heard the voice of Ormuzd continually, both by day and by night. Sometimes it was as though an inner voice spoke to him ; sometimes he was shown glowing symbols which were like the living thoughts of his God. Ormuzd instructed him concerning the creation of the world and the manifestation of the living Word in the universe,[2] the hierarchies or cosmic powers, the necessary combat with Ahriman, spirit of evil and of destruction, and how to vanquish him by prayer and the fire-sacrifice. He taught him the means of fighting

---

[1] In the Zend language Zend-Avesta means 'living word.'

[2] " In the Zoroastrian religion," says Silvestre de Sacy, "it is evident that everything has been created except time. Time is the creator, for time has no limits ; it has neither height nor depth ; it has always been and always will be. But in spite of all these excellent prerogatives possessed by time, nobody had ever named it the creator. And why ? Because it had created nothing. Eventually it created fire and water, and when they were put into contact with one another, Ormuzd came into existence. Thus time was both lord and creator, because of the creation that it had accomplished."

demons with vigilant thought, and the Turanians with consecrated arms. He told him of the love of man for the earth, and
of the earth for man who cultivates her, of her joy in being fer-
tilised and in the splendour of her harvests, and of her secret
forces which are poured forth upon the family of the labourer.
The whole of the Zend-Avesta is one long conversation between
Ormuzd and Zoroaster. " What is the thing that gives most
pleasure to the earth ? " " When a pure man walks upon her."
" What is the next most pleasurable thing to her ? " " When a
pure man builds a house where there is a fire, where there are
cattle, and fine flocks, where there is a woman and children.
For in such a house is abundance of righteousness." Through
the voice of Ormuzd, Zoroaster heard the promise made by the
earth to the man who respects and cultivates her : " Man, I will
forever sustain thee, and I will come to thee." And the earth
comes to him with her rich scents and odours, with her green
ears of wheat, and with her splendid harvests. In contrast to
Buddhist pessimism and to the doctrine of non-resistance, there is
in the Zend-Avesta a sane optimism and an energetic combative-
ness. Ormuzd condemns violence and injustice but upholds
courage as man's primary virtue. We feel, in the thoughts of
Zoroaster, the constant presence of the invisible world and of the
cosmic hierarchies, but the attention is fixed upon action, upon
the conquest of the earth, through spiritual discipline and exercise
of the will.

The prophet made a practice of recording his inner revelations
upon a sheepskin with a wooden pen charred in the fire, using
the sacred characters which Vahumano had taught him. Later
his disciples took down his thoughts from dictation, and so the
Zend-Avesta came into being, first written upon skins of animals
like the Koran, and kept in a kind of sacred ark in the cedar-forest
—a record of the cosmogony, the laws, the prayers and the ceremonies of the Zoroastrian religion.

CHAPTER III

WHEN Zoroaster returned to his native tribe, after ten years of solitude, his own people scarcely recognised him. A warlike flame burnt in his mysterious eyes, and his voice had a tone of sovereign authority. He convoked his own tribe and all the neighbouring Aryan tribes, to incite them to war against the Turanians, and at the same time announced to them the revelation that he had received, the living Word of Ormuzd. This Word, the Zend-Azesta, became the animating centre of his work. Purification, labour and combat were the three disciplines that it taught. *Purification* of the spirit and the body by prayer and the fire-sacrifice, fire being known as " the son of Ormuzd," the first breath of the God. *Labour* upon the earth with the plough, and the cultivation of sacred trees, the cypress, cedar and orange ; labour crowned by love, with the spouse for priestess at the fire-side. *Combat* against Ahriman and the Turanians. The life of the Aryans under Zoroaster was thus a perpetual armed watch, a ceaseless struggle, softened and made rhythmic by labour in the fields and by the joys of the domestic hearth. The hymns of Ormuzd were chanted at the daily fire-sacrifice. The primitive city founded by Zoroaster was a city on the march, a city of combat. Men sowed with bow in hand and javelin at the belt ; laboured on the battle-field ; gathered in the harvest on the days of rest. Progress was made step by step. On every piece of conquered land Zoroaster built a camp surrounded by palisades, the germ of a future city. In the centre stood the fire-altar under an arch-way, with cypress trees and often a spring near at hand. *Mobeds,* or priests, were instituted, and *destours,* or doctors of law. It was forbidden under pain of death to marry with the Turanians, or to give one's daughters to them in marriage. To his warrior-labourers Zoroaster gave sacred animals, to be their companions and helpers ; the faithful dog, the active horse, the watchful cock. " What does the cock say ? He says : Stand up, it is dawn ! He who first rises will enter into paradise." Like all true initiates, Zoroaster was aware of the law of reincarnation, but he did not speak of it. To reveal it was not a part of his mission, for it might have caused the Ayran race to turn aside from its immediate task, the conquest of the earth through agriculture and the establishment of the family. But he taught his adepts the law of Karma in an elementary form, i.e., that the next life is the consequence of this one. The impure go to the kingdom of Ahriman, the pure cross over the bridge of light built by Ormuzd, brilliant as a diamond, narrow as the blade of a sword. Upon this bridge a winged angel waits, beautiful as a young virgin, and this angel says : " I am your work, I am your true self ; I am your own soul, moulded by you." [1]

Within himself Zoroaster was always conscious of an unspeakable sadness. The terrible melancholy endured by prophets in payment for their ecstasies overcame him at times. His task was as vast as the horizons of Iran, where mountains rose behind mountains and plains stretched beyond plains. But Ahura-Mazda drew him ever nearer to himself, and the greatness of the prophet separated him ever more from the hearts of men, although he lived in the midst of their struggles. Sometimes in the autumn evenings, he would watch the women carrying home their harvest-sheaves. Some would kneel down and offer their sheaves to the prophet seated upon a rock near the fire-altar, and he would stretch out his hand and speak some words of blessing. He observed their strong arms and necks bronzed by the sun, and occasionally one among them would remind him of Ardouizur. But none had the dazzling fairness of the virgin of the blue spring, none had her royal features, her look as of a wounded eagle which pierced the heart like a sword, her voice in which one was drowned as in a crystal flood. He still heard her cry : " Save me ! " . . . and he had failed to save her. It was this terrible cry that had driven the passionate youth to the sage, Vahumano ; that had caused Arjasp to become Zoroaster. It was thanks to this cry that he had aroused his own tribe and the whole Aryan race to self-consciousness, and to a life-and-death struggle. From this cry of a woman in distress his life-work had been born. But she—Ardouizur—where was she ? Dead or living ? Zoroaster, who knew so much, knew not this. In spite of his prayers Ahura-Mazda had not revealed it to him. A dark cloud of sorrow veiled this secret from him.

After forty years of tumultuous fighting, and many wanderings,

---

[1] In the Zend-Avesta (translated by Anquetil-Duperron, discoverer of the Zend language and of the primitive Persian religion) there is an account of Zoroaster's being tempted by Angra-Mainyu (Ahriman), followed by a list of means for overcoming Ahriman by prayers and invocations. The chapter ends with a description of the judgment of the soul, as seen by Zoroaster in a kind of vision.

Zohak, king of the Turanians, who had never ceased to harass the conquerors, was killed, and his fortress taken by the Aryans. Zoroaster proclaimed Lorasp king of the Aryans, and instituted the religion of Ormuzd at Baktra, after having the two serpents destroyed, and the cave which had been used for the infamous cult of Ahriman filled up with sand and blocks of stone. Having now accomplished his task, he desired to retire to his mountain cavern, to learn from Ormuzd the future destiny of his race and to transmit this knowledge to his followers. He ordered his three foremost disciples to rejoin him at Mount Alborj in a month's time, to receive his last instructions. For Zoroaster wished to end his life upon the mountain where he had first heard the voice of Ormuzd; he knew that the God would there speak with him again. Before he left the world, however, he gave this recommendation to his people as conclusion and *resumé* of the Zend-Avesta : " Let those who have listened to me contemplate not Ahriman, the appearance of things and of shadows, but the original fire, the Word, Ahura-Mazda—that they may live. Those who listen not will repent at the end of time."[1]

When Zoroaster reached his cavern in the early days of spring, it was snowing upon the mountain, and a rough wind blew through the cedar-forest, below the snowy peaks. The herdsmen who had accompanied him made a fire, and left him alone. And the aged and weary prophet fell into deep thought as he watched the ruddy flames dancing around the resinous faggots. He looked back upon his own life and saw it as in a picture, like a winding river with many tributaries. He followed it from source to mouth, and saw how the clear streamlet became a brook, and the brook a wide river flowing over the sands, foaming against the rocks. Cities had grown up on its banks ; vessels had sailed over its surface ; and now the majesty of the river was to be lost in the immensity of the ocean. . . . The task was ended ; the Aryans were free. And what was next to become of his race ?

Night fell, and it was very cold. The aged prophet shivered beside his fire. Suddenly he cried out : " O divine Ormuzd, behold, I am near to my end ! I have despoiled myself, I have sacrificed all to my people, I have obeyed thy voice. In order to become Zoroaster, Arjasp renounced the divine Ardouizur —and Zoroaster has never seen her again. She has vanished into the limbo of space, and Ormuzd has not restored her to his prophet. I have sacrificed all to my people, that they might have free men

---

[1] *Ahura-Mazda*, the aureole of the sun, here represents the crown of divine spirits who created the sun, and who form his aura, of which Ormuzd is the animating essence. This spiritual aureole is, in a sense, the living soul of the sun in Zoroastrian thought.

and noble women, but none of them has the beauty of Ardouizur, the golden flame that darted from her eyes. . . . Let me at least know what is to be the future of my race."

As he spoke these words, Zoroaster heard the rolling of distant thunder, accompanied by vibrations like the clattering of a thousand brazen shields. The sound increased as it came nearer; the mountains trembled, and the voice of the angry God seemed as though it would uproot the whole chain of Alborj.

Zoroaster could only cry out: "Ahura-Mazda! Ahura-Mazda!" and then fell fainting to the ground. Soon he beheld Ormuzd in all his glory, as on the first day of his revelation, but without the surrounding *ferohers* and *amschapands*. The three sacred animals, the bull, the lion and the eagle, supported the fiery throne, and the voice of Ormuzd rolled through space and echoed in the prophet's heart.

"Why desirest thou to know that which pertains only to thy God? No prophet can know all the thoughts of the divine Word. Do not doubt Ahara-Mazda, O Zoroaster, best of men, for I carry in my scales the destinies of all beings, and thine own also. Thou wouldst know the destiny of thy race? Behold then what the peoples of Asia will make of the three animals who uphold my throne."

The blazing vision disappeared, and Zoroaster was transported in spirit into the future. Flying through space, he saw plains and mountains rapidly unrolled at his feet like the pages of a great book. He saw the Caspian Sea, the Taurus Mountains, the Caucasus, and the Persian Gulf. He saw a horde of Turanians retake the fortress of Baktra and profane the temple of Ormuzd. Then on the banks of the Tigris, he saw proud Nineveh arise, palaces, towers and temples. A gigantic winged bull with a human head, symbol of power, looked down upon the town, and Zoroaster saw this bull change into a wild buffalo which ravaged the plains and trampled the people underfoot, while the pure Aryans fled towards the north. Next he saw a still greater city arise on the banks of the Euphrates, Babylon with its mighty walls and its pyramids. In one of the sanctuaries there slept a huge coiled serpent, which was attacked by the eagle of Ormuzd from above. But the serpent drove the eagle away with hissings and fire, and then went out to breathe its poisons upon all the people in the city. Finally, Zoroaster saw the winged lion marching victoriously at the head of an army of Medes and Persians; but the lion suddenly changed into a ferocious tiger which devoured the people and destroyed the priests even within the Sun-temple on the banks of the Nile.

The prophet awoke from his dream with a cry of horror.

" If such is the future of the Aryans, the race of the pure and strong, I have fought in vain ! If this is the truth, I will gird on my sword which has hitherto remained free of the stain of blood, and will plunge it up to the hilt in the blood of the Turanians. I, old man though I am, will go forth alone to Iran, to exterminate the sons of Zohak, that they may not destroy my people—even though I become the prey of Ahriman, like the noble Ardouizur ! "

Then the voice of Ormuzd arose with a gentle murmuring, as of a breeze in the boughs of the great cedars, and said : " Stay, my son ! Stay, Zoroaster ! Thy hand shall never again grasp a sword. Thy days are ended. Climb to the mountain-top, where the sun can be seen rising above the peaks of Berezaïti. Thou hast seen the future through human eyes ; thou shalt now see it through the eyes of the gods. On the heights the justice of Ormuzd reigns, and the Angel of Victory awaits thee ! "

So Zoroaster climbed the mountain, and seated himself, exhausted, under a cedar-tree to await the dawn. When the sun appeared behind the ranks of snow-capped peaks a great shuddering seized the body of the old man.

" It is death ! " said the voice of Ahriman in the shadowy ravine.

" It is resurrection ! " said the voice of Ormuzd in the sky.

Then Zoroaster beheld an arch of light which seemed to spring from beneath his feet and to stretch across the sky. It was narrow as the blade of a sword, and brilliant as a diamond. . . .

His soul, swept out of his body as though on the wings of an eagle, rushed across it . . . and on the highest point of the bridge there stood a woman, veiled in light. She radiated superhuman joy and pride. Two wings, like lightning shafts, rose from her shoulders ; and she held out to the prophet a golden cup brimming over with sparkling liquid. It seemed to Zoroaster that he had known her for ever ; yet he could not name her, so dazzled was he by her marvellous smile.

" Who art thou, O marvel ? "

" O, my master, dost thou not know me ? I am Ardouizur. . . . Thou hast created me. I am more than myself ; I am thine immortal soul. It is thou who hast saved me, thou who hast restored me to life. When in horror and rage I had killed him who ravished me, the Turanian chief, when his brothers had me stabbed to death, my soul wandered long in the realm of shadows. I was the shade that haunted thee. I persecuted thee with my despair and remorse, with my desire . . . but thy prayers and tears gradually lifted me out of the kingdom of Ahriman, until borne on the incense of thy love, on the wings of thy thought, I also was able to approach the glory of Ormuzd. And now we will drink the cup of immortal life from the source of light!"

So saying, the fair Ardouizur, transformed into the Angel of Victory, embraced Zoroaster as a wife embraces her husband, and offered him the foaming cup of eternal youth. It seemed to the prophet as though a wave of light and fire submerged his whole being. At the same moment Ardouizur vanished, but she had entered into her saviour, and now dwelt in his heart. She saw through his eyes, and he through hers, and both beheld the glory of Ormuzd. Henceforth they were one. Zoroaster understood that Ardouizur could fly far away without being separated from him, or merge into his essence without ceasing to be herself.

And suddenly, looking down upon the earth, the prophet saw the Aryan tribes advancing in long caravans. At their head was Ardouizur, leading them towards the west—Ardouizur, now become the Soul of the white race.

When the three disciples sought to rejoin their master, he was nowhere to be found. In the cavern there remained only his pilgrim's staff, and the golden goblet which he used for pouring fermented liquor on the fire. On the mountain-top there was no trace of him. They searched everywhere, in vain.

Above the valley the great eagle hovered, and, when it approached the entrance to the cavern, it beat its wings and seemed to be searching for the sharer of its solitude, the only man who had dared, like it, to behold the sun face to face.

BOOK V

MANIFESTATIONS OF THE SOLAR WORD

II

A CHALDEAN PRIEST IN THE TIME OF THE PROPHET DANIEL

At the summit of the Tower of Babel
a virginal bed awaits the Saviour. . . .
In the infernal depths Lucifer
awaits deliverance through Ishtar,
the human soul. . . .

A CHALDEAN PRIEST IN THE TIME OF THE PROPHET DANIEL

THE application of the Divine Revelation to human life, and the conquest of the earth through reason—such was the mission of the race of Semitic Aryans and of all the sub-races with which it mingled. This conquest began in Persia with the organisation of agriculture and the establishment of the family, under the ægis of the Word of Ormuzd. It was continued in Chaldea and Assyria by the development of the science of mathematics, mistress of all other sciences, applied on the one hand to the observation of the stars and their influence upon humanity (astronomy and astrology), and on the other to architecture and the industrial arts.

Assyria and Chaldea were twin civilisations, essentially realistic, that played an important rôle in history despite their savage politics. They bequeathed to succeeding civilisations instruments of labour and the arts of craftsmanship. Thus the Chaldean world provided Egypt, Greece and Rome with ashlar, cement, and set-squares with which to build their cities, temples and acropoli.

The ethnical composition of the Assyrians and Chaldeans was very complex. As the Biblical legend has it, Babel produced a chaotic drama of confused tongues and races. The Semitic-Aryan element predominated in Assyria, the Turanian in Chaldea ; hence the war-like power of Nineveh, the genius of observation of Babylon. Queen of architecture and mother of industry, Babel gave birth to a massive and colossal art : huge temples, gigantic bulls, sturdy giants wrestling with lions.

From the point of view of religious inspiration, and of the spiritual influences which affected Assyria and Chaldea, these civilisations are of peculiar interest. The armies of Nineveh and Babylon were the rod and scourge of the Jewish people, rod of fire and scourge of steel, wielded by fierce and implacable kings. But, through oppressing the children of Israel without being able to destroy them, Assyria and Chaldea were also the means of raising up the great prophets, Isaiah, Ezekiel and Daniel, who unceasingly preached the resurrection of their enslaved and exiled people. At the same time the priests of Chaldea, strongly influenced by the Zoroastrian tradition, and creators of a special mythology, were powerful forces in the moulding of the Hebrew religion, which they provided with new cosmogonal data and with more precise knowledge concerning the celestial hierarchies. The fact that the prophet Daniel was made " chief of the governors over all the wise men of Babylon " by Nebuchadnezzar, and was retained in this office by Belshazzar, is in itself extremely significant. Though the cuneiform inscriptions ignore it, the whole subsequent history of the Jewish people is, so to speak, a counter-proof of it, for from that time forward their religion bears the ineffaceable imprint of the Chaldean initiation.

These historical data once established, let us take the viewpoint of *divine evolution*—that is to say, of the cosmic forces and spiritual influences acting upon humanity ; let us raise our thoughts to the Invisible which is reflected in the visible ; and we shall find that Babylon is one of the most important intersecting points of the two contrary currents that have, from the beginning, conspired and conflicted in the development of the earth-planet and of man. I mean *the current of the Solar Word*, which ends in Christ, and *the Luciferian current*, which ends in the modern world.

The narration that now follows is placed in the period when this intense struggle, this occult conflict, had reached its height, at the fateful hour when Babylon had been taken by Cyrus and when the prophet Daniel dwelt in that city.

CHAPTER I

THE SETTING SUN OF BABYLON

THE high hill of Borsippa rose to the south-west of the great city of Babylon, between the outer and inner ramparts—Imgur-Bel and Nivitti-Bel—which were separated by half a league one from the other.[1] In the wide space between these walls, the kings of Babylon were in the habit of encamping the large crowds of foreign captives whom they deported from time to time. At the moment thousands of Jews were living there in their brick and clay houses, some of which were surrounded by cultivated fields. The hill of Borsippa stood in the region where tradition has placed the fabulous Tower of Babel, where a certain Accadian king named Khammurabi[2] had formerly built a temple to the Sun-god. Nebuchadnezzar, at the height of his power, raised upon it the marvel of the age, a pyramid of seven temples[3] built one upon the other, the whole being (Two hundred and fifty feet in height.)

A terrace twenty-five feet high, with a massive brass railing, formed the base of the pyramid or *zigurat*. Not a soul was to be seen there. It was the morrow of the taking of Babylon by the Persians, and men feared the reprisals of Cyrus for the cruelties of the Chaldean kings in Media. Everybody was hiding. Even the seventy priests who served in the temple of Bel had fled.

One sole living creature was cowering before the bronze door of the lower temple, between the two lintels of brick covered with

---

[1] Herodotus, who visited Babylon in the fifth century, has left us a detailed description of it. " The city stands on a broad plain, and is an exact square, a hundred and twenty furlongs in length each way, so that the entire circuit is four hundred and eighty furlongs. While such is its size, in magnificence there is no other city that approaches to it. It is surrounded, in the first place, by a broad and deep moat, full of water, behind which rises a wall fifty royal cubits in width and two hundred in height." (Book I., chap. 178.) A furlong being one-eighth of a mile, the sides of the city would measure 15 miles each, and the whole outer boundary 60 miles. The main features of its topography have been fixed by the excavations of Oppert.

[2] His code of laws is preserved on a green marble tablet in the Assyrian museum of the Louvre.

[3] A cuneiform inscription of Nebuchadnezzar concerning Borsippa is reproduced in Vol. IV. of Lenormant's *Ancient History of the East*.

black bitumen.   It was the guardian of the sacred serpent of Saturn, whose worship had been permitted to continue up till now, because the people thought the safety of the town depended on it.

Suddenly a man who had mounted the staircase from below appeared upon the terrace.   He was wearing the purple tunic and scarlet mantle of the priests, embroidered with eagles' wings ; and on his head the golden coronet with seven balls set with precious stones.   But as a sign of national mourning he had covered his gorgeous apparel with a transparent black veil which enveloped him from head to foot, but through which could be seen his arched nose, hawk-like eyes, and the long false beard which Chaldean priests and kings alike were obliged to wear.

He approached the figure crouching before the temple of Saturn, and said in a tone of bitter contempt and disdain :

" So thou art still guarding thy dead serpent ? "

The Accadian, who was wrapped in ashen-coloured rags, did not move, but answered with a sardonic smile on his frog-like mouth :

" I am only waiting for the Persian he-mule to come with his acolyte, the cursed Jew, the sorcerer, and kill me."

" Useless to insult them," said Nabu-Nassir shortly.   " They are conquerors.   But why dost thou kneel before this great sword rusty with black blood ? "

" It is the sword with which the traitorous Jew cut off the head of the serpent before the king who had defied it.   He threw the weapon away in disgust, but I will never part from it until I have revenged my god ! "

" Give it to me," said the priest.   " I will be responsible for vengeance."

" Thou wouldst avenge our gods as I would ? " cried the Accadian, rising to his feet.

" I am going to spend the night in the upper temple, and invoke the Supreme God against the Adversary.   What will happen I know not . . . but I know that to-morrow one of us must die—he or I.   Thou wilt serve the survivor."

" If it is thou—always !   If it is he—never ! " said the serpent-guardian, handing him the sword.   Then he again seated himself on the ground, and remained motionless as a statue.

Nabu-Nassir fastened the sword to his belt and hid it beneath his mantle.   Then he made a tour of the terrace, from which could be seen the greater part of Babylon, the vastest city the world has ever known.   Close at hand were the rounded brass roofs of the three Temples of the Moon.   Above the houses crowded together in the valley, the eye followed the two parallel ramparts of Imgur-Bel and Nivitti-Bel, which stretched far out of sight in a straight line, like two royal roads.   A chariot drawn by four horses could easily be driven along either of these ramparts.   To the north, beyond the inner wall, lay the winding Euphrates, its waters gleaming here and there amid the streets and houses which enclosed it, as the scales of a serpent gleam among the bushes.   Beyond it could be seen the temple of Zarpanit, and the hanging gardens of the Queen Amytis, a pyramid of verdant greenery.   The horizon was marked by the long line of the royal city, a fortress of palaces, with its bastions, towers and pavilions, its doors of cedar-wood and bronze, its gold and silver roofs, its marble battlements.

The sun, plunging into a saffron-coloured mist, now lit up all these buildings with a sinister orange and purple glow, making them stand out from the shadowy depths of the town like urns of fire above a dark tabernacle.

Nabu-Nassir looked up at the pyramid of the seven temples which he now proposed to ascend for the first time.   It too flamed in the setting sun, like the other monuments of proud Babylon— flamed with all the colours of the rainbow, for the seven temples were covered with sheets of metals and minerals of many different tints.

The six lower temples were square, the topmost one circular, and, counted from above downwards, they symbolised the seven days of the week.   Counted from below upwards, they signified, according to the doctrine of the priests, the ascension of the human soul throughout our planetary evolution, from the chaos of the Saturnian period, through many metamorphoses, back to the divine solar ray.   And the pyramid itself, a chameleon of changing colour, seemed to participate in this gradual purification, for it rose from the blackness of Saturn to the marble whiteness of Venus, and passed through the pale rose of Jupiter, the shimmering blue of Mercury, and the deep crimson of Mars, to spire upwards like the pistil of a flower in the silver temple of the Moon and the golden chapel of Bel.

Nabu-Nassir measured the pyramid with his eye, while his soul prepared itself for the ascent to consult the gods in this time of distress.

He placed his foot on the outer staircase which mounted from stage to stage, encircling the whole *zigurat*.   As he climbed, he saw neither the sun disappearing behind the tawny Mesopotamian plains, nor the huge city whose contours became more and more indistinct in the gathering darkness.   Reaching the highest platform, he found himself on the threshold of the small chapel of Bel. The sun had vanished ; in a few seconds night had fallen upon the city.   From this height, Babylon was no more than a dark chaos from which arose, here and there, gigantic edifices like pallid citadels.

It might have been born from the womb of Erebus for the purpose of defying heaven.   But above the dark circle of the horizon the starry firmament stretched in all its splendour, the indigo Mesopotamian sky whose blue depths have the transparency of crystal. There revolved at prodigious distances globes of yellow, red and blue, keeping their innumerable rhythms in one vast harmony.

Under this sky, his own special domain of investigation, Nabu-Nassir brought his wisdom to bear upon recent events. He weighed his science in the balance with destiny—and it was indeed a sublime science.   For untold thousands of years[1] the magi and their predecessors, the Manus, had studied the movements of the stars.   They had fixed, through their investigations, the regular revolutions of the celestial clock, with all its complicated machinery. They had discovered certain influences, not only of the sun and moon, but of the five planets, upon human destiny, according to their respective positions in the sky, at such a place, in such a year, day, or hour.   To them the whole planetary system was a living body which had originally formed a homogeneous mass, and of which each planet represented a necessary organ.   The lives of men and of nations were affected by these various influences, and it was possible to foresee triumphs and defeats, but not to foretell the details of events, these depending upon an incalculable combination of human liberty and divine action.   The influence of the stars upon the lives of men and nations was like the frame, or warp, showing the weaving of events, but not the infinite weavings of men and gods.   Thus Nabu-Nassir had foreseen that Babylon was menaced by catastrophe, through the conjunction of Mars and Saturn in the sign Scorpio, but he had not foreseen the greatness of the downfall, or that the whole power of Chaldea would be overthrown, so that the Jewish prisoners shouted the predictions of their prophets in the streets, and insulted the passers-by in words such as these : " Come down, seat thyself in the dust, daughter of Babylon ;   seat thyself on the ground and not upon a throne, daughter of the Chaldean !   Take mill-stones and grind the corn ; doff thy veils and lift up thy robe ; show thy nakedness that all may see thy shame ! "

Now Daniel knew the science of divination ; by communing with the Invisible he could foretell the future and rule both kings and crowds, while the priests had lived for centuries in their observatories, without power over the souls or destinies of the people, useless contemplators of fatality.   For more than three thousand years they had been incapable of restraining the ferocity

---

[1] According to Diodorus of Sicily, the tradition of the magi dated back for 50,000 years.   This figure may be exaggerated, but it proves what antiquity the Greco-Roman world attributed to astrology.

of the kings of Nineveh and Babylon, who exhibited, despite their egoistic piety, all the passion and cupidity of Ahriman together with the savagery of the yellow Turanian race. If the priests ventured to oppose them they were massacred, and so they had finally confined themselves to speculative science, and to the observation of the sky and its periodic revolutions. The kings only came to them for horoscopes, and woe to them if these were not favourable! The priests had been able to control neither the tigers of Nineveh nor the bulls of Babylon; neither Teglath Phalasar, who strewed a whole mountain-chain with severed heads of Moschians; nor Assur-Nazir-Pal, nor Sargon, nor the terrible Sennacherib, devastator of Judea; nor Assurbanipal, the destroyer of ancient Babylon, who with his own hand flogged the rebel satraps upon the tomb of his grandfather.

And Nabu-Nassir seemed always to see before him the ascetic Jew, with his gentle but indomitable gaze, the ruler of souls whom none could resist, the lamb stronger than lions, the prophet of misfortune. Had not this Daniel charmed even Nebuchadnezzar, the fiercest of tyrants, by interpreting his dreams to him? Had he not received from him the title of Archimage, to the confusion of all the Chaldean priests? Had he not, to crown all, predicted, and perhaps even plotted, the fall of Babylon? At this thought the priest relived in spirit the stupefying scene which had preceded the death of Belshazzar.

Below the great gallery of the royal palace, with its cedar-panelled walls and ceilings, at the end of the suite of rooms whose walls were covered with bas-reliefs of Babylonian wars and victories in terracotta on a black ground, in the heart of this abode of pride and luxury, there glowed in the ruddy torch-light the king's favourite retreat. There Belshazzar was enthroned, half reclining upon a sumptuous couch, with his women grouped voluptuously around him, and the officers of his court forming an outer circle. The king was melancholy. He had had the sacred vessels from the temple at Jerusalem brought to him, and had drunk heavily in defiance of the enemy and his God.

Suddenly the loud laughter is stifled, a whispering runs through the crowd, and the women's arms are extended in horror towards the opposite wall, on the other side of the table with its seven-branched candle-stick. Belshazzar looks, and sees a luminous hand tracing three words upon the frieze of the wall. He rises and cries:

"Nabu-Nassir, canst thou tell me the meaning of these three words?" The priest has to confess that he does not even know the characters of the writing. "Let Daniel be brought," orders the king. And, as though forewarned, Daniel appears, pale and impassive. He reads and pronounces in a clear voice the three words written by the luminous hand of an angel or spirit, which can still be seen, like a divine signature, beneath the final letter.

" *Mene, Tekel, Peres*—that means in earth-language, Number, Weight, Measure ; in divine language, Wisdom, Justice, Economy. O Belshazzar, thou like thy predecessors hast lived foolishly in injustice and disorder. Thou hast been weighed in the balance and found too light. That is why thy kingdom has been given to another."[1]

During this speech, the writing and the hand had faded away. Suddenly a guard rushes into the chamber, crying : " The Persians have entered the town by the Euphrates ! They are marching on the palace ! " Belshazzar trembles ; the terrified women fling themselves upon him, but he shakes them off, and tearing himself from their embraces, demands his sword. As he leaves the room he is killed by his guards who have already gone over to the enemy.

And now the prophet, become the most powerful man in the city, had gone to the camp of Cyrus to negociate for peace in the names of the court authorities. What would be his report ? Would Babylon have to submit to the fate of Nineveh ? Would the city be sacked and razed to the ground, so that the plough could pass over it and the wild beasts make their dens in its ruins ? Would the conquerors abolish the college of priests, and condemn their chief to death ? Anything might be expected.

But Nabu-Nassir did not give himself up to defeat. He also was conscious of an incalculable power behind him, a magic power drawn by the stars from the depths of infinity, and harnessed by three hundred centuries of science. He would fight to the end, even though he be annihilated by the unknown God of the Jews and by his prophet !

With this defiant resolve, he extended towards the north the naked blade of the sword with which Daniel had cut off the serpent's head. For an instant he held it motionless, above shadowy Babylon, below the immutable constellations blazing in the sky, and invoked the two ever-beneficent planets, Jupiter and Venus. At the same time he projected his will far out into the night, against the invisible adversary.

---

[1] See Chapter V of the Book of the Prophet Daniel. The Book of Daniel, and even the existence of Belshazzar, have been dismissed as legendary, but the latter is confirmed by the cuneiform texts, in which he is called Bel-sur-Assour. As to the three enigmatic words, they are part of the sacred language of the ancient temples. Mene, Manas, or Man, signifies in all Indo-European languages the human intellect in its universal or divine aspect. See the beautiful interpretation of these three words given by Saint-Yves d'Alveydre in his *Mission des Juifs*.

CHAPTER II

THE MYSTERY OF PARTHENOGENESIS

SUDDENLY Nabu-Nassir remembered the object of his solitary expedition.

Having been head of the *zigurat* for a short time only, he had not yet penetrated into the uppermost temple of the pyramid, the chapel consecrated to the Sun-god. The high-priest of the temple had the right to enter it once a year, and to pass the night there, at the spring festival of Ishtar. At other times, he could enter only in the event of Babylon being in distress and the temple threatened, when he might consult the god Bel and the goddess Ishtar, and expect a sign from them. This moment had now arrived. Nabu-Nassir was about to penetrate into the Holy of holies, to behold with his own eyes the secret of the temple and to seek the solution of its mystery.

He slipped a key into the bronze door and pushed it open. The circular chapel was lined throughout with unornamented gold. From the roof hung an alabaster lamp, in the shape of a white dove, whose light was never extinguished, being fed from a reservoir of oil contained in the cupola. The flame within the lamp rendered it luminous, and lit up the golden chapel. The eye was at once attracted by an empty couch, encrusted with ivory and draped in purple, beside which there stood a phial upon a gold table. Behind it, on the black wall, was a sculptured design representing the goddess Ishtar, white and slender, raising her arms to hold back a winged genius carrying a torch which was flying from her like a storm-cloud chased by the arrows of the sun. Nabu-Nassir remembered that his predecessor, before his death, had explained to him the secret meaning of the myth of Ishtar, known only to the high-priest of Bel. Ishtar was Babylon's favourite goddess, the goddess of the moon, like the Chaldean Venus ; but in the secret tradition she had a deeper meaning, and was connected with Adar-Asshur, a mysterious and little-known god, the Chaldean Lucifer. Long before the creation of the earth, at the time of the formation of the planet Jupiter, Adar-Asshur (Lucifer), the rebel archangel, by the force of his desire had evoked from the mysteries of the Word Lilith, Mylitta, the astral Eve, the first Eve. He desired to espouse Lilith, and to rule the world with her ; but, for having violated the mysteries of the All-Powerful and forestalled His will, he was flung into the planetary abyss, while Lilith, separated from her celestial lover, became the earthly Woman, the half of Man, the soul of Humanity. This cosmic power, the Eternal-Feminine, was worshipped by the peoples of Asia under the name of Mylitta, Ishtar, or Astarte.

To this immemorial tradition a recent but enigmatic prophecy was now added. The high-priest had related it to Nabu-Nassir. In this suffering and cruel humanity created by the desire of Lucifer, there was to be born some day, of a virgin, a God who would be the saviour of the human race. This was why in certain of the solar temples, in that of Bel in Babylon, in that of Ammon-Ra in Egypt, the birth of this God was expected. This was why a bed was prepared for a virgin in the uppermost temple of the *zigurat*. She was to come of her own accord, driven by sacred fervour, walking like a somnambulist in a magic sleep, to pass a night in the temple and be mysteriously fecundated by the solar god, at the spring festival. But this virgin had not yet arrived.[1]

Nabu-Nassir was moved by disturbing emotions as the strange details he had heard from his predecessor passed through his mind while standing before the empty couch in the silent sanctuary. He did not understand the meaning of the prophecy, which filled him with a kind of fear ; but he understood the meaning of the myth of Ishtar, which corresponds to the deepest mystery of the Chaldean religion. He felt bitterly that the protecting power of his race and religion had been overthrown, and that the fate of Babylon was

---

[1] See the description given by Herodotus (Book I. chap. 181-182) :

" On the topmost tower there is a spacious temple, and inside the temple stands a couch of unusual size, richly adorned, with a golden table by its side. There is no statue of any kind set up in the place, nor is the chamber occupied of nights by anyone but a single native woman, who, as the Chaldeans, the priests of this god, affirm, is chosen for himself by the deity out of all the women of the land. They also declare—but I, for my part, do not credit it—that the god comes down in person into this chamber, and sleeps upon the couch. This is like the story told by the Egyptians of what takes place in their city of Thebes, where a woman always passes the night in the temple of the Theban Jupiter. In each case the woman is said to be debarred all intercourse with men."

We see from this passage that the idea of parthenogenesis haunted the priests of Babylon and Thebes in the fifth century B.C. But what is the real explanation ? Eastern and western esoteric tradition both affirm that the physical bodies of the great prophets and Messiahs were born of a man and a virgin, thrown into a magnetic sleep. The universal law of nature is not suppressed, but the mystery of generation is accomplished in a state of ecstasy which excludes carnal desire. It may be said that in such cases the man and woman remain morally virgin, because they remember nothing on awaking. The mystical nature of their astral union endows the body of the child with a particular purity. This is the meaning of what in the Catholic Church is called the ' Immaculate Conception.' But, however it may be interpreted, humanity must preserve before this holy mystery the profound veneration which is due to the highest manifestation of the Divine in the Human through the sacrifice of incarnation.

linked with his own. Involuntarily he murmured, " O Ishtar, beloved goddess, captive of the lower gods, mayst thou find thy light once more ! Tell me thy secret and I shall know how to overcome the Adversary ! "

On the golden table beside the bed there was a gilt phial. The priest lifted it, and cried, " Whether this liquid contain life or death, I must know its secret ! "

He drank the contents of the phial, and the aroma of the liquid rose to his brain like the spiral stem of a richly perfumed flower. Turning round, he saw near the entrance door a porphyry griffon carved upon the wall. Its head touched the domed ceiling ; its forepaws formed a seat. Nabu-Nassir seated himself between them, and at once fell into a deep slumber.

CHAPTER III

FOR a long, long time he was drowned in a black gulf of unconsciousness, and knew nothing. Minutes contained centuries; time moved backwards. He felt himself being transported into the outermost regions, before the formation of the earth. Dark Saturn revolved on the edge of the planetary circle; Jupiter emerged from the shadows like a phantom globe. In a sphere nearer to the sun, Nabu-Nassir perceived Lilith, the first Eve, Ishtar, with Lucifer, at the moment when the creative gods, the Elohim, tore her from the arms of her spouse and threw the rebel archangel into the abyss. The dazzling whiteness of the goddess grew paler, and for a long time she floated, fainting, in the orbit of a destroyed planet. When she regained consciousness she gave a cry of horror and plunged downwards like a comet, in search of her spouse; but in vain.

Then the wheel of time rushed forward with lightning rapidity.

In the midst of awe-inspiring convulsions of Fire and Water, the star of sorrow and effort, the Earth, had taken shape, and now smiled seductively, covered with a carpet of verdure. Ishtar threw herself upon it, and as she alighted on its mountain-peaks she found herself face to face with an initiate-king, Istobar, who dwelt in a high valley. She appeared before him in her most alluring splendour, and said, " Thou who knowest all things, canst thou tell me where to find my spouse, Lucifer? If thou wilt tell me, I will take thee up in my marble chariot with wheels of gold, and thou shalt see the gods."

Istobar replied, " Do penance, O goddess, and address thy prayers to the sun. Only he can give thy spouse back to thee."

" The sun? " said Ishtar. " It was his murderous darts, directed by the Elohim, that precipitated Lucifer into the abyss. Since neither Earth nor Heaven can give him back to me, I will seek him in the depths of hell."

And Nabu-Nassir saw the goddess, with disordered hair,

---

[1] The legend of Ishtar, which I have here tried to reconstruct in its deeper significance, has come down to us in an exoteric but very suggestive form in the cuneiform inscriptions. See Oppert's *Scientific Expedition to Mesopotamia* and *Babylon and the Babylonians*.

plunging from deep to deep, from darkness to darkness, and crying, " Where is my spouse ? Lucifer ! Lucifer ! "

At the entrance of the first sphere a swarm of shadows met her, and whispered, " Take off thy radiant crown, or thou shalt not pass ! "

She gave them her crown, and pressed onwards, trembling, for she felt herself losing the memory of her divinity. At the second sphere, a swarm of darker shadows stopped her, and cried, " Give us thy wings, or thou shalt not pass ! "

She gave her wings, and pressed onwards. But she shuddered, for it seemed to her that she had lost the power to reascend. At the third sphere a swarm of monsters assailed her, and howled, " Discard thy luminous robe, or thou shalt not pass ! "

She tore off her robe, and was seized with horror, for her body had become opaque and hard.

Then from the centre of the abyss there rose a cone of crimson fire, from which issued a commanding voice : " What desirest thou of me ? "

" Where is Lucifer ? "

" Far from here, in the inaccessible limbo of space. Thou seekest him in vain, for I am thy spouse and thou shalt never escape from here."

" Thou liest ! " cried Ishtar. " I have dared all and lost all, to find him. My love is great enough to break thy power, and to make the gates of thy hell fall down like straws."

Within the fiery cone the flames crackled as though in mirth, and the voice said : " All that enters my sphere belongs to me, and it is thy secret desire that has brought thee here. Already thou lovest me . . . or thou wouldst not have come. Already my breath has touched thee . . . When thou seest me in my true form thou wilt find me more beautiful than Lucifer ! For he is bound and miserable, while I am free and all-powerful in my kingdom ! "

" It is not true," said Ishtar. " I hate thee ! . . . Thou canst not prove thy words."

" Wouldn't thou see thine archangel ? " said the voice. " I can summon him, for he is my elder brother, and I can cause his phantom to appear to thee. Promise me, if I show him to thee, that thou wilt be mine ! "

Ishtar hesitated ; for it seemed as though the flames issuing from the cone licked her body like fiery serpents' tongues, and penetrated to the marrow of her bones. But taking courage, with a sudden glow of hope, she cried, " When I see him, he will carry me off in his arms. Make him appear ! "

Then the voice that issued from the fire spoke :

" By the power that the immortal gods have given to the Abyss which is their pedestal and without which heaven could not exist, appear, Adar-Asshur ! Appear, Lucifer ! "

A phosphorescent cloud rose up, and within it Ishtar saw the sorrowful archangel appear, with pinioned wings, sublime in heroic suffering and indomitable pride. Tears of light fell from his eyes, sparkling drops of blood ran down his limbs. His eyes were fixed on Ishtar with a look of love . . . but he remained silent.

Ishtar tried to rush towards him, but her body seemed petrified, and she could only murmur, " Adar-Asshur, take me from here ! "

But the apparition vanished, and Ahriman emerged from the cloud in the form of a monstrous dragon, trying to dart his fiery tongue upon his victim. But the goddess escaped from him, and her voice echoed through the shadows, sweeping all before it : " I have lost my crown and my wings and my luminous robe. I have given all for my love . . . But I still have a heart that thou hast not conquered, and that none—not even the gods—can hinder in its flight. With it I will cleave the gulfs of darkness, and go back to the world of men. They will show me the way to Lucifer ! "

Great was the anguish of Nabu-Nassir in his dream. He felt that if Ishtar, the divine Eve, were to perish, the magi and their science would perish also. For what would Science be without the divine Love which is also Wisdom ? An instrument of suicide and death. Nabu-Nassir felt as though he himself were plunging into the depths of the earth, while overhanging masses of black and yellow rock closed above him. He gave a cry of distress : " Ishtar ! Ishtar ! "

And suddenly it seemed as though he half awakened from his dream . . . He found himself again in the chapel of Bel, seated between the fore-paws of the griffon. The white dove still lit up the golden sanctuary, but between the priest and the sculptured goddess wavered a red flame . . . Was it Ahriman ? . . . Nabu-Nassir leapt up with a cry. Before him stood Daniel in his scarlet archimage's robe with its golden collar—and the prophet's eyes were fixed upon the priest of Bel with a gentle but indomitable gaze.

CHAPTER IV

THE MINISTRY OF THE PROPHET DANIEL

NABU-NASSIR had automatically raised the sword that he carried at his belt, but Daniel, quite unmoved, smiled at him and held out his hand.

Then Nabu-Nassir, conquered by a higher power, and scarcely knowing what he did, let the sword fall, and gazed at the prophet, who had come to him like a divine messenger after his terrible dream.

Daniel was bare-headed, and his black, curling hair made an aureole around his lean, emaciated countenance. Under the wide brow the eyes of a visionary shone with mild but steady fire. From his whole person there emanated a magnetism so powerful that the Chaldean was moved in the very fibres of his being. He was stupefied—and fascinated. Then Daniel spoke :

" Blessed be the name of the Lord from one generation to another, for in Him are wisdom and power. Thou thinkest me thine adversary, Nabu-Nassir, but I come to thee as a friend, on behalf of Cyrus, king of the Persians and ruler of Babylon. He respects the Chaldean gods, knowing that among them is worshipped his own, the god of Zoroaster. He will uphold the priests, guardians of the science of the stars, and promises them his protection if they show themselves worthy of their ancestor, Zoroaster, the prophet of the Solar Word. I, Daniel, the exile, the humble prophet of Israel, give thee this message and bring thee peace."

Overcome by these words, Nabu-Nassir stretched out both his hands to the prophet.

" Blessed be thou, in the name of the sovereign God whom we call Iliu, and of the God who spoke to Zoroaster through the sun. I see that thou comest in Their Name. But the ancient gods who reigned here are vanquished. The world has turned on its axis. Through a power that is greater than mine thou hast penetrated into this sanctuary which only the high-priest of the temple should enter, and where I have passed a night of agony. Canst thou explain the fearful dream that I have had? I saw the descent of Ishtar into Hades ; I heard her cry of distress, as she called for Lucifer—a cry that is lost in infinity and whose echo remains in my desolate heart. Canst thou explain this mystery, and that of the mystical marriage-rites foretold by this empty couch, above which hangs the white dove, symbol of the Eternal-Feminine ? Canst thou do this, O thou who knowest how to read the dreams of men and the blazing thoughts of God ? "

Daniel answered : " O priest of Chaldea, thou who canst read the stars, hear the truth which is sister to thine own. The invisible gods, the powers of above and below, the creative gods with their feminine counterparts, emanations of their love, those whom we call Seraphim, Cherubim, Elohim and Archangels, reign in turns over the world and the nations. They succeed one another from age to age ; but one single God inspires and rules them. It is in His Name that the prophets of Israel speak ; it is in His Name that I humbly speak to thee now ; for we are but the servants of His Voice . . . Thou hast seen in thy dream the first causes of all that has taken place during the bloody reign of Nineveh and Babylon. Ishtar, the first Eve, the astral queen of the human soul, the seeker for love, is dazed with blood, voluptuousness and death. She is sunk in lethargy . . . And all the prophets declare that she can never again find Lucifer, her lost archangel, until a God has been born of a Virgin."

" Is not that miracle to happen here ? " said Nabu-Nassir. " Is not that the meaning of the bed of ivory, and the white dove ? "

" Yes, your priests have also foreseen the great mystery. But not here will be born the Son of Man in whom the Living God will be manifested ; not here will be incarnated the Solar Word which spoke to Zoroaster . . . It is in the nation of Israel, in that captive and exiled nation, that the divine Man will be born. And all the peoples of the earth shall be subject unto Him."[1]

" Then what does my science mean ? And my temple ? "

" The science of the stars and the vision of the soul are both divine, when ruled by the Eye of the Spirit which is the Love of Wisdom and the Wisdom of Love. Guard thy science for future ages. When the science of the stars and the vision of the soul are united, there will be only one God and one nation upon the earth. That is why Cyrus has bestowed upon thee, Nabu-Nassir, the rank of Archimage."

" I, Archimage ? " said the Chaldean, recoiling a step. " Then what wilt thou be, Daniel ? "

The prophet calmly unfastened his scarlet mantle and let it fall to the ground, revealing himself clothed in the white linen robe of the high-priest of Jerusalem. On his breast was the pectoral

---

[1] See the Book of Daniel, vii, 13, 14 ; and ix, 25, 26.

in which blazed the twelve precious stones symbolising the twelve tribes of Israel and the twelve signs of the zodiac.

The priest reverently fell upon one knee before the prophet, who in divesting himself of his rank of Archimage seemed to increase in stature, while his eyes glowed with a light of ecstasy.

Dull sounds and far-off cries echoed from without. The priest and the prophet left the chapel and descended to the terrace overlooking Babylon. In the East, dawn was spreading her saffron fan above a copper-coloured mist. The metallic roofs of palaces and temples gleamed with a sinister radiance above the still darkened town. The line of dust and orange-brown mist that marked the horizon where soon the sun would rise, seemed already threatening to overwhelm Babylon with the cloak of the desert that was later to enfold it and efface it from the earth's surface. But from the valley into which the priest and prophet were looking there rose the sound of a solemn psalm chanted by the voices of men and women. Daniel pointed out to his companion a white house whose terrace was lit up by branched candlesticks. It glowed like a lantern amid the surrounding shadows. "Listen!" murmured Daniel, and the Chaldean knew enough Hebrew to understand the words of the psalm.

"If I forget thee, O Jerusalem, let my right hand forget her cunning.

"If I do not remember thee, let my tongue cleave to the roof of my mouth : if I prefer not Jerusalem above my chief joy."

"Thou hearest!" said Daniel. "Hope is not dead in the hearts of the exiles. In those hearts the future Jerusalem lives."

Meanwhile the crimson disk of the sun had risen above the barrier of the horizon and was flinging its pointed darts into swarming Babylon, whose labyrinth of streets became as animated as a human ant-heap. Soldiers hurried to and fro, women came out upon the roofs. The Persians were making their formal entry into the capital of Chaldea. Along the wide, straight rampart of Imgur-Bel the royal chariot slowly advanced, drawn by twelve white horses, harnessed in fours. Behind it marched the Median guards, with their long hair and sparkling armour. Before it, a soldier carried a red standard embroidered in gold with the Persian lion and the sun of Zoroaster. A tremendous shouting, like the sound of the sea, arose from within the city :

"Glory to Cyrus, king of the Persians and of Babylon ! "

BOOK VI

MANIFESTATIONS OF THE SOLAR WORD

III

The Death of Cambyses and the Sun of Osiris

CHAPTER I

CYRUS was the greatest monarch of Asia, a just king, and a true son of Zoroaster. He played a leading part in the destiny of the world, and his actions had a decisive influence on the future of the white race. Without him, history would have taken a different course.

As conqueror of Babylon he spared the capital of his vanquished enemies, and allowed the priests to maintain their wisdom, the foundation of future sciences. By repelling the Scythian invasion he preserved the Mediterranean civilisations from destruction by the Barbarians, and drove the northern races back towards Scandinavia, whence they were to descend, eight centuries later, upon the Roman Empire, and bring about the rejuvenation of Europe. On the other hand, in authorising the Jews to regain Palestine and rebuild the temple at Jerusalem, he was the preserver of Israel, the keystone of monotheism and cradle of the future Christ.

But although Cyrus held, during his life, all the threads of the future in his powerful hands, and was able to unravel their Gordian knot, he could not prevent the gangrene of vice and the epilepsy of pride, always on the watch for absolute power, from developing in his own family.

The contrast between Cambyses and his father was appalling. He was the jackal that follows the lion and prowls in his footsteps. Farewell, Wisdom, Mercy and Courage ! Farewell, virtue of the soul and genius of the spirit, who had descended from the mountain of Zoroaster to float as winged victories above the armies of the conqueror of Babylon ! Cambyses, idle, cruel, envious and brutal, wallowing in luxury and perversity, carried his tyrannous frenzy to the point of actual crime. He was scarcely on the throne before he had his younger brother, whom he considered a dangerous rival, secretly murdered. Then he turned towards Egypt.

For more than a thousand years the kingdom of the Pharaohs had been an imposing rival to all the empires of Asia, and a protecting wall against universal anarchy. In spite of invasions from without and rebellions within, the Pharaohs had remained disciples of the Theban wisdom. Among them initiation still existed, and impressed royalty with a sense of justice, and all social functions with the seal of the divine hierarchies. Egypt had resisted the attacks of Nineveh and Babylon. Nebuchadnezzar had ravaged it without reaching the sacred city of Thebes; Cyrus had respected it; Cambyses wished to destroy it. All tyrants instinctively hate other powers which limit their own, and any moral and spiritual power which surpasses them has the effect of arousing their anger. In the wisdom and theocracy of Egypt the young King of the Persians sensed an unconquerable foe, and the consciousness of danger exasperated him and drove him to extreme measures.

Cambyses was superstitious, and at the same time delighted in sacrilege. His uneasy mind wavered between panic terror and measureless pride. When the fear of death overcame him, he would grovel before the vilest sorceror; when the madness of power possessed him, he thought himself the equal of Ormuzd, and burned to contend with him. But at this epoch the Persian priests had lost the power of evoking the light of Ormuzd, and Phanes of Halicarnassus, the Greek general who had deserted from Amasis, King of Egypt, to Cambyses, said to him: "The priests of Egypt are wiser than yours. Their God Osiris is the most powerful of all, and the same as Ormuzd. They know how to evoke him, for the name Osiris holds a great secret. He who knows it, they say, has the power of resurrection and no longer fears death. I will undertake to lead your army to the banks of the Nile. If you become master of the priests and temples of Egypt, and obtain the favour of their god, you will be master of the world."[1]

"Take me to Egypt," said Cambyses.

The desert and the swamps formed a bulwark between Syria and the Egyptian delta, but, through the intervention of Phanes, the Arab sheik who held the coast placed caravans with three days' provisions along the route, thus enabling the Persian army to invade the delta. A great battle took place at Pelusium, and on both sides the struggle was a desperate one. On the morning of the engagement, the Carians and Ionians in the army of Pharaoh slaughtered the children of Phanes the traitor, but this cruel and senseless sacrifice brought no good fortune. Towards evening the Egyptian army gave way, and was put to flight. The king, Psamatik III, took refuge in Memphis, but had to surrender, and at the same time Upper Egypt announced its submission. The war had only lasted a few weeks, and the powerful empire of the Pharaohs, which for two thousand years had ruled the Mediterranean and held back Asia, collapsed under the first blows of the son of Cyrus.

Cambyses was delirious with triumph. He began by asking

---

[1] Concerning Egyptian initiation, see the chapter on *Hermes* in *The Great Initiates* and that on *Ancient Egypt* in *Sanctuaires d'Orient* (by Edouard Schuré).

the priests of Memphis if they could invoke the god Osiris for him, and reveal his secret.   They replied : " It is not we who know this secret, it is the priests of Thebes.   You must go to them."

Cambyses was so infuriated that he indulged in unrestrained violence, and had all the chief priests of the temple of Ptah executed.   Not only did he condemn the unfortunate king Psamatik to death, but he forced him first to witness the murder of his children. After this he violated the tomb of Psamatik's father, King Amasis, and burned his mummy, a terrible sacrilege in the eyes of the Egyptians.   Arrived at Thebes, he called together the priests in the temple of Ammon-Ra.

" I am the ruler of Egypt," he told them, " and I claim for myself what the Pharaohs claimed from you. Can you show me the most sacred of your gods ? Can you reveal to me the secret of Osiris ? Your temples, your treasures, your archives, and your lives, are in my hands.   If you wish to preserve them, see that your supreme god looks on me with favour."

The chief pontiff of Thebes replied :

" What thou askest, O king, is beyond our power. We can invoke our god and pray him to pardon thee the blood that thou hast spilt, and to allow mercy to enter into thy heart, but we cannot force him to manifest himself to thee. It is not we who command our god ; it is he who commands us ! Thou canst bring Egypt into subjection, violate the tombs of our kings, burn their mummies . . . Thou canst overthrow the pillars of our temples and the obelisks on which our victories are engraved . . . Thou canst reduce to ashes the papyrus-rolls on which our secret wisdom is written . . . . Thou canst kill all the priests of Egypt and break the statues of our gods in pieces . . . but—thou will not see our god, thou wilt not discover the secret of Osiris, who speaks to the initiate from the depths of the Eternal and the Invisible. He can be approached only in the white robe of the neophyte, after years of penitence and purity, not in a king's blood-stained mantle, with a sword reeking of crime."

Cambyses was abashed by this speech.   The solemnity of the words, the dignity of the pontiff, the calmness of the priests of Ammon-Ra, each robed in white linen with a panther-skin thrown over the left shoulder, had filled him with involuntary awe. He left the sacred building with oblique and sullen looks, like a wild boar escaping from the hunters ; but he had scarcely re-entered the palace of the Pharaohs before he sent his guards to massacre the pontiff and all the priests of Ammon-Ra.   Then he went through the temple himself, and had the statues broken, the obelisks overturned, the crypts ransacked, the treasures pillaged, and all the papyri covered with sacred writings burnt. Finally he tried to destroy the temple by fire, but the great hall with its massive columns withstood the flames, and the enormous statues of Osiris, in grey granite and black basalt, remained upright, with their double crowns bearing in front the erect serpent of the uræus.

Cambyses next departed to conquer Nubia, but he suffered a severe defeat, and he and his army almost perished of thirst in the desert. He returned to Thebes, beaten, ill at ease, and disconcerted.

As he walked through the temple of Ammon-Ra, blackened by fire and desolate, he noticed a scribe squatting in a cell. It was a copper-skinned Nubian, who was copying hieroglyphics from a stela, with a reed dipped in red ink, on to a long roll of papyrus which fell in coils around his feet.

" What dost thou there ? " asked the king.

" I am copying the Book of the Dead for a noble citizen of Thebes, whose mummy is to be taken to his sarcophagus in the valley of the Tombs of the Kings."

" Thou knowest," said Cambyses, " that I have ordered the destruction of all the temple papyri, and that thou hast risked the death-penalty by writing on this one."

The scribe, crouching in a corner of his cell, did not seem to be moved by this threat. His face had the naïve expression of a scarab ; an enigmatic smile curved his thick lips, and his eyes sparkled with malice.

" Take this papyrus," he said, " and burn it. O great king, I give it to thee. But how wilt thou burn all the papyri in the thousands and thousands of tombs of all Egypt ? For every man of good faith has one buried with him. Thousands of years hence those who can read these hieroglyphs will find in them the science of our priests and the secrets of their wisdom."

" What is there in this Book of the Dead ? " asked Cambyses, becoming attentive.

" Instructions for the soul that travels to the Beyond ; magic words to guide him through the realm of Amenti, and across the great River of Forgetfulness ; warnings to avoid the evil pilot, the black Double, and to recognise the good one, the white Double ; rules for finding grace in the eyes of the implacable Judge who awaits the dead . . . down there. In fact this book contains the magic formula for regaining the divine memory, entering the barque of Isis, and reaching the *Sun of Osiris*."

" The *Sun of Osiris* ! What is that ? " cried Cambyses, trembling. He seized the scribe's bony arm and shook it violently. But the same enigmatic smile passed over the Nubian's lips, and the same malicious light sparkled in his eyes.

" I know nothing of it," he said, " for I have not seen it. But it is said that the dead see it, when they are good . . . O, very good . . . when they are pure . . . O, very pure."

" Is there no one who can make the living see it ? "

" Only the high-priest of Thebes could do so—and thou hast killed him."

" Is there no one else who knows the secret ? "

The scribe scratched his shaven head behind the ear, and placed his first finger on his forehead.

" There is one—the pontiff Osaharrisinti, high-priest of Saïs, in Lower Egypt. He has a drink made from the flower of nepenthes, a few mouthfuls of which will plunge the initiate into a lethargic sleep and cause him to travel to the other world. Perhaps Osaharrisinti can make thee see the nocturnal star of Osiris . . . the sun of the dead that rises upon a world of shadows . . . the sun of midnight. But he will risk his life—and thou also."

" What matter ? I shall know how to compel him. To thee, scribe, because thou hast told me the means of discovering the great secret, I will allow thy life ; and if I see the sun of Osiris, I will make thee chief pontiff of all Egypt."

" I pontiff—and thou god ? " said the Nubian, with the same sly expression. Then he added, " Dost thou see this little scarab of green marble from Syene ? "

Cambyses took the scarab and examined it. There were twelve signs graven upon it.

" Those are the twelve great gods of the universe," said the scribe. " Together they constitute the Soul of the World. Every man carries them within himself, and all beings are a reflection of them, like this scarab. The papyri may be burnt, but the sacred wisdom which comes from the Soul of the World cannot be destroyed. It would be reborn from a scarab. Accept, O great king, this souvenir of a scribe of Egypt ! "

For a moment Cambyses, half fascinated, gazed at the marble insect. Then he laid it on the stela in a kind of panic, and took his departure hurriedly. He was afraid of some enchantment. Several times he looked fearfully behind him ; for it seemed to him that the Soul of the World that he had tortured was following him in the form of a scarab with a mocking smile.

On the day when Cambyses returned to Memphis, the festival of spring was being celebrated with dance and song. The Persian king thought the people were rejoicing in his defeat, and ordered a fresh massacre of the priests. Next he stabbed his own sister whom he had forced to marry him in defiance of the law of Persia, and who had denounced his crimes with indignation and horror. Untouched by remorse, but full of fear, Cambyses presented himself before the pontiff of Saïs, in the temple dedicated to the goddess Neith, the nocturnal Isis, identified with the Universal Soul, and demanded immediate initiation and the vision of Osiris.

" Thou comest here stained with the blood of the priests of Egypt," said Osaharrisinti, an old man, humble and timid. " O great king, how should I obtain for thee what I have not been able to obtain for myself, after a life of purity and mortification ? "

" Thou canst. Thou hast a liquid which plunges one into a lethargic sleep, and enables one to descend to the world of the dead in order to remount to the sun of Osiris."

" But know well, O Cambyses, that if thou shouldst succeed in seeing the sun of Osiris it would destroy thee ! . . . Have a care lest it be not thine end."

" I fear nothing and no one," replied the king, in whom opposition only provoked excessive pride. " I have braved Ahura-Mazda, and I still live. I defy Osiris to harm me, provided I retain my sword, my cuirass, and my royal crown."

" Let it be done according to thy will," said the priest. " I will first invoke for thee Zoroaster, the prophet of thy race. If he comes, he will tell thee whether thou art ready to see the sun of Osiris."

He then led the king through a long avenue of sphinxes to the interior of the temple. They passed through a series of chambers before reaching a retired part of the sanctuary, where stood an empty sarcophagus. The vast colonnade, dimly lighted, seemed to vanish into dark shadow. Having drunk the narcotic beverage, the king lay down in the sarcophagus, girt with a cuirass, and with his sword beside him and his crown on his head. Meanwhile the priest threw perfumes into a brazier which stood on a tripod, and pronounced his invocations aloud.

At first Cambyses experienced a strange sensation. It seemed to him that his body became heavier and heavier, and sank into a bottomless gulf, while his spirit rose through space, light and trembling. Then he felt himself dissolved into nothingness, and lost consciousness. When he became conscious again he was in the same chamber, but it seemed to have increased enormously in size. A thick smoke rose from the tripod. The pontiff was on his knees, praying, with outstretched hands ; and a majestic old man, whose beard was a river of silver and who wore a sparkling sheepskin over his linen robe, gradually appeared, veiled in golden mist, and leaning upon a staff. Cambyses trembled, for he knew that it was Zoroaster.

In a deep voice the prophet of the Aryans spoke.

" Why dost thou call me up, degenerate son of the Aryan race, king of iniquity, stained with many horrors ? Thy purple is dyed with innocent blood ; thy breath exhales the odour of crime as the jackal's that of decaying flesh. Traitor to thy father, thy race and thy god, perverse offspring of Ahriman, wouldst thou dare to contemplate the glory of Ahura-Mazda whom the priests of Egypt call Osiris? Do not attempt this sacrilege. Thy days are numbered. The time approaches when Ahura-Mazda will be incarnated in a man, who will offer his body as a sacrifice for the manifestation of the Word. When the Son of God walks alive upon the earth, thou and all who resemble thee will be swept away like dust before the wind. Hide thyself in a cave like a serpent. The sun of Osiris is not for thee."

Having pronounced these words the phantom of Zoroaster faded away, and his speech ended in a peal of thunder. Cambyses awoke in a cold sweat. He stepped,s huddering, out of the sarcophagus, and groped his way towards the priest, who was still praying.

" Hast thou seen thy prophet ? "

" Yes."

" What did he say to thee ? "

" He threatened me with death if I evoked the sun of Osiris. He told me that soon Ahura-Mazda, called Osiris by the Egypt.ans, would incarnate as man, and that then the all-powerfulness of kings would be ended. But I do not believe it. This Zoroaster was perhaps only a phantom created by thee. My cuirass is still around me, my sword by my side, and my crown on my head. I do not fear either Zoroaster or his god. It is the hour of darkness —there is no light save from the fire upon the tripod—none sees or hears us—on pain of death therefore, evoke for me the sun of Osiris, the sun of midnight ! To thy incantations, priest ! "

"Follow thy destiny," said Osaharrisinti. "May the eternal thought of the gods emerge from the limbo of the future for thee, like a sword from the sheath ! "

Cambyses took a second draught of the liquid, and lay down once more in the sarcophagus. This time it seemed to him, in losing consciousness, as though his soul were driven out of his body like the smoke from a bundle of straw that is being consumed by fire. When he awoke from nothingness, a trembling ghost, he saw, as at an infinite distance, a brilliant star at the end of the gallery. The star became a golden sun whose rays strove to embrace the universe. As it came nearer, a black cross appeared upon the face of the sun, and on the cross the body of a crucified God. And the Crucified One increased in size till the whole of the solar disk was hidden. His limbs were bleeding, and in His dead face was all the sorrow of the world. But suddenly He lifted His head and opened His eyes. A slender ray of light issued from them, and rested upon the brow of Cambyses. It was a look of love and pity, but such was its piercing strength that it seemed to penetrate the king's body with sharp agony, as though the very marrow of his bones were melting away. At the same time a wonderful harmony filled all space; trumpets of brass and sounding harp-strings, thunderous voices of the spheres and archangelic choirs. And all these voices said:

"Tremble, O Ahriman! Kneel, O Kings! Priests, burn your incense! He prepares to come, He descends from heaven, the Lord of Lords, the Radiant Son of the Supreme God, the Master of gods and men! He shall walk the earth; He shall be crucified. He shall die through love to arise again in glory. . . . The tyrants are vanquished; the heavens open; the dead arise. Glory to the Christ! In the heart of death He has found eternal life!"

During this chant, which throbbed like a great symphony above the cosmic thunder, the Crucified One had become glorious, clothed in a shining robe. From the end of the colonnade the gigantic Christ advanced upon Cambyses. Behind Him, all the victims of the tyrant were rising transfigured in the rays of His solar glory; and the face of the resurrected God shone like the lightning, and His glance pierced the heart of the king like a sword.

Then Cambyses awoke in unbearable anguish. The felicity of his victims caused him to suffer all the tortures he had inflicted on them. Under the gaze of the victorious God, the point of his own sword had entered his heart; his cuirass stifled him; his crown burnt his temples like molten lead. He leapt from the sarcophagus with a cry of horror, and flung himself upon the priest, who had fallen with face to the ground before the smoking tripod.

"Help me, help me! I am burning!" cried Cambyses.

The pontiff rose to his feet, and repulsed the king as he tried to cling to him.

"I told thee, O king, not to ask to see the sun of Osiris."

"Take from my eyes this light that is blinding me," the king stammered. "The night was better. Give me back the darkness!"

But the priest, who now also seemed transfigured by the superhuman vision, replied, "Thou hast evoked the light that kills when it does not revive. It will never release thee again."

Then Cambyses, seized with madness, threw from him his crown, his sword, and his cuirass—and fled. He died soon afterwards upon the coast of Syria. Herodotus recounts that his sword pierced his thigh when he was mounting on horseback, but according to the inscription of Behistan it seems that he killed himself in a fit of despair.[1]

---

[1] See Rawlinson's *Records of the Past*, vol. ii, p. 112—"Inscription of Darius on the rock of Behistan."

Such was the tragic end of Cambyses, one of the most savage incarnations of Asiatic tyranny.

The vision of the sun of Osiris, spoken of in the Book of the Dead, and in the sacred tradition of Egypt, was for the priesthood of the Nile a foreshadowing of the solar mystery of the Cosmic Christ (the Logos), and a presage of the historic Christ (Jesus) who was to put an end to the apotheosis of absolute power, and to change the face of the world and the character of initiation.

BOOK VII

THE HELLENIC MIRACLE

APOLLO AND DIONYSUS—THE ELEUSINIAN MYSTERIES—
THE BASIS OF TRAGEDY.

Happy are those who have experienced
the Mysteries. They know the beginning
and the end of life.

PINDAR.

The Beautiful is the splendour of the
True.

PLATO.

CHAPTER I

THE GORDIAN KNOT

THE part played by Greece in human evolution can be summed up through the main idea with which she enlightened the world, and this idea can be formulated as follows : *The work of Greece was the perfect realisation of the Divine through the Human in the form of Beauty.* In the Greek world we contemplate a powerful incarnation of Divine Beauty, and its harmonious expression in civilisation and in art. We are still living, so to speak, on the remains of this work and the reflections of this idea—but do we know anything of their origin and historical significance ? In other words, can we organically link up the Greek revelation with those which preceded it, and with that which followed it ?

In this respect Greece is uniquely situated, and plays a leading part. She marks the transition from the ancient cycle of polytheistic religions to Christianity. She is the Gordian Knot in which are entangled all the secret threads that run from Asia to Europe, from the East to the West.

Have we unravelled this distaff ? Have we penetrated to the inner sanctuary ? In spite of all our researches and discoveries, we are too far away from this world and its radiant mysteries.

Alas ! the spell is broken ; the smile of the gods that illuminated the world like a rosy dawn has faded away. Never since then has any nation seen it ; never has man rediscovered that marvellous equilibrium of body and soul, that exquisite penetration of matter by spirit, which gave wings to the athletes of Olympia and to the words of Plato. To-day, the austere shadows of Christian asceticism, the formidable framework of a civilisation founded upon machinery and the laborious constructions of materialistic science, combine to rear themselves like an impassable mountain-range between us and the luminous Arcady for which we yearn with homesick longing.

Two thousand years of history hide sacred Greece from us, and we have lost the secret of her divine ecstasy, so rich in wisdom and subtle delights. On the other hand, we must recognise that she is always the half of ourselves, since to her we owe our arts, our philosophies, and even our sciences. But this only makes the Greek genius seem more and more of an inexplicable prodigy.

We can thus speak of a *Hellenic miracle* as of a *Christian miracle*, and there is no better symbol of its marvels than the myth of Prometheus, audacious stealer of lightning, who, in bringing men the fire from heaven, bestowed on them art, science and freedom.

Up till now historians have sought the explanation of the Hellenic miracle in the race and country of the Greeks, and these two factors certainly provided the indispensable conditions for it. If Europe seems like a ramification of Asia, Greece, terminated by the Peloponnesus and surrounded by her islands, seems the most delicate branch, and the flowery bouquet, of Europe. Gulfs and capes, leafy valleys and barren hills, all the outlines of sea and mountain, merge into a rich and sober harmony. The steep, snow-clad peaks of Thessaly might have been hewn by Titans to form the thrones of the Olympians ; and were not the ivy-hung grottoes of Cythera made for gods who loved the women of earth, and the springs and myrtle-groves of Arcadia for nymphs and dryads ? Did not the plains of Elis, Argos and Attica seem to await heroic combats and the gallop of centaurs ? Did not the foam-fringed Cyclades, strewn upon the violet sea like shells or dewy flowers, invite the dances of the nereids ? Did not the rock of the Acropolis demand the Parthenon with its virgin goddess whose brazen helmet could be seen shining from so far away ? And finally, did not the gloomy chasm of Delphi, below the white peaks of Mount Parnassus, seem a place predestined for the tripod of the Pythoness, who vibrated to the voice of the Abyss and to the whisperings of Heaven ?

Here, without doubt, was a marvellous setting ; but the cradle, however beautiful, does not make the child.

Do the various peoples—Thracians, Ætolians, Achaians, Lydians, Æolians—who met and mingled with the ancient Pelasgians in Hellas, suffice to explain, together with the beauty of the land, the miracle of Greek religion and poetry ? At their head we find two types that synthesise the qualities of the whole race—the Ionians and the Dorians. The Ionians came from Asia, and were called *Yavanas* by the Hindus, meaning worshippers of *Iona*, the feminine principle of the divinity and the receptive principle of nature. To the masculine gods these people preferred goddesses—the earth-mother, Cybele, the voluptuous Astarte, the changeable Hecate. They represent the feminine side of the Greek soul—grace, quickness of mind, and versatility, together with a certain indolence ; but also passion, orgiastic genius, and enthusiasm. In Hellas they found themselves confronted by the Dorians, a rough and warlike race from the plains of Scythia beyond the Thracian mountains. These were barbarians. Their sturdy bodies had been bathed in the icy waters of the Strymon, but in their brave hearts and reddish hair they carried the rays of their hyperborean Apollo, whose memory was preserved at both Delos and Delphi. They represent the masculine element in the Greek genius ; their gods are those of the sky, Vulcan, Zeus, Apollo—fire, lightning and light ; their heroes are Hercules, slayer of monsters, and the Dioscuri, Castor and Pollux, tamers of horses.

The strife between the Ionians and the Dorians, culminating in the rivalry between Athens and Sparta, and in the disastrous Peloponnesian War, forms the groundwork of Greek history, which is filled with its bloody records. But it fails to account for the poetry and religion of Greece. How comes it that these appear, from the very beginning, like a harmonious edifice that neither poetic license nor fantasy could cause to tremble ? Whence came the unity of the Greek Pantheon, and its glorious hierarchy, rhythmic as the dance of the Muses, or as the flight of Iris between earth and heaven ? (We must note that this hierarchy was identical in the Ionian Homer and the Dorian Hesiod.) From what authority emanated the Amphictyonic Council, which gave its sanction to a national unity that should overrule all internal dissensions ? And who bestowed supremacy, from prehistoric times, upon the male genius of the Dorians over the passional and orgiastic genius of the Ionians—not to spoil or destroy it, but rather to bring about its finest blossoming through wise cultivation ?

The Greek poet recounts that Jupiter, enamoured of the fair Europa, took the form of a magnificent bull, and carried her on his back across the azure seas, from the sunny shores of Asia to the rugged Isle of Crete—a story suggestive of the Ionian emigrations and of the many abductions of women in that rough and joyous age. But—to follow the delightful symbolism of the myth—when Jupiter, in a cavern of Mount Ida, had reassumed his human form, through which the god was visible, by what charms, what lightning glances, what fiery caresses, did he succeed in transforming the gentle maiden into a powerful woman who was to display in turns the seductiveness of Aphrodite, the impetuousness of Pallas, and the seriousness of Melpomene ? For Greece holds us captive not only by her smile ; she also enchains and challenges us by the tragic fire of her gaze. Whence has she this power and this magic ? That is the enigma.

The land and the race may serve as explanation of the lighter Greece, laughing, intelligent and refined, so well described by Taine and Renan, but having neither the Ionian passion nor the

Dorian grandeur.[1] Very charming is this Greece of sailors and
shepherds, of amiable pirates and graceful artists. She plays, in
a superior fashion, with life, thoughts and gods, savouring them a
little mockingly. She makes us understand Theocritus, Aristophanes, the Anthology, and Lucian ; the rhetoricians, the sophists ;
the demagogy of Athens, the fierce politics of Sparta. But by
the side of this profane and sportive Greece, there is another,
deeper and more serious—the Greece of Homer and Hesiod, of
Pindar and the great lyric poets, of Phidias and Praxiteles, of
Æschylus and Sophocles, of Empedocles, Heraclitus, Pythagoras
and Plato. The soul of Greece, as manifested in these great
individualities, can be explained neither by the soil, the race, nor
the age, but only by the superhuman inspirations that called it to
life. The decadent Greece, too often presented to us in place of
the true one, was that of later times—the surface dust of her
decaying genius.

Like all great nations, the Greeks had a prehistoric religious
revelation, adapted to their nature and their mission—a revelation
which has left its traces in their legends and institutions, a well-
spring of light and life which nourished their masterpieces and did
not dry up until after these had come to birth. In a word, *behind
the visible Greece there is an invisible Greece ;* and only the second
can explain the first, which it created and organised. Its secret
is hidden from us in the Mysteries, guarded by the vow of silence,
and by the penalty of death which the Areopagus enforced upon
any who violated it ; but, nevertheless, the Orphic fragments,
the allusions of Plato, the treatises of Plutarch, the indiscretions
of the Alexandrian philosophers, the polemics of the Church
Fathers, the topography of the ruins of Eleusis and their characteristic inscriptions, permit us to gain some idea of the essence and
symbolism of this secret religion.[2]

Let us bravely enter the shadows of the two most venerated
sanctuaries of Greece—Delphi and Eleusis. We shall there find
the two divinities who were the two opposite poles of the

---

[1] See Renan's " Study of the Religions of Antiquity " in his *Essais d'Histoire
Religieuse* and Taine's *Philosophie de l'Art en Grèce.*

[2] The best description of the Eleusinian Mysteries—not of the personal
initiation given to the pupils of the Eumolpidæ, but of the festivals celebrated
annually—is to be found in *La Symbolique de Kreuzer,* translated and added to by
Guigniant under the title *Les Religions de l'Antiquité.* See also the remarkable
work of M. Foucart, *Recherches sur l'Origine et la Nature des Mystéres d'Eleusis*
(1895), and the excellent study of *Les Fouilles d'Eleusis* by M. Diehl in his
Excursions Archéologiques. There are vivid descriptions of Delphi and Eleusis
in the charming book by M. André Bernier, *Le Sourire d'Athéna.*

Greek soul, and who will give us the key to it—Apollo and Dionysus.

Apollo, the Dorian god *par excellence*, inspirer of wisdom and divination, master of the conscious and disciplined individuality, is the Solar Word of Zeus, conceived as the Eternal and Infinite God, and the revealer of the Archetypes of all things. When Apollo speaks, whether in light or in sound, through the bow or the lyre, in poetry or in music, he is the direct manifestation of his Father, the language of pure Spirit to spirits. Brilliant messenger from the impenetrable azure and the uncreated light that slumbers within the primordial darkness, beneficent to those who worship him, terrible to those who deny him, impenetrable to human thought, he soars above time and space in immaculate splendour.

Dionysus is the other Word of Zeus—but how different is this son of Semele and the lightning ! We find in him the manifestation of the same God in the visible world, his descent into matter, and his circulation throughout terrestrial nature, vegetable, animal and human, in which he becomes infinitely dispersed and divided. He is the god of sacrifice and of revelry, of death and of rebirth, of incarnation and of dis-incarnation. By his dispersion and immersion into the many souls that make up the great Whole, he overflows with joy and sorrow at the same time ; he pours forth floods of ecstasy, suffering, and enthusiasm. He is terrible, yet gentle ; sublime yet unfortunate. For if he is fruitful of creations, so is he of metamorphoses, of sudden changes and turnings ; and his unbridled desire that plunged him into the depths of matter can cause him to rebound with a prodigious spring to the pure ether of Zeus, where distant suns are seen shining alone beyond the archetypes of the worlds.

To sum up, Apollo is *the static god of Revelation*, and Dionysus *the dynamic god of Evolution*. Their encounters, their conflicts, and their temporary alliances, form the history of the soul of Greece, from an esoteric standpoint.

This history has three stages : primitive Orphism, the Eleusinian Mysteries, and Athenian Tragedy. In each of these luminous points we find displayed a victory of the Apollonian principle over the Dionysian principle, followed by a reconciliation between the two. Left to himself, Dionysus unchains passion, or loses himself in infinity, but under the discipline of Apollo he exhibits marvellous charms and powers. So it happens that Greece marks an epoch unique in history—the epoch when the cosmic forces, which in all other nations were engaged in unequal combat, had attained a perfect equilibrium and a harmonious fusion. The pact between

Apollo and Dionysus is the *chef d'œuvre* of the Hellenic religion and the secret of the invisible Greece.[1]

Thus there is presented to us, twisted and twined into an inextricable tangle by the most mysterious powers of the universe, the Gordian Knot of the Greek genius. Would that I had the sword of Alexander with which to sever it ! I shall at least try to disentangle a few threads. Through the visible Greece we will seek to penetrate into the invisible ; after a glance at the many-coloured façade of the temple, resplendent with statues and trophies, we will enter the sanctuary. There perhaps we shall see at work the Powers who ordain the marvels that we have beheld outside.

---

[1] We must here render justice to the discoverer of the psychological significance of Apollo and Dionysus in Greek æsthetics. Greece herself, though she realised it in her Mysteries, and illustrated it vividly in her myths, did not express it through the mouth of her philosophers. Perhaps she *lived* it too thoroughly to be able to formulate it. Among the moderns no one has suspected it, save only Nietzsche, who divines it in that work of genius, *Die Geburt der Tragœdie aus dem Geiste der Musik*—(*The Birth of Tragedy from the Spirit of Music*). Having remarked on the radical antagonism between the Apollonian and Dionysian elements in all Greek literature, he classified the first as the phenomenon of *dream*, and the second as that of *ecstasy*. Dreaming brings visions of beauty, ecstasy produces a fusion of the soul with the souls of the elements and all beings. For this reason, Nietzsche calls Apollo *the principle of individuation* and Dionysus *the principle of identification with Nature*, or of the return to the Great Whole. From this profound conception he draws novel and striking deductions, first concerning the contrast between the contemplative serenity of the Greek epic rhapsodies and the tumultuous passion of the lyrics, and next, concerning the primitive nature of the dithyramb and the origin of tragedy, in which the two principles meet and are synthesised.

In fact, Nietzsche has classified perfectly the psycho-physiological effects of the Apollonian and Dionysian forces, and has shown their action upon Greek art, but his mentality and philosophy did not permit him to rise as far as the *cosmic powers* of which the Apollonian dream and the Dionysian ecstasy are merely reflex actions. Not admitting the existence of a spiritual world above the physical, the Apollonian vision of the Archetypes could be to him only a poetic hallucination, and the Dionysian ecstasy only a return to nothingness or to the unconsciousness of the elements. Upon his retina, inflamed by the philosophy of Schopenhauer, the light of Apollo and the flame of Dionysus became transformed into the black spot of pessimism. But this makes his discovery all the more remarkable, for it required a singularly acute intuition to penetrate to the very threshold of the Mysteries and to lift a corner of the veil, in the absence of complete illumination and a knowledge of esoteric tradition.

CHAPTER II

THE VISIBLE GREECE—THE DELPHIC APOLLO

FROM the time of the ancient Pelasgians, Zeus-Jupiter had reigned alone upon the hill-tops of Thrace and Thessaly. He had a sanctuary at Dodona, and others in Arcadia and in Crete, on the slopes of Mount Ida. He was a sublime god, but inaccessible and awe-inspiring. For ministers he had priest-kings who dwelt upon fortified heights, and who ruled through force and fear in the name of the conqueror of the Titans, the son of Uranus and of the Saturnian night. His oracles were obeyed without being comprehended. Men invoked him by night in the innumerable eyes of heaven ; they quailed before his rolling thunder ; they heard him roaring in the branches of the oak-trees. Through the decrees of his priest-kings he ruled imperiously over the people, who lived in groups within cyclopean walls for the safety of their flocks. But this Uranian god was scarcely interested in the miserable race of mortals ; he tolerated rather than loved them. His power protected the domestic hearth, and vows and compacts. But who was he, the inaccessible one ? Who would ever see him ?

It was a veritable revolution when the Dorians descended upon Hellas. They were clothed in animal skins, armed with long bows and arrows, and followed by their red-haired women, who, like druidesses, invoked Helios before the battle, with loud cries, in a kind of sacred ecstasy. The solar god that they brought with them in their brilliant blue eyes, in their quivers, and in their hymns, was not a distant god, but a god who was present everywhere. The sun was merely his outward sign, his heavenly chariot. This son of Zeus spoke directly to the heart of man in a new language, through weapons of war, through the lyre and the song. Soon a great vibration of light and melody passed through the soul of Hellas. Let Jupiter thunder on the hill-tops —Apollo reveals himself in the beauty of bare bodies and in hymns of joy ! It seemed as though the rhythm of the stars were then communicated to human limbs and human speech ; to the strings of the lyre, to the phalanxes of the warriors, to the processions of the virgins ; and became crystallised in the growing columns and architraves of the temples. The Solar Word of Apollo was to create the harmonious man, the harmonious city. That was his first miracle.

The echo of all this is to be found in the Homeric Hymn to Apollo.[1] If the Greek genius localises and anthropomorphises its gods, one can still find in its poetry the echo of distant cosmic happenings.

"It is by thee, O Phœbus," says the poet, "that songs are inspired, whether in the islands or upon the mainland where the heifers feed. The high rocks hymn thee, and the mountain summits, the rivers flowing seawards, the ports, and the promontories that jut out into the sea." Thus the earth herself sings a hymn to the god, with all her fauna and flora, a lively response to the beams that fall upon her. The poet then celebrates the birth of Apollo. The chief event of our planetary system, the emergence of the sun from the Saturnian night, seen by the Indian *rishis* in its true cosmogonic aspect, in vast circles of shadows and light, takes in Greek imagination the form of a graceful story, lit up by profound symbolism. It is the Dorian idea rendered by an Ionian rhapsodist. Leto, kneeling before the palm-tree at Delos and embracing it, gave birth to the god.

"All the goddesses raised a cry. . . . Nor did his mother suckle Apollo the golden-sworded, but Themis with immortal hands first touched his lips with nectar and sweet ambrosia, while Leto rejoiced, in that she had born her strong son, the bearer of the bow.

Then Phœbus, as soon as thou hadst tasted the food of Paradise . . . no bonds could bind thee, but all their ends were loosened. Straightway among the goddesses spoke Phœbus Apollo: "Mine be the dear lyre and bended bow, and I will utter to men the unerring counsel of Zeus."

So speaking, he began to fare over the wide ways of earth, Phœbus of the locks unshorn, Phœbus the Far-darter. Thereon all the goddesses were in amaze, and all Delos blossomed with gold, as when a hill-top is heavy with woodland flowers." [2]

The author of the hymn then describes the magical effects of the cult of Apollo at Delos.

"With Delos, Phœbus, art thou most delighted at heart, where

---

[1] The hyperborean priestesses of Delos, the Delian Virgins, of whom the Homeric Hymn speaks, and whose tombs M. Homolle found at Delos, were one consequence of it.

[2] English prose version by Andrew Lang.

the long-robed Ionians gather in thine honour. . . . Whoso then encountered them would say that they are exempt from eld and death, beholding them so gracious, and would be glad at heart, looking on the men and fair-girdled women, and their much wealth, and their swift galleys. Moreover, there is this great marvel of renown imperishable, the Delian damsels, hand-maidens of the Far-darter. They, when first they have hymned Apollo, and next Leto and Artemis the Archer, then sing in memory of the men and women of old time, enchanting the tribes of mortals. And they are skilled to mimic the notes and dance music of all men, so that each would say himself were singing, so well woven is their fair chant." [1]

Does not this picture show us the blossoming of a new religion? To the strains of Apollonian music boats from all parts arrive at the sacred island. Men and women mount to the temple in groups, to the sound of lyres, and there is something chaste and solemn about this human architecture. It is the imprint of Apollo upon the Ionian race. Under his influence the Greek cities are ranged in rhythms of beauty. Many centuries later, after the victory of Platæa, when the Greeks were building an altar to Jupiter-Liberator in that town, they desired that the first fire for it should be brought from the sanctuary at Delphi, which had not been defiled by the barbarians. A young man named Euchidas offered to make this twenty-league journey without letting the fire be extinguished. On arrival, like the runner of Marathon, he fell dead. It was the homage of virile youth to its god.

But though Apollo presided over the organisation of the cities, his most subtle and noble influence was manifested through poetic inspiration. From the wave of inspiration which the Solar Word caused to flow from Hellas to Ionia and back from Ionia to Hellas in innumerable rhapsodies, there arose the Iliad and the Odyssey, Homer and Hesiod, epic poetry and theogony, and the various cycles of mythology and heroic legend, all of which cross and re-cross one another in great circles without confusion, like the ripples on a clear pool. What is the primitive nature and character of this inspiration? Lucretius has said somewhere that men first saw the sublime forms of the gods during sleep, and the opening portion of Hesiod's theogony confirms this hypothesis. It is near the violet fountain of Hippocrene, in the dense shade of the great oak-trees, that Hesiod has his vision of the Muses. In his dream he sees them descending, light of foot, from snowy Olympus.

---

[1] English prose version by Andrew Lang.

"Wrapt in misty air they pass swiftly through the night, raising their lovely voices in praise of stormy Zeus and honoured Hera who walks in golden sandals, and the daughter of Zeus, clear-eyed Athena, and Phœbus Apollo and joyous Artemis with her arrows. . . . 'Shepherds who sleep in the open air,' they cry, 'vile race, mere fleshly appetites, we can tell many lies that are like truths, but we can also, when it pleases us, speak truth unveiled.' So spake the very daughters of great Zeus, and they gave me a sceptre, a green branch of well-grown laurel, and inspired me with a voice divine, that I might tell things past and future, and give praise to themselves and to all the race of immortal gods."

On awaking from this dream Hesiod recognised his mission. "Why remain here with the oaks and the rocks?" he cried. The herdsman had become a poet.

Such was the Apollonian vision in its original and authentic simplicity. Modern criticism may discuss it as nothing but an allegory, or the play of an over-excited imagination; but the science of the spirit, free from all scholastic or popular superstition, sees in it a relic of the ancient clairvoyance, a higher inspiration adapting itself to the mind of the seer. Like Homer, Hesiod calls the Muses the daughters of Mnemosyne, a word which should be translated as the Wisdom of Memory, for Mnemosyne really represents the universal memory of nature, the astral light, subtle and ethereal, in which float all the images of the past. The nine muses of Hesiod are like intelligent messengers of this light, gentle awakeners of the higher human faculties, subtle sowers of the arts and sciences in the human brain. It goes without saying that the free imagination of the poets, beginning with Homer, has considerably altered these primitive ideas, but as a whole, and in essentials, Greek epopee and mythology represent very clearly the astral vision which the Greeks called the light of Apollo.

But Apollo, as well as being the ruler of cities, the model of youthful beauty, and the inspirer of poetry, was also the god of divination and wisdom. These last two attributes make him the chief of the pan-Hellenic gods, the spiritual head of the tribunal of Amphictyons, the supreme arbitrator for the Greek people. In all these ways he intervened in the destinies of individuals and of nations. This was his most obvious and most important rôle, for in it he showed himself present and active in the whole of the ancient world. Numbers of strangers—the tyrants of Sicily and Lydia, and even the Pharaohs of Egypt—came to consult him, but his oracles were given only through his priests and priestesses in the sanctuary.

Athens was the brains of Greece, but Delphi was the beating heart. Let us go then to Delphi.

We are now far from the city of Pallas, whose citadel dominates the Attic plain, between the distant, smiling sea and the perfumed slopes of Hymettus. The situation of Delphi is magnificent and tragic.

In the sombre gorge of Phocis, at the end of a valley of perpendicular rocks, the mount of Apollo cowers beneath the high ramparts of Parnassus like an eagle scared by lightning. From a distance it appears small, because of the colossi that surround it; from a nearer viewpoint, it seems to become gradually larger. Beside it, between Parnassus and Mount Kirphis, winds the sinister torrent of Pleistos, roaring amid a chaos of rocks. No horizon; a dry, cracked soil; and everywhere the menace of overhanging peaks, from which the tremblings of the earth cause huge blocks of stone to roll. In these summits towering heavenwards, as in these yawning gulfs, the earth here bears witness to her own volcanic power of creation and destruction.

Why should the god of light have chosen this terrible place for his abode? Like modern travellers, the ancient pilgrims, winding in long processions across the plain of Krissa, suffered from a sense of oppression. But it lifted and grew lighter as they approached their goal, and were dazzled by the far-off shining of marble and bronze. They passed through the outskirts of Marmaria, shadowed by ash and olive, and entered on the Sacred Way. There they saluted the Marathon memorial, with its brass combatants and mythical Athenian heroes, and, facing it, the monument recording the victory of Aigos-Potamos, erected by the Lacedæmonians as though in defiance of their rivals, and showing Zeus crowning King Lysander. The pilgrims climbed steadily up the broad road that winds between thickets of laurel and myrtle, and were filled with diverse emotions at the sight of the treasures from enemy cities forced into reconciliation before the common god. They saluted the column of the Thyiades, the treasure of Rhodes, the tripod of Platæa, the Messenian Victory, and the graceful caryatides of the Cnidians.

When they had passed the silver fountain of Castalia, gushing from a hollow in the rocks, they at last found themselves before the temple of Apollo, hung with shields and trophies, and uniquely placed between the Phædriades, or Shining Crags, which the setting sun dyes with crimson and violet tints. Then the pilgrims, with deep emotion, intoned the Hymn of Praise, thinking of the myth according to which Jupiter's eagle, ordered to find the centre of the world, came soaring over the heights of Parnassus, and, dropping into the gorge, alighted upon the sacred mount.

Was not this eagle the temple itself, flanked by its two rocks as by outspread, flaming wings, and bearing within its heart the Word of Apollo, inspirer of all marvels?

CHAPTER III

THE PYTHONESS

APOLLO prophesied at Delphi through the Pythia, an institution which dated from time unknown. Certain authors attribute its origin to the disturbing effect of vapours rising from the cleft of a grotto in which the tripod of the Pythoness was placed, and where she pronounced her oracles in the midst of violent convulsions. A shepherd, taking refuge by chance in this place, might have begun to prophesy, and the experiment, successfully repeated, would confer popularity on the primitive sanctuary. This is quite possible.

In any case it is certain that from time immemorial there had been prophesying at Delphi. Æschylus says, at the beginning of the *Eumenides*, that, before Apollo, oracles spoke at Delphi in the names of three other divinities, the Earth, Themis and Phœbe—which means centuries for each of these cults. To the most ancient Pythoness, the priestess of Phœbe, the Greeks gave the name of Sibylla, and they attributed these strange words to her : " When I am dead, I shall be in the moon and I shall take her face for mine. I shall be in the air, like a breath. With the universal sounds and voices I shall go everywhere."

The establishment of the cult of Apollo at Delphi brought an organisation more skilled in prophecy. The Pythonesses were chosen in childhood by an assembly of priests, and were brought up in the sanctuary like cloistered nuns, the most rigorous chastity being enforced. Rustic and simple natures were preferred, but their receptive psychic faculties were cultivated, and the priest of Apollo who bore the name of prophet generally interpreted their oracles. But the practice of this art and the source of this wisdom remained an impenetrable mystery to the public.

Plutarch, priest of Apollo at Chæroneia, and Platonic philosopher of the second century A.D., gives some glimpses of the secret, and, so to speak, of the invisible mechanism of divination, when he remarks that as the body employs many organs, so the soul in its turn employs the body and the members of the body ; and that *the soul is the instrument of the god*. But this instrument is necessarily imperfect. The thoughts of the god are revealed

in a form that is not his, and, being produced through an intermediary, are impregnated with the nature of this intermediary.
When the god uses the soul (of the Pythia) it cannot remain quiet
and in its natural state, but is agitated by its own emotions and by
the passions that trouble it, as though tossed about in a stormy
sea. He adds that the god of Delphi uses the Pythia to make
himself heard, even as the sun uses the moon to make itself seen.[1]
This is equivalent to saying that the oracle of the Pythia is
a weak reflection of the visions that pass before the eyes of her spirit
with the rapidity of lightning-flashes followed by black darkness.

To gain an idea of what this kind of divination was, we must
read the forceful description given by Lucan, in his *Pharsalia*,
of the prophetic delirium of Phemonoë, the priestess of Delphi
consulted by Appius after Pompey had been appointed commander-
in-chief.

" Our age is deprived of no greater blessing of the Deities
than that the Delphic seat has become silent, since monarchs
have dreaded events to come, and have forbidden the Gods of
heaven to speak. . . .

Thus does Appius, an enquirer into the remotest secrets of
the Hesperian destiny, make application to the tripods for a length
of time unmoved, amid the silence of the vast rocks. The priest,
requested to open the dreaded seats, and to admit to the Gods
a trembling prophetess, seizes Phemonoë, roving amid the streams
of Castalia and the recesses of the groves, and compels her to burst
open the doors of the temple. The maid, inspired by Phœbus,
dreading to stand within the awful threshold, by a vain stratagem
attempts to wean the chieftain from his ardent longing to know the
future. . . .

The deceit of the maiden is manifest . . . and her very fear
imparts confidence. Then does the wreathed fillet bind her
locks in front and her hair streaming down her back a white head-
dress encircles, with Phocæan laurel. She, dreading the fate-
foretelling recess of the deep-seated shrine, in the first part of the
Temple comes to a stop, and, feigning the inspiration of the God,
utters from her breast, undisturbed beneath, fictitious words,
testifying a spirit moved by no divine frenzy. . . . Her words
broken with no trembling sound, her voice not sufficing to fill
the space of the capacious cavern, the laurels shaken off, with no
standing of her hair on end, and the summits of the Temple
without vibration, all these betrayed that she dreaded to yield
herself to Phœbus. Appius beheld the tripods unoccupied, and

---

[1] See Plutarch's *Morals.* (Theosophical Essays.) *On the Pythian Responses*
(xxi.)

raging, exclaimed : " Impious woman, thou shalt both pay the deserved penalty to me and to the Gods of heaven, whom thou art feigning as inspiring thee, unless thou art hidden in the caverns, and, consulted upon the tumults so vast of the trembling world, dost cease thyself to speak."

At length the affrighted maiden flies for refuge to the tripods, and led away within the vast caverns, there remains, and receives the Deity in her unaccustomed breast, who pours forth the spirit of the rock, now for so many ages unexhausted, into the prophetess. . . . He banishes her former mind, and throughout her whole breast bids the mortal give way to himself. Frantic, she rages throughout the cave . . . shaking from her upright hair both the fillets of the god and the garlands of Phœbus . . . and throws prostrate the tripods that stand in her way . . . enduring thee, Phœbus, raging with wrath. . . . All time comes in a single mass ; and ages press upon her afflicted breast. Such a vast chain of events is disclosed, and all the future struggles for the light of day. . . . At last voices resound, the maiden now overcome :

" O Roman, thou dost escape from the vast threatenings of war, free from dangers so great ; and alone shalt thou take thy rest in the wide valley of the Eubœan quarter." The rest Apollo suppresses and stops her speech. . . .

Then smitten by the breast of the prophetess, the doors open, and she leaps forth from the Temple. Her frantic fit still lasts ; and the God whom as yet she has not expelled still remains in her, not having said the whole. She still rolls her fierce eyes . . . ; a fiery blush tints her face and her livid cheeks, and a paleness exists, not that which is wont to be in one who fears, but inspiring fear. Nor does her wearied heart find rest ; but, as the swelling sea after the hoarse blasts of Boreas moans, so do sighs relieve the prophetess. And while from the sacred light by which she has beheld the Fates she is being brought back to the sunbeams of ordinary day . . . hardly come to herself, she falls to the ground."[1]

But the scene described by Lucan represents only the decadence of the prophetic art. When the Pythia had to be dragged by force to the tripod, and the vision induced by artificial means, the true source of inspiration had long been exhausted.[2] In the account

---

[1] English translation by H. T. Riley.

[2] More than all the other occult arts, divination lends itself to charlatanism and superstition, and in spite of the severe discipline and acknowledged piety of the priests of Apollo, these vices were not unknown at Delphi. The story of Cleomenes, king of Sparta, who succeeded in corrupting the Pythoness in order to obtain the removal of his colleague, Demaratus, is celebrated. In that case the intrigue was discovered, and the priestess dismissed, but there are other analogous instances in the Delphic records. This, however, is no reason for altogether denying the clairvoyance of the Pythonesses, or for seeing only a clever exploitation of

given by Herodotus, with reference to the battle of Salamis, the Pythoness appears again in all her majesty. It is the fateful hour, the decisive moment, of the Median wars. Xerxes has crossed the pass of Thermopylæ, and is on the point of invading Attica with his immense army. The Athenians must find out whether to remain within the walls, or to abandon their city to the enemy. After the usual ceremonies, the Athenian deputies take their places within the temple at Delphi. The priestess Aristonika comes forward, robed in white, hollow-eyed and pale as death beneath her laurel crown. Her loosened hair escapes from its fillet and falls in disorder upon her shoulders. Her whole body is shaken by violent shudderings. Stressing her solemn words like verses, she cries aloud :

" O unfortunates, why are you seated here ? Fly to the ends of the earth ! Abandon your dwellings and the high summits of your city, for neither the head shall remain, nor the body, nor the feet and hands, nor any of the members. Destruction shall efface them. Upon the city shall fall flame and the impetuous Mars that accompanies the Syrian chariots. The immortals sweat within their temples, and from their roof-tops flows black blood.—Leave the sanctuary ! Meet your afflictions with courage ! "

After this prophetic outpouring, the Athenians throw themselves upon the ground and beg for mercy. One of the Delphians advises them to return with suppliant boughs in order to obtain a more favourable reply. They do so, and the Pythoness once more emerges from her grotto, and speaks as follows :

" Pallas cannot appease Olympian Jupiter. Again I repeat his inflexible word. Of all that is inclosed within the limits of Cecrops and the caverns of divine Cithæron, nothing shall resist. Only a wooden fortress shall remain impregnable. Do not await the enemy. . . . O, divine Salamis, thou shalt be fatal to the son of Woman ! " [1]

We know what meaning the brave and clever Themistocles saw in this oracle, and how the Athenian ships destroyed the Persian fleet at Salamis, and so saved Greece. Here history attains the

---

credulity in an institution which retained the veneration of the ancient world for more than a thousand years. It should be noted, above all, that thinkers of the first order, such as Pythagoras and Plato, honoured it with their faith, and that they considered the ' divine madness ' ($\mu\alpha\nu\iota\alpha$, $\dot{o}\rho\mu\dot{\eta}$; L. *furor divinus*) as the highest and most direct means of obtaining knowledge. The positive and scrupulous Aristotle himself acknowledged that there is an ' epoptic philosophy '—that is to say, a science of spiritual vision.

[1] See the account given by Herodotus, Book vii, chapters 140–141.—We may remark that for the Dorian priestess of Apollo, Xerxes represented the feminine cults of Asia. That is why she calls him ' The son of Woman.'

grandeur of an Æschylean tragedy, and the voice of the Pythoness is charged with divine import.

Such were the great days of Delphi, and such was the part played by Apollo in the destiny of Hellas. He was then all-powerful, but his wisdom was hidden behind an impenetrable veil, and his nature remained an enigma. Let us suppose that, a little later, some young disciple of Plato, a son of the Athenian aristocracy—a Charmides or a Theages—were to come in his first ardour for knowledge to seek an explanation of the mysteries and a solution of his doubts from the prophet of Delphi. How would the pontiff of Apollo have replied to him? I imagine that he would have chosen, for this interview with the subtle and gracious Athenian, a nocturnal hour, when the temple had regained its calm after the noise of festivals and processions—an hour when the burning arrows of Helios had been succeeded by the caressing rays of Phœbe, who turned the foliage of the olive-trees to silver, and gave the buildings a phantasmal air by flooding them with her Elysian light.

In the peristyle of the temple the prophet showed the visitor the inscription over the entrance door : ' *Know thyself* ' ; and said to him : ' Fix these words in thy memory, and think often of them, for they hold the key to all wisdom.' Then he led him to the interior of the temple, dimly lighted by the dying flame on a tripod. They advanced to the statue of the god, placed in the *cella*, but invisible in the darkness. By the light of a torch the priest showed the young man the mysterious letter E inscribed on its pedestal, and added :

" The god addresses each one of us here, when approaching him, as if with a salutation, in the words ' Know thyself,' which is neither more nor less than ' Hail,' whilst we, in requital to the god, say ' Thou art,' as though paying to him the true, undying, and sole property of himself, the predicate of existence." [1]

The priest then explained to the inquirer that all beings, the earth, the sea, the stars, and man himself, in so far as visible and corporeal, had only a mobile and ephemeral existence, and did not exist *in reality*, but were constantly changing, to die and to be born without cessation. Only one Being exists always and fills eternity ; that is God, who gives life to all things with His breath, and also dwells within man. This is why Apollo says to his worshippers : ' *Know thyself.*' For the wise man can awaken this unknown God in himself, and if, having found traces of Him, he raises his thoughts towards Him, crying with full faith and

_____

[1] This passage is taken from Plutarch's treatise *On the* E *at Delphi*, xvii. (English translation by C. W. King.)

fervour, 'Thou art!' a light will flash across his soul and reveal the divine presence. This is the beginning of wisdom."

" O, holy priest," cried the Athenian, moved but not convinced, " thou speakest almost like my master, Plato, but I would know more than he tells me, and more than thou hast told me. Tell me the origin and the end of the soul, the secret of life, and what comes after death ; tell me the origin and the end of the gods themselves, who are called the Immortals ! "

"Dost thou know what thou art asking, imprudent one ? " the prophet replied. " Hast thou thought of the danger to thyself, if I should grant thy request ? Hast thou forgotten the fate of Semele, the beloved of Jupiter, who desired to behold the god in his divine glory, and died, consumed by that celestial fire ? Remember Icarus, who tried to follow the flaming chariot of Apollo in its heavenly course, and was cast into the sea ! Remember the hunter, Actæon, who wished to see Artemis bathing, and was changed into a stag by the goddess and devoured by his own hounds. Such would be thy fate if thou wert to penetrate without due preparation into the forbidden mysteries. Canst thou not live happily and virtuously in thy city, in the light of Apollo, and under the protection of Pallas ? Go and fight for thine ancestors, and know how to live again in thy children, awaiting with courage the hour when death shall call thee and make of thee an Elysian shade."

" A shade ? " murmured the young man. " We are then nothing but shades ! . . . This feeble hope does not satisfy me. Thou wouldst have me live like the grasshoppers on the banks of the Cephissus, who die after the summer without hope of rebirth or like the nightingales of Colonus who migrate to Egypt without knowing if they will ever return. Thou who knowest, give me the light ! I conjure thee by the Infernal Deities ! "

" Take care not to insult the God of Delphi ! " the priest replied. " Apollo does not love funeral libations, and has nothing to do with the dead. He hates the Styx like Zeus himself, and never departs from the light."

As he spoke he threw a handful of incense upon the ashes in the tripod, and a shower of sparks flew upward, revealing for an instant the statue of the Divine Archer, with his foot upon the python.

" Since thou art so audacious," continued the prophet in a low voice, " go to the priests of Eleusis, to the Eumolpidæ. There, the Great Goddesses, Demeter and Persephone, will show thee the descent to Hades, and thou wilt learn the mysteries of Dionysus, if thou art capable of making the journey."

" Concerning this journey," said the young man, " let the oracle of Apollo speak for me ! "

" Impossible ! Apollo and Dionysus are brothers, but their domains are separate. Apollo *knows everything*, and when he speaks, it is in the name of his Father. Dionysus knows nothing, but *is everything*, and his actions speak for him. By his life, as by his death, he reveals the secrets of the Abyss. When thou hast learnt them, mayst thou not regret thine ignorance ! "

A last glimmer of fire smouldering in the ashes . . . a metallic sound from the tripod like the groaning of a human voice . . . an imperious gesture of the high-priest . . . and the youth, seized with sudden fear, left the temple and descended by the Sacred Way.

The white statues of gods and heroes still kept watch upon their pedestals in the clear moonlight, but they seemed to have turned into phantoms, and the deserted Way lay silent beneath the cold rays of Selene.

CHAPTER IV

THE INVISIBLE GREECE—DEMETER AND PERSEPHONE

FROM earliest times, and up to the apogee of their civilisation, the Greeks had an intuitive awareness of the direct and intimate communion that exists between the outer life of the world and the inner life of the soul. The Greek genius did not separate the human soul from the Cosmos, but conceived them as an organic whole. If the spectacle of the universe awakens an inner world, this world enables man to understand and explain the universe. Hence the profundity and the incomparable charm of Greek mythology, whose magnificent fables playfully conceal the most sublime truths.

Despite this feeling of identity between the soul and nature, there were, in the most ancient days, two distinct religions in Greece —that of the Olympians, or Heavenly Gods (Zeus, Juno, Pallas, Apollo, etc.), and that of the Chthonians, or Infernal Gods (Demeter, Persephone, Pluto, Hecate, Dionysus). The first was the official religion, corresponding to the external and visible world ; the second was the religion of the Mysteries, corresponding to the inner world of the soul. It was in a sense the religion of the under-side of things, of the subterranean—that is to say, inner— realities, through which can be opened the door of the invisible world, of the Beyond. The first taught that the gods must be reverenced according to consecrated rules and rites ; the second introduced the soul of the mystic to awe-inspiring secrets, and renewed its forces at the primordial springs of being. Hence the name of " Great Goddesses," which was given only to Demeter and Persephone. Scholars of to-day refuse to admit that this religion of the Mysteries was not only the most sacred, but also the most ancient, known in Greece. They look on it as an artificial fabrication, grafted upon a purely naturalistic mythology, though this opinion is contradicted by the most solemn witnesses of antiquity—by the poets, from Homer to Sophocles, by the historians, from Herodotus to Strabo, and by the two greatest Greek philosophers, Plato and Aristotle. All these speak of the Mysteries as of the highest and most holy religion ; all of them trace it back to prehistoric times, and speak of an ancient sacerdotal religion which reigned in Thrace and is borne witness to by the legendary, but eloquent and significative, names of Thamyris, Amphion, and Orpheus. The arbitrary theories of modern historians and mythologists, who carry the yoke of materialistic preconceived ideas, cannot prevail against such authorities, still less against the marvellous and suggestive poetry which these old myths are found to contain when one dares to face them and to be inspired by their undying magic.

Demeter, the divine and universal Mother, was the oldest of all Greek divinities, for the Pelasgians of Arcadia worshipped her in the form of a goddess with the head of a horse, holding a dove in one hand and a dolphin in the other. This signified that she had given birth to the animals of the earth, the birds of the air, and the fishes of the sea. She thus corresponded to what we call Nature. When a man of to-day speaks of Nature, if he is an educated man he visualises a landscape of sea, trees or mountains ; if he is a scientist, he sees the instruments used in physics and chemistry, he imagines the movements of the stars and the grouping of atoms, he dissects the corpse of the Cosmos, of which he has only a lifeless, mechanical conception, and stirs up its dust. Very different was the feeling of the Greeks towards the living world. Neither the uncouth Pelasgian idol, nor the abstract word Nature, can give us an idea of the overwhelming emotions that filled the soul of the Greek at the mere name of Demeter. This sacred name awoke in him not merely the thought of Nature in visible form, but all the mystery of her creative power, and her perpetual bringing forth of new life. It rang through his heart like the echo of a sonorous voice in a deep cavern, and enveloped him like a wave of the sea. Demeter was the power that reclothed the earth's surface with luxuriant verdure ; Demeter gave life to all the watery legions of the ocean ; heavenly Demeter, spouse of Uranus, shone also in the million-eyed, starry sky. Was she not the universal and beneficent Mother ? And man felt himself to be the legitimate son of this mother, for had she not given him the ears of wheat and the fruits of the earth ? Had she not taught him, through the succession of the seasons, the art of agriculture and the holy laws of the domestic hearth ? The cult of Demeter dates back to the primeval ages of the Aryan race, when the three currents of Religion, Science and Art, now separated, acted upon man as one single power. This unique power passed through the human soul like a torrent, and made it conscious of its own universal life. It was a unitive civilisation, in which all forces were joined together in religion—a strong religion that bestowed powers and created forms. Religion and Art constituted a whole, for Art was worship, and dwelt with Religion, its mother.

This religion had a strong influence upon men; it was of such a kind that its ceremonies and the voices of its priests awakened the wisdom of the gods in the hearts of men. Consequently, when the primitive Greek laid a sheaf of corn or a wreath of wild flowers on the altar of Demeter under the luminous sky, he experienced the joy of a child whose mother takes him upon her knee, and who sees love in her eyes and draws life from her gentle caresses.

But the primitive Greek also knew that from this great Demeter was born a mysterious maiden, an immortal Virgin, who was none other than the Human Soul, descended from the heavenly Light through innumerable generations and strange metamorphoses. He knew that, separated from her mother by inevitable fate and the will of the gods, she was destined to rejoin her periodically amid the labyrinth of her deaths and rebirths, her many journeyings from earth to heaven and from heaven to earth. He knew this through a deep and irrefutable intuition, and sometimes perceived it in vision, as though reflected in the mirror of his own soul. Hence arose the moving story of Persephone, which has been called the primordial drama—the tragedy of the Soul torn between earth, hell and heaven—which sums up all human tragedies in three impressive acts, Birth, Death and Resurrection. In this drama the devouring flames of desire, the shadows and terrors of forgetfulness, the poignant glory of divine recollection, embrace all the joys and sufferings of terrestrial and heavenly life.

Let us recall the Homeric Hymn to Demeter. Ceres has left her daughter in the company of the nymphs—elementary beings as pure and primitive as herself. She has begged her not to gather the narcissus, the dangerous flower of temptation created by Eros, since its starry whiteness conceals a subtle desire and its strong perfume can efface the memory of heaven. But in spite of the pleadings of the nymphs, Persephone is tempted by the magic flower which spreads its snowy petals before her and reveals its golden heart. She gathers it, and breathes in the intoxicating scent that dulls the senses and dims the sight. At this moment the earth is reft open and Pluto appears, seizes the maiden, and carries her off across the ocean in his chariot drawn by dragons. Persephone, distracted, sees earth, sea and sky disappear, and is engulfed with her ravisher in the dark abyss of Tartarus. It is a striking symbol of the soul losing its divine memory through incarnation.[1]

From very early times, this story, which is impressively

---

[1] See the account of this scene, which served as prologue to the drama of Eleusis, in the chapter on Plato in *The Great Initiates* by E. Schuré.

recounted in the Homeric Hymn, was represented symbolically every autumn, when women would go to a promontory overlooking the sea, and indulge in mournful lamentations over the loss of Persephone, and her descent to the infernal regions. The family of the Eumolpidæ, whose head, Eumolpus, was probably initiated in Egypt, took this rural mystery-play and developed it into an organised series of ceremonies and dramatic representations. They thus founded the Eleusinian Mysteries, and their hereditary privileges were retained for over a thousand years. The part of Demeter was always played by the high-priestess, wife of the hierophant, and that of Persephone by a young seeress specially chosen for the tragic festival. Demeter was the principal character, and only she and the hierophant, who represented Zeus, pronounced the sacramental words. The rôle of Persephone was played in silent, but expressive, pantomime. As in the later tragedies, choruses of nymphs, demons, shades and blest spirits, played an important part in the sacred drama.

In the second act, the despair of Demeter, and her vain search for Persephone, were portrayed up to the moment when Hecate, goddess of metamorphoses, was permitted by Zeus to reveal to her her daughter's fate. Persephone was then seen imprisoned in Tartarus, seated on a throne with Pluto in the midst of ghosts and demons; and finally, her return to her mother and to the Olympic regions, accompanied by the songs of divine heroes, was represented.

Beholding these different scenes, the spectator at Eleusis experienced a variety of sensations, human and divine, which distressed and delighted him by turns. Through the magic of words and music, through the beauty of the settings and the impressiveness of the gestures, evoking the Invisible in plastic form, he was borne from the flowery carpet of earth to the ruddy shades of Acheron, or to the limpid ether of the Uranian regions. When the Greek saw the pale Queen of the Dead in her violet veil, crowned with narcissi, opening wide her tear-filled eyes and unconsciously stretching out her arms in longing for her lost mother; then falling back upon her throne, menaced by the sceptre of her terrible spouse, and, fascinated and overcome, drinking from a black cup the pomegranate juice which binds the senses to the lower world—when he saw this, it seemed as though he saw his own soul, and he was filled with longing for the spiritual sight that he had lost, and for direct communion with the gods.[1]

Through a profound and infinitely delicate intuition, Greece

[1] See the complete reconstruction of the drama of Eleusis, and its adaptation to the modern theatre in *Sanctuaires d'Orient* by E. Schuré.

had conceived Persephone, the immortal Soul, as remaining eternally virgin throughout her migrations, in spite of the embraces of Pluto and the flames of infernal passion, which enveloped without corrupting her. Though Pluto could compel her to taste the red pulp of the pomegranate, symbolising carnal desire, which, once savoured, engenders a myriad rebirths through its innumerable seeds ; though he might clasp her in his black arms and burn her with his fiery mantle, she still remained the Impenetrable, the Untouchable, as long as she preserved within herself the divine imprint, the germ of her final liberation, the sacred image, the remembrance of her mother. So comes it that Persephone, she who crosses the abyss, is also called Soteira, who she saves.

One may feel some vague reflection of these sublime emotions before the Eleusinian bas-relief preserved in the Athens Museum, of which there is a reproduction in the *Ecole des Beaux-Arts* in Paris. Demeter is gravely presenting to Triptolemus, the eponymous founder of the temple of Eleusis, the grain of corn symbolising immortality, while the chaste Persephone, standing behind him and holding the torch of the Mysteries, crowns him by placing her first finger on his head, to instil the divine will into him. These noble figures in their archaic draperies are full of religious feeling— the calm majesty of the mother of the gods, the gentle profile of her daughter, the humble yet dignified attitude of the young man. The most ordinary commonsense suggests that we are witnessing a scene of initiation of the deepest significance ; yet there are actually mythologists who see in Demeter only the goddess of agriculture and in her daughter only a symbol of spring ! [1] Thank God, we can surmise to-day that the Mysteries of Eleusis were something more than an agricultural meeting embellished by a prefect's discourse and an electoral manifestation—though this would doubtless represent an ideal civilisation to those who wish to extirpate all sense of the divine.

---

[1] The spiritual significance of Persephone is luminously clear in the legend for those whose eyes and ears are not closed by a materialistic fanaticism. The cult of which she was the object proves it no less eloquently. At her festival, in the spring, the tombs of the dead were wreathed in flowers. What could be clearer ? At the time of earthly blossoming the Mysteries celebrated the reunion of Persephone and her mother, and the return of souls to heaven.

CHAPTER V

DIONYSUS OF THE MYSTERIES

THROUGH Demeter and Persephone we touched the primitive psychic foundation of the Mysteries of Eleusis. To reach their intellectual and cosmogonic foundation, we must look into the heart of the veiled god who was introduced later, and who became the arcanum of the doctrine of the Eumolpidæ, and the crown of the sacred drama. In contemplating Dionysus with close attention, we shall find in him not only the mainspring of the whole of Greek mythology, but also the motive-power of Greek evolution.

The Hellenic genius summed up its conception of the universe in four great gods, who are eternal Cosmic Forces—Zeus, Poseidon, Pluto and Dionysus. These gods are found again in the constitution of man, who re-creates them by reflecting them, and who could not comprehend them if he did not contain all four within himself.

When the Greek, to whom every movement of nature was a spiritual gesture, beheld the atmospheric phenomena, the colours of daylight in the sky and the clouds, dawn and sunset, lightning and thunder, and the radiant miracle of the rainbow, he was transported into the higher regions of his being, and he took all these things for the thoughts and messages of a god. For just as thought springs from the depths of the soul, so did these signs spring from the depths of the universe, to speak with him. He called this god of the sky and the atmosphere, Zeus; and the dawn, the thunder and the rainbow manifested the thoughts of Zeus, like the hope, anger and joy which he himself experienced.

Quite different was the impression made on him by the ocean. With its dark, deceptive depths and its ever-changing surface, million-coloured, chameleon-like, this uncertain, capricious and fantastic element, surrounding the earth and creeping into the gulfs, seemed like a great reservoir of apathy and dream. But at the least breath of heaven the sleeper became terrible ; as soon as the wind was unchained, there arose the furious tempest. And yet from the ocean, the father of rivers, came all the life of the earth. This god the Greek called Poseidon, feeling him to be like the blood that ran in his own veins, and like the hidden life where his deeper

memory slept, which yet was stirred and raised to heaven by all
the passions of the heights and depths.

No less powerful was the impression received by the Greek
from the soil of earth herself, bristling with rocks and mountains ;
or from descending into caverns ; or from seeing the volcanoes
belch forth liquid fire. These gave him a sensation of solidity,
concentration and power. He imagined the interior of the earth—
the bed of the Styx, colder than death, the burning heart of fire,
and the magical centre of attraction which holds the globe together
in a compact mass. And he called this power Pluto. He made
Pluto the centre of gravity of the Cosmos, just as he felt his own
body to be the centre of gravity of his being, absorbing and
condensing the centrifugal forces.

Zeus, the astral aura of the world ; Poseidon, the vital (or etheric)
body ; Pluto, the physical body : thus were revealed, through the
sole virtue of contemplative intuition, the cosmic trinity and the
human trinity. But the essential thing was still lacking—the
organic principle, the Creative Spirit, which unites the parts into
a homogeneous whole, inspires them with its breath, and makes
life circulate through them. The consciousness, the ' self,' was
lacking. And for the Greeks, the cosmic Self whence the
human self proceeds, the god in action in the universe, was
Dionysus.

According to the temple tradition, it was Orpheus, a Dorian
from Thrace, initiated in Egypt, but inspired by the genius of his
people and by his own *dæmon*, who founded the Mysteries of
Dionysus and spread the worship of this god abroad throughout
Greece.

Orpheus was the son of a priestess of Apollo. Born within the
walls of a cyclopean temple, overlooking a wild expanse of forests
and mountains, and having triumphantly passed through the
formidable tests of the Theban initiation, he had imbibed from
the highest sources the male conceptions of divine unity, and of the
transcendent spirituality of the sovereign God. But if his brain
sometimes froze under the influx of the divine ether, his heart
burned with an immense love for the Eternal-Feminine who manifested in the multiple forms of Demeter-Adama, the Great Mother,
Eternal Nature. Flowers, trees and animals were so many children
of this Demeter, conceived and formed by her under the influence
of the gods. And in woman—whom he contemplated from the
depths of his inner sanctuary—Orpheus saw the divine Persephone,
the suffering one, shy and gentle. The simultaneous double intuition that he had of the Eternal-Masculine and the Eternal-
Feminine, whose work is the Universe, is expressed in the line
attributed to him by Onomacritus :

Jupiter is the eternal Male and Female.

Inspired by this double revelation, Orpheus vowed that he would cause the glories of Uranus, and of all the gods, to descend into the warm gulfs and hollows of Nature, whose labyrinth of verdant and winding valleys lay spread at his feet. It seemed to him that the gods would thus become more human, and the earth more fair ; and this was the task he set himself. He became the living lyre and the mouth of gold through which the divine torrent flooded all Greece with dionysian waves, making it one great Temple of Beauty. But, in order to accomplish his design, he had first to overcome the ferocity of the Thracian kings and the dangerous priestesses of Bacchus.

The Bacchantes were the druidesses of prehistoric Thrace. They worshipped a bull-headed god called Bacchus, whose barbaric image symbolised brutal instinct and the generative forces of nature. They made blood-sacrifices to him and performed libidinous rites. Through blood and lust they beguiled the barbarian kings, and induced them to adopt this lewd and cruel religion. Orpheus, however, conquered them by force of charm, melody and grace. He introduced the fascinated Bacchantes and the pacified barbarian chiefs to the religion of the Olympians ; he taught them about the gods of the sky—Zeus, Apollo, Artemis and Pallas ; he spoke to them of Poseidon, king of storms and of the sea, and of Pluto, judge of the dead, reigning in Tartarus. Being well informed of the divine hierarchies, he was able to bring order, clearness and harmony into the chaos of Hellenic divinities. This was the popular religion.

But to his disciples and initiates Orpheus taught the most profound and moving things—the hidden marvels of Dionysus ! Dionysus, he told them, is the heavenly Bacchus, the powerful generator who passes through all the kingdoms of nature to incarnate and fulfil himself in man. And in order to make this idea clear to them, he told them the story of a dream that he had had. " Zeus, in the form of the astral serpent, was united to the Soul of the World, conceived as the increate Virgin, and called by the same name as Persephone (Koré). Their divine child, destined to universal domination, bore the name of Dionysus-Zagreus, or Dionysus dismembered. One day the child was regarding himself in a mirror and became lost in contemplation of his own fair image. Then the Titans—the unbridled elements or lower forces of nature—threw themselves upon him and rent him into seven portions, which they then boiled in an immense cauldron. Minerva-Pallas, the divine wisdom, born of the pure thought of Zeus, saved the heart of Dionysus and took it to her father. Zeus placed it in his bosom, to generate a new son, and destroyed the Titans with lightning. From their burning bodies, mingled with the vapours that arose from the mangled body of Dionysus, humanity is born. But from the purest part of the heart of Dionysus, renewed and remoulded in the ethereal bosom of Jupiter, are born heroes and men of genius ; and from it will also be born the new Dionysus, in whom the souls scattered throughout the universe will recognise their divine model. Thus the god, dismembered into suffering humanity, will regain his radiant unity in Dionysus resurrected ! "

By means of such plastic dreams and vivid images, Orpheus strove to make his disciples understand the double origin, terrestrial and celestial, of man, through the action of the cosmic forces ; the multiplicity of his successive incarnations ; and the possibility of his return to divinity in spotless beauty and splendour. This was the central idea of the doctrine of the Greek Mysteries. As a blazing torch, lighted in the depths of a cavern, illuminates all its dark walls and winding passages, so does the Mystery of Dionysus illuminate all other Mysteries. It terrified the weak, but the strong found in it courage, the joy of strife, and undying hope. Magnificent cults and luminous philosophies were to arise later from this revelation, and we shall presently see Tragedy emerge from it, armed from head to foot, like Minerva from the head of Jupiter.

In this way there was formed, on the one hand, the public religion of the Olympians ; on the other, the secret religion of the Mysteries ; the first for the masses, the second for the initiates. They did not contradict, but explained each other reciprocally. The secret religion was the foundation, the internal organism, of the outer religion, which in its turn was the coloured surface, the plastic expression, of the former on the physical plane.

Tradition—perhaps symbolical, perhaps true—relates that Orpheus suffered the same fate as his god, and died, torn to pieces by the Bacchantes, like Dionysus by the Titans. They would have thus revenged themselves for his persistent love for the lost Eurydice, and at the same time would have realised, ironically, his Mystery in their bloodthirsty religion. It is a suggestive legend. Perhaps they also resented the fact that Apollo's son had momentarily awakened in themselves the sleeping Persephone, and had disdained their fair bodies draped in fawn-skins, when they passed through the leafy woods of Thrace with serpents entwined around their arms. However this may be, Orpheus, dying, knew that sacred Greece would draw life from his breath, and his severed head, carried down the river with his still vibrating lyre, is truly the symbol of his work.

The religious cult of the Eumolpidæ became enriched by the Orphic doctrine and tradition, whose lofty spirituality and wide cosmic outlook supplied the completion of their Mysteries. This happened, doubtless, about the sixth century B.C., at the time when the popular and orgiastic cult of Bacchus, flowing back from Phrygia like a wave of madness, swept over Greece, spreading as far as Thebes, and to the heights of Cithæron and Parnassus. Delirious processions of men and women, brandishing thyrsus-wands and crowned with vine-leaves, created a new kind of passionate lyricism, unknown in the days of Homer, and a stirring music with the beating of cymbals and the shrill calling of the double flute, while everywhere the cry " *Evios ! Evohé !* " resounded, as though to draw forth the god of wine and revelry from the depths of the woods and the mountain caverns. It was to check this movement, and to oppose it with a higher initiation, that the priests of Eleusis adopted the Orphic Dionysus and introduced him into the worship of the Great Goddesses. At the same time, the discipline was made more severe, and the teaching given to the initiates more profound.

The religion of Eleusis did not consist only of ceremonies, dramatic representations, and periodic festivals. In its flowering-time, before the Median wars, the essential part of it was the instruction given concerning the secret wisdom. This was communicated to the candidates, who came to live for a time in the temple precincts. Spiritual ecstasy was sought by means of fasting, meditating on the nature of the soul and the gods, and clear concentration of thought before sleeping and on awaking, in order to retain a definite impression of the dreams which the ordinary man rarely remembers. The object of this initiation was to transform the *mystes*, or veiled one, into an *epopt*, or seer, and to enable him to behold Dionysus. But Dionysus was a multiple god, scattered throughout the whole of humanity, and he manifested himself differently to each disciple. At Eleusis he was recognised in three forms, representing three degrees of initiation. The first, accessible only to the abstract intelligence, was that of Dionysus-Zagreus, the Orphic Dionysus, existing in all beings. It was said to the candidate : " Know that the supreme Spirit, the divine Self, manifests through sacrifice, and is divided up among innumerable souls. He lives, suffers, breathes and aspires in thee as in others. The vulgar know him not, but the initiate must reconstitute him completely within himself. That is not done in a day. Look into the depths of thine own spirit. Seek him and thou shalt find him." The *mystes* plunged himself in meditation, looked within himself, and found nothing. Usually he could not understand this god, existing in all things, one and yet many, sublime and yet humble, powerful and yet miserable. It was the first test, and the easiest, but still painful—the doubt of the soul before insoluble contradictions unilluminated by reason. The hierophant then said to the troubled candidate : " Learn to understand the necessity for contradiction that lies at the root of all things. Without suffering there would be no life, without struggle no progress, without contradiction no consciousness. Dionysus would remain for ever hidden in the bosom of Zeus, and thou thyself would'st be but a drop of water diffused in a nebula. There was once an age, it is true, the far-off age of Atlantis, when primitive man was so mingled with nature that he saw the forces hidden in the elements and spoke with them. The Egyptians called this age that of Shesu-Hor, when the gods reigned upon earth. Dionysus, though divided among men, was then still united in their consciousness, for the men of that epoch were seers, and the gods dwelt with them in changing etheric forms of every kind. There was another epoch much nearer to our own, when the divine spirit incarnated in those whom we call the Heroes. Their names were Hercules, Jason, Cecrops, Cadmus, Theseus, and many another. Among these divine men who founded our cities and our temples, there was one who left Greece in order to conquer India, and returned to Thrace through Arabia and Asia Minor, with his train of followers, spreading everywhere the religion of wine and joyfulness. We call him the second Dionysus. He was not born of the uncreated light, the celestial Demeter, like the first, but of a mortal woman whom the Greeks call Semele. Rashly desiring to behold her god in his full glory, she died from the touch of his lightning-fires, but she had first conceived a divine child by him. Now learn what this story is meant to teach us. If man to-day were suddenly to demand to see, with his physical eyes, the gods—that is to say, the foundations of the world and the cosmic powers among which the Atlantean moved naturally, being differently constituted—he would not be able to endure this terrifying sight, this whirlwind of fire and light. He would die, like the too temerous Semele. But her son, Dionysus, who formerly trod the earth as a man of flesh and blood, lives eternally in the spiritual worlds. It is he who guides the initiate ; it is he who shows the way to the gods. Persevere—and thou shalt see him ! "

And it came about that one night, sleeping in his cell in the temple of Eleusis, the aspirant had a dream, and saw the god crowned with vine-leaves pass by, accompanied by his train of fauns, satyrs and bacchantes. This Dionysus had, strangely, not the regular features of an Olympian, but rather the face of a Silenus. Nevertheless, from his eyes and brow there streamed rays of light and ecstasy, which betrayed his divine nature. And the dreamer said to himself : " If a demi-god once had this form, what have I been myself and what am I still, with all my passions ? " Then he saw writhing before him a monster that seemed to be a mixture of bull, serpent and dragon, and that filled him with fear and horror. But an implacable inner voice commanded him : " Look well, for it is thyself."

When he related his vision to the hierophant, the latter replied : " Thou hast found Dionysus and he has shown thee the Guardian of the Threshold—that is to say, thy lower self, that which thou hast been in numberless former incarnations, that which thou still art in part. Thou must now learn to endure the sight of the monster, to know it, to control it, to bring it into subjection. If thou dost not enchain thy Cerberus, thou canst not enter into Hades, the land of shadows." Many of the candidates rebelled indignantly against this idea, and even derided it. They would not consent to recognise themselves in the monster, and turned away from it in disgust. They thus proved their unfitness · for the methods of Eleusis, and were allowed to pursue their initiation no farther. Those, on the contrary, who were able to familiarise themselves with phenomena of this kind, grew to see the meaning and object of them more and more clearly. The second Dionysus became their instructor, and, lifting veil beyond veil, revealed to them secrets ever more marvellous. Some few chosen ones succeeded in seeing the third Dionysus,[1] at the heart of the divine world which opened itself to them from within, like a limpid dawn. This was in reality the first Dionysus—who was torn in pieces by the Titans, and divided up among all beings—but reconstituted and resurrected in higher form through a kind of transfiguration. In him the advanced *epopt* saw the human archetype in its Greek form, having attained fulness of life and consciousness—the divine pattern of a future humanity. This Dionysus was of a perfect and translucent beauty, faintly suggested in the marble of Praxiteles. An ambrosial dew gleamed on the ethereally moulded limbs ; the golden curls might have been smoothed by a celestial Demeter ; the sad and gentle gaze seemed to respond to the longing of some far-off Persephone. Ah, how could the seer forget this gaze of Dionysus, measuring the length of the road that he had travelled ? It contained all the rest . . . But at the same time the initiate saw the docile lions and panthers licking the god's hands, and the shining serpents coiled at his feet in luxuriant vegetation. His magical breath animated all nature, and nature, fully content,

---

[1] He was worshipped officially under the name of Iacchos, and his statue was carried in state from Athens to Eleusis on the sixth day of the festivals, before the 'sacred night.' The god Iacchos was represented as a child because he was looked upon as a renascent god, in a state of growth.

breathed through him. Was it not he of whom Orpheus had said :
" The gods are born from his smile, and men from his tears ? "

Then an inner voice spoke to the ' veiled one ' who had become
the ' seer' : " One day . . . perhaps . . . thou wilt resemble him ! "

We have now penetrated to the heart of the Dionysian mystery.
From this burning centre radiated the other mystical phenomena
of vision and ecstasy that were a part of the Eleusinian discipline.
Out of all these experiences grew the religious doctrine that, by
means of vivid imagery and forceful epitome, linked up human
destiny with the life of the Cosmos. It was a question, not of
abstract theories, but, as Aristotle perfectly expressed it, of an
experimental, emotional philosophy, based on a series of psychic
happenings. The periodic festivals of Eleusis, which terminated
in phenomena of a different kind, described by Porphyry, were
merely the sumptuous setting—a dramatic transposition of what
the candidates for initiation had individually experienced.

We know that the drama played in the temple ended in the
symbolic marriage of Persephone to the resurrected Dionysus.
This union was given the name of $\zeta\acute{\epsilon}\rho o s \ \gamma\acute{a}\mu o s$ (sacred marriage).
It exteriorised, so to speak, the inward phenomenon experienced
by the initiates. Each of these had travelled to another world,
through plunging into the depths of the subconscious, and in this
Hades had found the monsters of Tartary and all the gods—
Demeter, the primeval mother ; Persephone, the immortal soul ;
and Dionysus, the cosmic Self, the transcendent Spirit, evolving
towards the truth through all his metamorphoses.

Now the *epopt* relived these things through the medium of
art, in an assembly of souls tuned to the same diapason as his own.
What rapture, what renewal, to discover within himself the powers
that the visible universe hides beneath her veil, and to draw energy
from them ! What bliss to become conscious of his intimate relationship with the Cosmos, and of an invisible thread linking his
soul, through all other souls, to the unfathomable God !

Like all religious institutions, the Mysteries of Eleusis had their
florescence, their maturity and their decline. After the Median
wars, and the excesses of democracy, they became vulgarised through
opening their doors to the crowd. Serious tests were no longer
imposed, the discipline was relaxed, and outward ceremonies finally
replaced the genuine initiation ; but the Mysteries never lost
their unique charm. There is more than one voice of antiquity
to celebrate the grandeur, the holiness, and the benefits of Eleusis.
It is well to recall these witnesses, neglected by modern criticism
because they would turn it from its beaten track. Let us first
hear the ancient rhapsodist in the Homeric hymn to Demeter.
He speaks of " her rites . . . her goodly mysteries, holy mysteries

which none may violate, or search into, or noise abroad, for the great curse from the gods restrains the voice. Happy is he among deathly men who hath beheld these things! and he that is uninitiate, and hath no lot in them, hath never equal lot in death beneath the murky gloom."[1]

The greatest of the Greek lyric poets, Pindar, exclaims: "Happy are those who have been initiated into the Mysteries; they know the beginning and the end of life!" The traveller Pausanius, who visited and described all the sanctuaries, halts respectfully before that of Eleusis. He had had the intention of describing it, but, unfortunately for us, was prevented by a dream. His conclusion, however, is significant, and perhaps worth more than a description. "As far," he says, "as the gods are above men, so far are the Mysteries of Eleusis above all others."

But all this is not to say that the institution of the Eumolpidæ was without danger for the Greek cities and the Hellenic civilisation. Every mystical centre arouses, within a certain circumference, hostile forces which flow back upon it, just as positive electricity develops negative electricity at its opposite pole. The popular orgiastic religions which periodically invaded Greece, the Corybants and Mænads, are an example of this. The Eumolpidæ knew it well, and forestalled the danger by increasing the severity of their discipline, and by proclaiming, through the Areopagus, the death-penalty against any who betrayed the secrets of the Mysteries. The danger nevertheless existed, for fragments, only half understood, of the Eleusinian doctrines and dramatic performances transpired in spite of all precautions, and circulated among the public under strange travesties. We can understand that the priests of Apollo and the *archons* of Athens feared lest these profanations might affect the religion of Greece as a whole; for a coarse and false interpretation of secret doctrines threatened the popular belief in the gods, and the very existence of the ancient city.

"*Eskato Bebeloi*! Back with the profane!" cried the herald of Eleusis, when he visited Athens for the opening of the great autumn festivals. But that did not prevent the profane from saying strange things among themselves. Among other tales, it was related that within the Eleusinian temple with its basalt columns, in the sanctuary of Hecate, a place of darkness like to that of Tartarus, the priest gave voice, by torchlight, to sacrilegious statements such as these: (1.) Man is a collaborator with the gods. (2.) The essence of the gods is immutable, but their manifestation depends on time and place, and their form is partly the work of man. (3.) The gods themselves evolve and change with the universe.

---

[1] Prose version by Andrew Lang.

" And shall then man, created by the Immortals, become their equal ? " queried in Aristophanic style the sophists and dandies of the stadia and the gymnasia. " And have the gods, like actors, a dressing-room where they change their costumes in order to deceive us ? And do the gods evolve according to human caprice ? Then it must be man who has made them. As well say that they do not exist at all ! "

These subversive comments and frivolous babblings, in which the superficial minds of all ages have indulged concerning the mysteries of religion and the conceptions of the divine wisdom, alarmed the governors of the Greek cities. In this mocking incredulity they sensed something that might overthrow the god of Olympus, the Zeus of ivory and gold made by Phidias, as well as great Pallas, the divine Virgin with eyes of precious stones, who stood in the Parthenon leaning upon her sword, and holding the winged Victory in her hand. So the Eumolpidæ redoubled their vigilance, and the Areopagus its severity. The death-penalty was rigidly enforced against the treacherous and the profane.

In spite of all, the ideas of Eleusis went on their way through the world. We shall see how there arose from them, as though by contraband, and in a manner totally unforeseen, the most vital and wonderful of the arts, the Greek theatre, ancestor of the theatre of to-day. Tragedy was, in the beginning, nothing else than a refugee from the Mysteries, an intruder into the cities. This strange phenomenon, so highly significant that the whole enigma of life and evolution seems to be expressed through it, has up to now been so little understood that it is necessary to insist upon it.

CHAPTER VI

THE BASIS OF TRAGEDY

SIDE by side with the mysteries of Demeter, Persephone and Dionysus, which date back into the night of time, the popular worship of Bacchus never ceased to stir and fascinate Greece. Frenzied corybants in Phrygia, dishevelled mænads in Thebes, joyful satyrs in Attica, were all so many impetuous manifestations of enthusiasm for the hidden forces of nature, through which often glimmered certain secrets of the sanctuaries. All that was possible was done to check this, but the forces of Dionysus, once let loose, are not easily mastered. When the Megarian peasants heard how the God Bacchus had been torn in pieces by the Titans, and how he had emerged from this misadventure by being reborn—as the grape each year from the vine-stock, and the clear wine from the foaming vat—they were charmed by the piquant mystery and tragedy of the story. Perhaps some vague intuition told them that this fable contained a world-secret. They had heard also that, in the Mysteries, Bacchus was accompanied by satyrs, and so, devout and mischievous at the same time, they thought of disguising themselves as these hybrid beings, goat-footed and horned, and of praising their god with enthusiastic hymns to the sound of flutes and cymbals. This was the *dithyramb*, which soon spread over the whole of Greece. Next a rural poet, Thespis—a bold impresario—thought of mounting upon some planks and himself impersonating the god, in the midst of a chorus of satyrs, who replied to his sad or gay recitals in rhythmic strophes. The experiment was an immense success, and immediately another poet, Susarion, a sprightly jester, imitated it—but, instead of representing the serious side of the story, he introduced all the laughable details that could be added by transforming it into an everyday reality. Thus were born simultaneously—tragedy and comedy.

The psychic essence of this phenomenon—the most surprising in the whole history of art, and the most fruitful in consequences—merits investigation. In Greek mythology the satyr represents primitive man, nearer both to the beasts and to the gods, because he is still in direct, instinctive communion with the divine powers of nature. In him is expressed sexual energy, for which the Greeks had a kind of religious respect, as for a creative power ; but he also manifests spontaneous divination, with sparks of wisdom and gleams of prophecy. In a word, the satyr is a recollection and a revivification of the Atlantean in whom clairvoyance existed naturally.

This is the basic reason for the emergence of tragedy from a chorus of satyrs. In their Dionysian exaltation, the crowd of revellers, disguised as fauns and satyrs, mourning and praising their dead or resurrected god, calling to him in songs and hymns, ended by experiencing a hallucination of his presence—the climax of the dithyramb. When the ingenious poet impersonated Bacchus, spoke in his name, described his adventures, and conversed with the chorus—who acclaimed the recital of his martyrdom with funereal chants, and of his resurrection with delirious joy—he was only giving reality to the desire of the over-excited crowd. From this sudden reduplication of the self, this projection of the inner vision into living action, tragedy is born. Dionysus has sprung, full of life, from the enthusiasm of the dithyramb. He has only then to scatter himself abroad in the multitude of gods and men— and we have drama, human and divine. The theatre is established for all time. It would be easy to suppose *a priori* that drama was originally an imitation of actual life ; but this was not the case. The most powerful of all the arts arose from the desire of god and man alike to return to their source. It was only after having seen his god that man laughed at his reflection ; that is, at himself.

One can imagine the effect of these performances, with their many violent and contradictory emotions, upon an intelligent audience. In the country places, the Dionysian revelries developed into dramatic representations, accompanied by dances and the emptying of innumerable wine-skins. When Thespis brought his performance to Athens, a veritable madness swept the town. Men and women, the ignorant and the cultured—all alike were carried away. It caused the magistrates some anxiety, and not without reason. Plutarch relates in his *Life of Cimon* that Solon called Thespis before him, and inquired " if he were not ashamed to present such great lies to the people ; " but the sage who then ruled the city must have feared not so much the innocent illusion of the scene as the profanation of the Mysteries by the gross distortions of them that were presented by the first tragedians. The torrent, having burst open the flood-gates, could not be arrested, but it was finally dammed, and here was shown the wisdom of the Areopagus illuminated by the teachings of the Eumolpidæ. Dramatic authors were permitted to take the subjects of their pieces from the mythological traditions which had their source in the Mysteries, but they were forbidden, on pain of death, to divulge their secret meanings or to defile them with low pleasantries. The chief citizens of

Athens, nominated by the Archons and the Areopagus, were directed to choose the plays, and thus developed the annual festivals in honour of Dionysus. Tragedy ceased to be a rustic diversion for drunken peasants, and became a public cult for the city of Athens. By this masterly stroke, a dangerous game was transformed into a beneficent revelation. Pallas extended her protection to the refugee from the Mysteries, and made her the most powerful of all the muses, the priestess of the art of initiation and salvation. So, under the ægis of Minerva, and with the help of the seers of Eleusis, Melpomene developed—she who was to give humanity a new thrill, and to draw from the human heart floods of divine tears.

We have seen that all the creations of the Greek genius, which provide to this day the essential elements of our own culture, grew out of the Mysteries. In tragedy we may recognise the last and not the least astonishing of their miracles.

With Æschylus, the organiser and true creator of tragedy, it advances towards us still bearing the torch of initiation. Son of a priest of Eleusis, he may be called the great pontiff of tragedy. His successors had other merits, but were far from attaining his majesty and profundity. Æschylus draws with both hands from the sources of the ancient wisdom, and it is by their light that he descends into the obscure depths of human life. Poet, musician, architect, engineer, costumier, chorus-leader and actor, wearing the *cothurnus* and the tragic mask—Æschylus is still one of the Eumolpidæ. The human material that he digs up in great spadesful is the same as that of Homer, and even more massive. His seventy tragedies, of which only seven have been preserved, embrace the whole horizon of the cyclic poets, and the whole of Greek legend.

But what a gulf between Æschylus and Homer ! The one unfolds Olympian adventures and terrestrial catastrophes like an airy dream. The other transports us, through scene, characters, words and gestures, to the very centre of human will and consciousness. We are in the cavern where destinies are forged. Whether the chorus in a drama of Æschylus be composed of old men or virgins, of *erinyes* or *oceanides*, it is always in the presence of the gods, and as though vibrant with their breath. In the *Choephoræ* the slaves of the palace of the Atrides swarm like a flock of doves around the tomb of Agamemnon. Electra and Orestes, who dominate the group, invoke the spirit of their father for the work of vengeance, and the leader of the chorus, spreading wide her veils like wings, pronounces this imprecation, which is repeated by the rest :

" O that I might one day chant the funeral oration over a man struck down by the sword, or a dying woman ! Why should I seek to hide the divine impulse that fills all my soul ? It will nevertheless escape, and the anger of my heart, the hatred that rages within me, will be shown upon my countenance ! O when will Zeus stretch forth his vengeful hand ? Strike, O great God, the guilty heads ! "

Rising to such heights of vehemence and exaltation, the chorus is not an accessory ; it is the very soul of the action.

Above these semi-clairvoyant beings plunged in a kind of dream-state, stand the heroes of the trilogy—Agamemnon, Clytemnestra, Orestes. By the grandeur of their characters and the energy of their wills, they exceed ordinary human stature, but they abound with true passion. In them we can study the psychology ot crime, passing through the collective soul of a family from generation to generation. It is customary to say that the ancient drama is founded upon the blind fate which enfolds man through the action of the gods, like the net in which Clytemnestra enfolded her husband in order to murder him. The modern critic thinks he has found the true basis of this conception by substituting for divine arbitration the law of atavism, which, according to him, explains everything.

Nothing could be narrower or more false than this idea. The meaning of Æschylus is very different.

The structure and *dénouement* of his dramas prove that he was fully conscious of the three powers that dominate human life and balance one another—Destiny, Providence, and Freewill. Destiny, or Fate, is nothing but the chain of passions and calamities accumulating from generation to generation. Human freewill has made them possible, but man, aided by divine wisdom, can react. We see in Orestes the sense of responsibility growing out of the fatality in which he is entangled, through suffering and effort of will. The *erinyes* that attack him do not represent objective remorse only. They are occult forces created by the sins of humanity throughout the ages. By his sanguinary deeds man himself has flung these vengeful furies into the atmosphere, and they can victimise all who for any reason whatever have committed a crime. Orestes, who was driven through the destiny of his family to murder his mother, purifies himself with the help of Apollo and Minerva. The latter institutes the tribunal of the Areopagus, thus replacing the law of retaliation by a more merciful system, which allows the guilty one who acknowledges his sin to free himself. The *erinyes* continue to be dreaded powers, a terror to criminals and a warning to all, but they no longer represent vengeance without pity. At the end of his trilogy Æschylus shows us a procession of young Athenians conducting the Furies, now transformed into beneficent Eumenides, to their subterranean temple at Colonus.

The words, the dramatic situation and the setting, give this *dénouement* a serene magnificence. On the one hand, the terrors of nature conquered, reconciliated, changed into benevolent powers : on the other, the happy city protected by the gods. Night herself, the ancient Night of Chaos, falls away before the Eleusinian torches, and hymns of joy fill the soul with superhuman rapture. It is a genuine scene of initiation, transformed into a religious drama and civic festival.

In his *Prometheus*, Æschylus went further still. His titanic temperament did not always respect the limits imposed by the law. Driven by his genius, he had the audacity to half-reveal one of the greatest secrets of the Mysteries—a step which appears to have cost him dear. It was taught at Eleusis that man, the offspring of the gods, became their associate, and in a measure took their task in hand, as he developed, and that the gods, the cosmic powers, on their side, evolved through and with man. This was not in any sense a denial of their existence, but merely placed them under the great law of universal evolution, recognising man as their heir who had attained creative power by his own efforts. Such was the fundamental idea of *Prometheus Bound*, a veritable cosmogonic drama, in which the hero constantly speaks of the thousands of years he has yet to live. Prometheus took pity on men when Jupiter wished to destroy them, and saved them by stealing the heavenly fire, father of all the arts. Hence his struggle with the chief of the gods. The colossal image of the Titan, chained by Vulcan with great hammer-strokes to the mountain-summit, enduring his agony in disdainful silence ; then, when alone, invoking all the divinities of the universe as witnesses of his voluntary martyrdom ; the captive of the gods consoled by the Oceanides before Jupiter's lightning-stroke precipitates him to the depths of Tartarus : this symbol is graven in the mind of man as the type of suffering genius and noble rebellion.

Never has so much meaning been contained in any strongly individualised poetic figure. Prometheus is, in a sense, the sub-consciousness of the gods and of the Cosmos—speaking through man who has reached his prime—in which dwells the great idea of universal Justice, primordial and final, ruling the universe and the gods, victorious over Fate, daughter of Eternity. As interpreter of this subconsciousness, Prometheus is indeed the highest dramatic incarnation of Dionysus, the god divided up into hundreds of heroes. Here all the heroes are gathered into one, who seems to wish to speak the final word on all things, and whose voice causes Olympus to tremble.

We can well understand that the Athenian public also trembled, and that thousands of uninitiated spectators would shudder at the words spoken by the poet himself in the part of Prometheus—words concerning the national God of all the Greeks : " And yet this Zeus, despite the pride that fills his soul, shall one day be humbled. The *hymen* that he prepares shall cast him down from the height of his power ; he shall fall from his throne ; his empire shall be ended ! "

According to the scholiasts, this boldness roused the crowd to indignation. The stage was rushed, and the author threatened with death for such sacrilege. He escaped the daggers of his assailants only by taking refuge in the orchestra and embracing the altar to Dionysus. Thus, by the refined logic of Fate, the ideal tragedy was on the point of engendering a bloody drama upon the stage, and the lot of the poet almost became that of his hero, at the very moment when he personified him.

Such a lot might have been almost enviable, since it was that of Orpheus, and of Dionysus himself ! As to the Areopagus, it would, according to this account, have condemned Æschylus to drink the hemlock, but for the intervention of the Eumolpidæ, who declared that he was not initiated and had sinned through ignorance. But, whether this story be true or not, no other dramatist has ever equalled the audacity of the Titan-Poet, born at Eleusis and dying in exile in the shadow of Mount Etna. His volcanic soul emitted its last flashes at the foot of the volcano.

Whether or no he was formally initiated, the works of Æschylus prove that he carried the imprint of Eleusis in every fibre of his being. No less closely is Sophocles linked to the Mysteries, though with him the Eleusinian ideas are much more veiled and transformed. His less dithyrambic choruses nevertheless preserve a religious character. His always noble heroes approach nearer to ordinary humanity. The interior action is more skilfully managed ; the characters, more clear-cut, more colourful, follow the laws of progression. Sophocles is the inventor of psychological evolution. If we study from this point of view his tragedies of *Œdipus* and *Antigone*, we find in them a veritable drama of initiation. The discipline of Eleusis consisted precisely in bringing about a metamorphosis in man, in causing a new soul to be born in him, purified and clear-seeing, which became his conscious genius, his dæmon, under the ægis of a god.

In the *Œdipus* of Sophocles this mystery is clothed in a transparent legend. Œdipus has become king of Thebes by delivering the country from a female monster, the Sphinx. Classical literature and tradition look upon this as a fabulous monster like the Hydra, the Chimera, and the innumerable dragons of all countries ; but in the ancient Mysteries the Sphinx was a great and powerful symbol. With its body of a bull, claws of a lion, and human head, it represented the whole animal evolution through which man had passed ; while its eagle's wings signified the divine nature which he carries in embryo within him. Sophocles took the Sphinx with which the popular Theban legend furnished him, and simply left its esoteric nature to be divined. Œdipus is not an initiate, or even an aspirant ; he is the strong, proud man who plunges into life with all the energy of his unbounded desires, and dashes himself against obstacles like a bull against his adversaries. The will for pleasure and power ruled in him. By a sure instinct he guesses the riddle that the Sphinx-Nature asks of all humanity on the threshold of life, and gives the answer as ' Man.' But, creature of passion and desire, he means a man like himself, having not the least idea of man divine and transfigured. Through the quick insight of a man of action he gains the advantage over the monster, masters it, presents himself to the people, and becomes king. But the gods are preparing the punishment incurred by his violence and presumption. Without knowing it, he has killed his father and married his mother, and the discovery flings him from the heights of prosperity into the lowermost abyss. The spiritual beauty of the drama lies in the contrast between the soothsayer, Tiresias, who, deprived of physical sight but endowed with spiritual vision, can unravel the web of destiny, and Œdipus who, with open eyes, sees only the appearances of things and runs like a wild deer into the snares set for him.

If *Œdipus Rex* shows us the punishment of presumption, *Œdipus at Colonus* presents, in the figure of the old man, a wandering fugitive weighed down by misfortune and led by his noble daughter, the purification of man through suffering heroically borne. Having suffered courageously and conscientiously, the blind and exiled king has himself become a spiritual seer, and his head is ringed by an aureole of hope and consolation, radiating divine grace. Œdipus thus transfigured is almost a saint. After this we are no longer surprised to behold in Antigone the exquisite flower of pure human love, a Christian in anticipation.

The *chef d'oeuvre* of Sophocles thus entirely justifies the wise conclusions of Fabre d'Olivet. " Derived as a whole from the Mysteries, tragedy had a moral significance that initiates understood. This is what placed it above anything that we can imagine to-day, and gave it an inestimable value. While the ignorant, dazzled only by the splendour of the spectacle, and carried away by the beauty of words and music, experienced a fugitive pleasure, the wise man tasted a purer and more lasting joy in the reception of truth from the very heart of the lying illusions of the senses. This joy increased in proportion to the greatness of the poet's inspiration, and to his success in making the allegorical meaning felt, without betraying the veil that covered it."

If all the power of the Mysteries shines through the work of

Æschylus and Sophocles, we find no further trace of it in Euripides, their illustrious rival and successor. The sacred torches which guide man to the blessed light are extinguished, and we grope amid the shadows of a blind destiny lit up only by the flames of passion and the ruddy fires of Tartarus. It is easy to find the reason for this sudden change. Although a contemporary of the titanic Æschylus and the divine Sophocles, as great a poet in his own manner, and their equal, perhaps their superior, in certain respects—his tenderness of feeling, his marvellous limpidity of style, and his inventive richness of imagination—Euripides belongs to another world, to our own much more than to that of antiquity, through the order of his mind and the nature of his soul. Not only has he no links with Eleusis, but he is an ardent disciple of Socrates, who refused to be initiated because, as he said, he did not wish to know things that were communicated under the seal of silence and that he would not have a right to discuss in public. Socrates firmly believed and taught that reason alone could attain to the truth, and that rigorous logic, without the aid of any other faculty, leads infallibly to virtue and happiness. He turned his back upon ancient prophecy, mother of the primordial wisdom and of all the religions of antiquity; he ignored intuition, the creator of synthetic philosophy; he smiled shrewdly at inspiration, the source of poetry and art. He saw salvation only in observation, analysis and dialectic. In consequence he was, truly and authentically, as Nietzsche has said, the father of intransigent rationalism and of modern positivism.

And Euripides, although a poet, and a poet of genius, is the most fanatical disciple of this master of doubt. It is as though he wrote only for this one spectator, for Socrates, who never visits the theatre, goes to hear the tragedies of Euripides. What a refined pleasure for him to hear the characters and choruses of his disciple reproducing his own syllogisms, wherein the mind is caught as in a mouse-trap, and paraphrasing his destructive scepticism! How his Cyclopean eye must have gleamed, and his Silenus-like countenance brightened! In vain the gods descend from heaven in their golden chariots and declaim pompous verses through their painted masks. In their contradictory discourses the untiring reasoner sees Olympus crumble into dust, and all the mythological phantasmagoria vanish away. And he applauds to the skies this passage in a chorus of the *Hippolytus:* " Indeed, the foresight of the gods, when it enters my thoughts, relieves my anxieties; but scarcely have I grasped it ere I renounce it at the sight of the deeds and the sufferings of mortals."

These words reveal the gulf that separates the works of Euripides from those of his predecessors. The same subjects, the same characters, the same scenes; all the Homeric legend; but the religious feeling and the deeper comprehension of life have disappeared. Despite the knowledge of human passions, despite the incomparable charm of language and the innumerable beauties of detail, we are no longer conscious of the wide outlook that embraces the whole of human destiny and pierces to its depths through penetrating the Beyond. The genius of the Mysteries is no longer there, and without it everything shrinks and withers and falls to pieces. The chorus has ceased to be the eye and the voice of the gods, and represents merely the people, the changing crowd, the common herd, the trembling and credulous crone, the citizen *Demos* of Aristophanes. As to his heroes, it has been justly said that Euripides " has put the spectator on the stage." All the great characters in whom mythology glorified the founders of the Greek civilisation, have descended one or two rungs of the social ladder. Hercules, type of the initiate with his Twelve Labours, has become a mere *bon vivant*, coarse and vulgar, but generous; Jason, the hero of the Golden Fleece, a snivelling coward; and Achilles, Orestes and Pylades barely retain their dignity. Euripides has created some exquisite maidens, but his male characters as a rule are feebly drawn. He is a pastmaster in the depiction of passions themselves, when they become rulers of the soul and take the place of the individuality—as in the fierce lovers, Phædra and Medea, and in tragic Hecuba, the tigress of maternal vengeance. There remains pathos—of which Euripides is the inventor. There is no one who can arouse pity and cause tears to flow as he can, but it is a weakening and fruitless pity, which leaves the heart devoid of strength or consolation. It may be said that the æsthetic of Euripides—the result of his philosophy—amounts to pathos without enlightenment, and a sense of the inexplicable tragedy of life. He has nevertheless dowered us with two masterpieces from which the modern theatre has drawn much inspiration—*Hippolytus* and *Iphigenia at Aulis*. In these he attains the height of emotion, but if we search them closely we shall find that they are an involuntary condemnation of the philosophy of which Euripides made himself the mouthpiece. Hippolytus, the chaste, proud youth, worshipper of Diana, unjustly accused of incest by his father and killed at his prayers by Neptune; Iphigenia, the gentle virgin, sacrificed by a savage father and a superstitious army—do not these two victims prove that a purely intellectual civilisation, which knows not the true gods, is forced to immolate its noblest children in order to survive?

Nothing could be more strange or more tragic than Euripides' own destiny. After a life of continuous success and glory, he was called to the court of Archelaüs, king of Macedonia. There he wrote his tragedy of the *Bacchæ*, which is a complete negation of his former æsthetic and of his anti-mystical philosophy. In it we see King Pentheus torn in pieces by the bacchantes, after having denied the divinity of Dionysus and the necessity for incomprehensible Mysteries. Was the magician-god of metamorphoses satisfied with this tardy recantation? It seemed not, if we are to believe the story rumoured in Athens, for it was said that the famous guest of the king of Macedonia was torn to pieces by a pack of hounds, when out walking alone. This was a fine opportunity for audacious comparisons on the part of the upholders of Æschylus. They declared that the tempestuous passions which Euripides had let loose upon the stage, and which he had so cleverly played with throughout his long life, had entered into the dogs of Thrace in order to attack their master, like wild beasts who in the end devour those who tame them. It was the final and consummate irony, they said, of the gods that he had offended !

Fabre d'Olivet, that great forgotten thinker, has passed a remarkable judgment upon Euripides. I quote it, despite its excessive severity, because it gives in a few lines an authoritative picture of the degeneration of tragedy after the abandonment of the rules and traditions of Eleusis. " If the laws had been carried out that were at first promulgated against those who, in treating tragic subjects, debased their occult meaning, Euripides would not have been permitted to depict so many heroes degraded by adversity, so many princesses crazed by love, so many scenes of shame, scandal and crime ; but the people, already degraded and verging on corruption, were carried away by these dangerous representations and ran to drink from the poisoned cup that was offered to them. It is to the very charm of these pictures, to the talent with which Euripides knew how to colour them, that the decadence of Athenian society and the first offences against the purity of religion, must be attributed. The theatre, having become a school for passions and no longer offering any spiritual nourishment to the soul, opened a door through which entered contempt and derision, doubt, audacious sacrilege, and entire forgetfulness of divinity, and these insinuated themselves into the very sanctuaries."

So tragedy, this living marvel of art, has been shown to us as the flower of the Hellenic miracle and the crown of the Greek national genius. I have pointed out how the myth of Dionysus gave birth to it, how the Mysteries of Eleusis inspired its masterpieces, and how it fell into rapid decadence as soon as it ceased to understand them. The connection between these two institutions points to a conclusion which opens up a new perspective of the true mission of the theatre and its possible future history.

Tragedy is, according to Aristotle, *a purification* ($\chi\acute{\alpha}\theta\alpha\rho\sigma\iota\varsigma$) *through terror and pity*. This formula is concise and perfect; but it requires explanation. Why should terror and pity, which in real life are depressing sensations, become in the great Greek tragedies consoling and purifying forces? Because they present to the spectator the *ordeals of the soul* which render it fit to assimilate sublime and consolatory truths, by freeing it from veil after veil. Without a clear comprehension of these ordeals, the emotional waves of terror and pity remain impotent; but the purgation of the soul which follows the thrill of tragedy, produces in it a calmness lit up by the rays of truth and unknown bliss. The object of the Mysteries of Eleusis was to communicate this truth and bliss to the initiate through personal experience, by lucid conceptions and vivid imagery. To those who could understand them, the festivals and the initiation ceremonies of Eleusis gave a key to the contradictions and terrors of life. Thus the two institutions completed and assisted one another. In Æschylus and Sophocles we can perceive peace and light beyond the terror and the pity. In Euripides the dialectician and sophist, belonging to the purely intellectual and rationalist civilisation of which Socrates is the mainspring, we find terror and pity without their transcendent efficacy—that is to say, without the spiritual appeasement and illumination which they possessed in the primordial drama of Eleusis, and which the drama of Æschylus and Sophocles had to a great extent preserved. In the works of Euripides man appears as the victim of chance or of divine caprice. It may be said that this view of life rendered terror and pity more poignant, but they lost through it their ennobling virtue and their educative power. One emerges rejuvenated and spiritually enlarged from a tragedy by Æschylus or Sophocles, but moved and overwhelmed from a melodrama by Euripides. In spite of his greatness as poet and artist, the divine afflatus is lacking.

The ideal of art should be to join, in fulness of life, to the salutary terror and pity of tragedy, the consoling revelations that Greece found in her Mysteries, and particularly in the Eleusinian drama. History, it is true, does not begin over again, and one does not swim twice in the same river, as Heraclitus has said; but in the course of ages things and ideas return in ceaseless metamorphoses and unforeseen forms. Though our material civilisation envelops us as in an opaque veil, it is not impossible for the Hellenic miracle yet to undergo surprising incarnations and renaissances.

New creations sometimes proceed from a deep and sorrowful desire for a past that is forever lost, and there still burns in our hearts to-day an inextinguishable nostalgia for Greek tragedy, over which hovers, like an immortal hope, the sublime radiance of Eleusis !

BOOK VIII

THE COSMIC CHRIST AND THE HISTORICAL JESUS

> One can always search more and more
> deeply into the mystery of Palestine, for
> behind it lies . . . Infinity!"
>
> RUDOLF STEINER.

CHAPTER I

THE COSMIC CHRIST

WE have now reached a crisis in human and divine evolution when it is necessary to look back to all that has gone before, in order to understand all that follows. For here the influx from above and the effort from below meet in a luminous point that throws its rays backwards upon the immemorial past, forwards upon the infinite future.

The coming of the Christ is the central, incandescent focus of history. It marks a *volte-face*, a change of orientation, a new and powerful impulsion. No wonder it appears like a baneful deviation to the hardened materialist, and to the simple believer like a sudden stroke of fortune which suppresses the past in order to rebuild the world anew. The truth is that the first is the victim of his own spiritual blindness, and the second of his own narrowness of outlook. For if the manifestation of the Christ through the Master Jesus is, on the one hand, a fact of incalculable import, it has, on the other hand, been led up to by the whole of precedent evolution. A network of invisible threads attaches it to all our planetary past. It is a beam of light descending from the heart of God to the heart of man, to remind the earth, daughter of the sun, and man, son of the gods, of their divine origin.

We will try in a few words to elucidate this mystery.

The earth with its kingdoms, humanity with its races, the spiritual powers with their hierarchies stretching to infinity, evolve through one and the same impetus, in simultaneous and continuous motion. Heaven, earth and man move together, and the only way to discover the meaning of their evolution is to contemplate all three together at their common task, and to consider them as an organic and indissoluble whole.

Let us, from this point of view, glance at the state of the world at the time of the birth of Christ, and concentrate our attention upon the two races who then formed the advance-guard of humanity —the Greco-Latin and Jewish peoples.

From a spiritual standpoint, the movement of humanity from the Atlantean to the Christian era offers us the double spectacle of recoil and progress. On one side, the gradual loss of vision and of direct communion with the forces of nature and the cosmic powers ; on the other, the active development of intelligence and reason, resulting in man's material domination of the world. Vision continues to be cultivated by a chosen few in the centres of initiation where the oracles are heard, and from these spring all religious movements and all the great impulses of civilisation. But vision and the faculty of divination diminish in the human race as a whole. This spiritual and intellectual transformation of man, more and more drawn to the physical plane, corresponds to a parallel organic transformation. As we look further back into his prehistoric past, we see his body becoming ever lighter and more fluid. Then it solidifies, and at the same time his etheric body, which formerly extended beyond his physical body, is more and more absorbed by it and finally takes its exact form. His astral body, or radiant aura, which was formerly spread out around him like an atmosphere and served as medium for his hyperphysical perceptions and for his communion with the gods, is also drawn more closely around him, and becomes no more than a narrow halo saturated with his own life-force and coloured by his passions. This development occupied many thousands of years, and included the second Atlantean period and all the civilisations of Asia, North Africa and Europe that sprang from it—Hindu, Persian, Chaldean, Egyptian, Greek, and that of the Northern European peoples. It was an involution of the cosmic forces into physical man which was indispensable to his completion and to the perfecting of his intellect. Greece represents the last phase of this *descent of Spirit into Matter*. In her case the fusion is perfect, and it ·results in a marvellous blossoming of physical beauty combined with mental balance. But this airy temple inhabited by semi-divine men is situated on the edge of a chasm swarming with the monsters of Tartarus. It is a critical hour indeed ; for since nothing stands still, and it is necessary to move either backwards or forwards, humanity must from now on either fall into bestiality and depravity, or mount, with a wider consciousness, to spiritual heights. The decadence of Greece, and still more the imperial orgy of Rome, offer a magnificent but repulsive spectacle of the descent of man into debauchery and cruelty— the fatal reaction of all great historical movements.[1]

" Greece," says Rudolf Steiner, " was able to accomplish her task only by letting the veil that covered the ancient powers of vision become gradually thicker. The Greco-Roman world, in its rapid decadence, marks the deepest descent of spirit into matter

---

[1] See the " Life of Jesus " in *The Great Initiates* (Edouard Schuré) for a description of this period.

in the course of human evolution. This was the price paid for the conquest of the material world and the development of positive science. The posthumous life of the soul being conditioned by its earthly life, average men did not go far into the spiritual world after death. They took most of their veils with them, and their astral existence was like that of shadows. Hence the lament of the soul of Achilles in Homer : " Rather would I be a beggar on earth than a king in the land of shadows." The mission assigned to post-Atlantean humanity inevitably removed it further from the spiritual worlds. It is a cosmic law that growth on one side is paid for, temporarily, by weakness on the other." [1]

A fundamental change of attitude, a reascension towards the heights of the spirit, was required, that the destiny of humanity might be fulfilled. But for this a new religion was needed, more powerful than all those that had gone before, capable of uplifting the sunken masses and of stirring the human soul to its ultimate depths. The former revelations to the white race had taken place on the etheric and astral planes, whence they acted strongly upon man and upon civilisation. Christianity, coming from a higher plane, and from further away, was to manifest through all the planes as far as the physical, which it was to transfigure and spiritualise, giving back to individual men, as to collective humanity, the immediate consciousness of their celestial origin and divine goal. There were thus not only moral and social, but also cosmological, reasons for the appearance of Christ in our world.

Sometimes in mid-Atlantic, the wind tears a rent in the cloudy sky, and one sees the clouds gather at one spot and drop towards the ocean in the shape of a horn. At the same time the sea rises up in a peak, to meet the clouds. It seems as though the whole mass of waters rushes to this liquid whirlpool, to be swirled round and caught up in it. Suddenly the two points, attracting one another, meet like two mouths. The waterspout is formed ! The wind sucks up the sea, and the sea drinks the wind. A living column, vortex of air and water, moves giddily above the tossing waves, and for a moment earth and sky are united.

The manifestation of the Christ, descending from the spiritual world, through the astral and etheric planes, to the physical, resembles this marine phenomenon. In both cases, the powers of heaven and earth are at work, collaborating to bring about a supreme union. But while the waterspout is formed in a few minutes by the violence of the tempest and the electrical currents,

---

[1] *Die Geheimwissenschaft im Umriss.* Rudolf Steiner.

the descent of the Christ to earth requires thousands of years, and has its primal cause in the arcana of our planetary system.

In this metaphor, which seeks to express the rôle of the cosmic Christ in our humanity, the Jewish people represent the earthly side, exoteric and visible—the base of the waterspout which rises upwards, attracted by the whirlwind from above. This nation goes contrary to all other nations. With its intolerance, its obstinacy, its one fixed idea, it overrides the nations as the waterspout overrides the waves. The monotheistic idea comes into being with the patriarchs. Moses seizes upon it, and makes use of it to mould a whole nation. As the simoom raises a column of dust, so Moses gathers together the wandering Bedouins to form the people of Israel. An Egyptian initiate, under the protection of an Elohim whom he calls *Jahveh*, he imposes his will through speech, sword and fire. One God, one Law, one Ark, one people to carry it ; and first forty years in the desert, amid famine and sedition, on the way to the promised land ! From this majestic conception, like the column of fire that moved before the tabernacle, there emerges the people of Israel, with its twelve tribes corresponding to the twelve signs of the Zodiac. Israel is to preserve the monotheistic idea intact, despite the crimes of kings and the attacks of idolaters ; and upon it is grafted, from the beginning, the Messianic idea. For the dying Moses had announced the final Saviour, the king of justice, the universal prophet and purifier ; and from century to century the untiring voices of the prophets proclaim Him, from the Babylonian exile up to the time of the iron yoke of Rome. During the reign of Herod, the Jewish people resembles a ship in distress, whose demented crew wish to set the foremast alight as a beacon to guide them amid the reefs. For at this moment Israel presents the strange spectacle of a nation crushed by fate, almost overwhelmed, which expects salvation through the incarnation of a God !

Israel had to be shipwrecked ; but the God became incarnate.

What is this complex game of Providence, human liberty, and fate ? The Jewish nation, in a sense, personifies and embodies the earth's appeal to the Christ. Through it, human liberty, shackled by destiny—that is, by the mistakes of the past—cries to Providence for its salvation. All the great religions had reflected this preparation as in a mirror, for though none of them expressed a clear idea of the Messiah, the initiates had long foreseen and proclaimed His advent.

To the Pharisees who question Him as to His mission, Jesus replies : " Before Abraham was, I am." To the Apostles who fear His death, He speaks astonishing words such as no other prophet had ever spoken, words which on any other lips would have sounded ridiculous : " Heaven and earth shall pass away, but My words shall not pass away." Such words are either the ramblings of an idiot, or they contain a transcendent cosmological meaning. According to the official Church tradition, the Christ, the second Person of the Trinity, left the bosom of the Father in order to incarnate through the Virgin Mary. According to esoteric tradition also, the Christ is a superhuman being, a God in the strongest sense of the word, the highest spiritual manifestation that humanity has known. But like all the Gods, manifestations of the Eternal, from the Archangels to the Thrones, He is passing through an evolution which lasts throughout the whole planetary life, and as He is the only one of all the Powers who has been completely manifested by means of a human incarnation, this evolution is of a special nature. To grasp its origin we must go back, far beyond the beginning of human history, to the formation of the earth and the first glimmerings of light in our nebula. For, according to the Rosicrucian tradition, the Spirit which spoke to the world in the name of Christ and through the lips of the Master Jesus, is closely related to the ruling star of our system, the Sun.

We have seen, in *Planetary Evolution*, the Cosmic Powers working upon our world through a wise and unique hierarchy. The types and elements, souls and bodies, outlined upon the spiritual plane, are reflected upon the astral plane, vitalised upon the etheric, and made concrete on the physical. Each planet is the work of a different order of powers, and gives birth to different forms of life. Each great Cosmic Power—or, let us say, each great God—has in his train legions of spirits who are his intelligent co-workers. Western esoteric tradition looks upon the Christ as the chief of the solar genii. At the time of the separation of the earth from the sun, the sublime spirits called ἐξουσίαι by Dionysius the Areopagite, *Virtues* in Latin tradition, and *Spirits of Form* by Rudolf Steiner, withdrew to the luminous star which had just thrown off its opaque nucleus. They were of too ethereal a nature to take any part in the heavy earthly atmosphere in which the Archangels had to struggle, but, concentrated around the aura of the sun, they acted from there all the more forcibly upon the earth, fecundating her with their rays and clothing her in her mantle of greenery. The Christ, becoming the regent of these spiritual powers, might be called the Solar Archangel ; but hidden among them, in His veil of light, He remained long unknown to men.

The nascent earth was under the influence of another God,

whose legions were then concentrated in the planet Venus. This Cosmic Power has been called Lucifer, or the rebellious Archangel, in Judo-Christian tradition. I have indicated his rôle in the first chapter of this book. He drove the human soul further into matter, and buried the self in the depths of the body; consequently he was the indirect author of evil, but also of passion and enthusiasm, which are the effulgence of divinity in man through the tumult of the blood. Without him we should have had neither reason nor liberty, and the spirit would have no spring-board from which to leap to the stars.

The influence of the Luciferian spirits predominated during the Lemurian and Atlantean epochs, but from the beginning of the Aryan period the spiritual influence emanating from the solar aura made itself felt, and was gradually augmented from period to period, from nation to nation, from religion to religion. Thus the Christ drew nearer, little by little, to the terrestrial world, through a progressive radiation. This slow and profound method of approach resembled on the spiritual plane what was to take place on the physical plane—the appearance of a star in the depths of the sky, whose disk would gradually increase in size as it came nearer to us. Indra, Osiris and Apollo rose upon India, Egypt and Greece as precursors of the Christ. He shines through these solar gods as the white light shines through red, yellow and blue cathedral windows. He appears also to rare initiates, as sometimes on the Nile one sees a distant star gleam through the rosy rays of the setting sun that stretch to the zenith. So He appeared, resplendent, to Zoroaster in the form of Ahura-Mazda, who showed Himself to him, in his great vision, as a God clothed with the Sun. He flamed for Moses in the Burning Bush, and flashed like lightning through the Elohim amid the thunders of Sinai, having there become Adonaï, the Lord, announcing His near approach.

But this was not enough. To free humanity from the grip of matter in which it had become entangled, it was necessary that this great Spirit should be incarnated in a man; that the Solar Logos should descend into a human body, walking and breathing upon the earth. To bring men back to the road leading to the spiritual heights, and to show them their heavenly goal, it needed nothing less than *the manifestation of the Divine Archetype upon the physical plane*. It was necessary that He should triumph over evil through boundless Love, and over death through a dazzling Resurrection, emerging whole, transfigured, and more glorious than before, from the abyss into which He had plunged.

The writer of the Gospel according to St. John is thus able to say in a sense both literal and transcendental : " The Word was made flesh, and dwelt among us . . . full of grace and truth."

Such was the cosmic reason for the incarnation of the Solar Word. Having seen the necessity for His earthly manifestation from the standpoint of divine evolution, we shall now see how human evolution prepared a vehicle worthy to receive Him.

CHAPTER II

THE MASTER JESUS—HIS ORIGIN AND DEVELOPMENT

IN attempting to depict the true Jesus, we are faced by a preliminary question—that of the relative value of the four Gospels. Those who are convinced through meditation and intuition of the intrinsic truth of these unique testimonies, will be inclined to reply to all the objections raised by critics concerning the authenticity of the Gospels, in the words of Goethe. Towards the end of his life a friend said to him, " You know, it has been discovered that the Gospel of St. John is not authentic." " What *is* authentic," replied the creator of *Faust*, " if not that which is eternally beautiful and true ? "

In these superb words, the old poet, wiser than all the thinkers of his time, disposed of the heavy constructions of the documentary school of criticism, whose pretentious ugliness has ended in masking from us the faces of Truth and Life.

But let us be more precise. It is acknowledged that the Greek Gospels were written long after the death of Jesus, and based upon Jewish traditions which could be traced back to the disciples and to eye-witnesses of the Master's life. Whether or no they contain certain contradictions of detail, and present the prophet of Galilee from different angles, in what does the authority and truth of these writings consist for us ? Is it in the date of their composition ? Is it in the mountains of commentaries that have been heaped upon them ? No. Their force and their truth depend upon the living unity of the person and teaching of Jesus which they reveal ; and we have for counterproofs the fact that this revelation has changed the face of the world, and the new life that it can still arouse in each one of us. This is the sovereign proof of the historical reality of Jesus of Nazareth and of the authenticity of the Gospels. Everything else is accessory. As to those who, like David Strauss and his imitators, wish to persuade us that the Christ is a myth, " a grandiose historical humbug," their grotesque pedantry demands from us a blinder faith than that of the most fanatical believers. Jean-Jacques Rousseau has well said that if the fishermen of Galilee, the scribes of Jerusalem, and the neo-Platonic philosophers of Ephesus, had entirely invented Jesus Christ, who has vanquished the ancient world and conquered the modern, it would be a miracle more illogical and more difficult to understand than all the miracles of Christ. These material miracles, to contemporary occultists, as to initiates of all times, are known and established facts, raised by Him to their highest power. They were necessary to convince the contemporaries of Jesus. But what impresses us much more to-day is the outstanding personality and the incomparable spiritual greatness of this same Jesus, Who is revealed ever more vividly in the Gospels and in the consciousness of man.

Let us then say with Rudolf Steiner : " Modern criticism of the Gospels throws light only upon the outer and material side of these documents. It teaches us nothing concerning their essence. So great a personality as that of the Christ could not be comprehended by any one of His disciples. He must have shown a different side of His nature to each of them, according to their faculties. If we take the photograph of a tree from one side only, we have but a partial likeness ; but if we took it from four different sides, the likeness would be complete.

It is the same with the Gospels. Each of them corresponds to a different degree of initiation, and presents to us a different side of the nature of Jesus Christ.

Matthew and Luke depict in preference the Master Jesus, that is to say, the human nature of the founder of Christianity. Mark and John describe chiefly His divine and spiritual nature.

Matthew observes the Master Jesus *from the physical standpoint.* He dwells upon His descent, His genealogical connections with the people of Israel, His most sacred title-deeds. Luke, the most poetic and visionary of the Evangelists, describes *the intimate life of the Master.* He *sees* the reflection of His true self in His astral body. He paints in moving images the forces of Love and Sacrifice that flow from His heart. Mark corresponds to *the magnetic aura that surrounds the Christ,* whose radiance extends to the spiritual world. He shows us above all the miraculous power and majesty of the Healer. John is the supreme *metaphysical Evangelist.* He is concerned with the Divine Spirit of the Christ. Less precise than Matthew and Mark, more abstract than Luke, he does not, like the latter, experience impressive visions reflecting events in the astral world ; but he hears *the interior and primordial message, the Creative Word,* which vibrates through every utterance and through the whole life of the Christ. He preaches the Gospel of the Spirit.

The four Evangelists are thus all inspired seers of the Christ, but each has his own limitations and his own sphere." [1]

The diversity, and at the same time the unity, of the inspiration of the Gospels, which complete and fit in with one another like the four stages of the human being, indicate to us their relative value. By connecting each with its special sphere, we gradually become aware of the lofty personality of Jesus Christ, which is related on its human side to the special evolution of the Jewish people and on its divine side to the whole planetary evolution. [2]

In tracing the genealogy of Jesus back to David and Abraham, the Gospel of Matthew aims at proving that He is descended from the chosen people of Judah, and that His physical body is the supreme flower of their race. What must be remembered concerning this genealogical tree is that Jesus had to be the product of a long process of selection, the final outcome of a whole race. But as well as the heredity of the body, there is that of the soul, for every human ego has had numberless former incarnations. Those of initiates are of a special and exceptional kind, in accordance with their degree of evolution. The Jewish prophets, the *nabi*, were usually dedicated to God by their parents, and bore the name of *Emmanuel*, or *God in him*. This meant that they were spiritually inspired. These children were brought up in a school for prophets, and afterwards led an ascetic life in the desert. They were called Nazarenes, because they allowed their hair to grow. The Boddhisatvas of India, taking into consideration all the differences of race and religion, resembled the Hebrew prophets who bore the name of Emmanuel. They were beings whose spiritual self (*Bodhi*) was sufficiently developed to be in touch with the divine world during their incarnation. Among the Hindus a *Buddha* was a Boddhisatva who had attained perfection in his last incarnation—a perfection which meant complete penetration of the body by the spirit. After such a manifestation, which had a purifying and regenerative effect upon humanity, a Buddha was no longer obliged to reincarnate. He could enter the glory of Nirvana, or Non-illusion, and could still influence humanity from the divine world in which he dwelt.

---

[1] This classification of the Gospels according to their spheres of comprehension is a *resumé* of various lectures given by Dr. Steiner. A short sketch of the subject will be found in the note at the foot of p. 445 of *The Great Initiates*, and these spontaneous intuitions are now strikingly confirmed by a seer and thinker of the first order. I have pleasure in expressing here my warm thanks to three well-known Swiss Theosophists, M. Oscar Grosheinz of Berne, and Mme. Grosheinz-Laval and M. Hahn of Basle, for their kindness in lending me valuable notes of private lectures given by Dr. Steiner.

[2] For the story of the early development of Jesus and the unfolding of His consciousness, the reader is referred to Book viii. of *The Great Initiates* by Édouard Schuré.

The Christ is more than a Boddhisatva and more than a Buddha. He is a Cosmic Power, the Chosen One of the Devas, the Solar Word, Who can only be embodied once, to give humanity a new and powerful impetus. A spirit of such vast extent could not be incarnated in the womb of a woman or in the body of a child. He could not—as other men must, even the greatest—pass through the narrow channel of animal evolution which is reproduced in the process of gestation. He could not undergo the temporary eclipse of divine consciousness which is the inescapable law of human incarnation. A Christ directly incarnated in the womb of a woman would have caused the mother's death, as Jupiter caused the death of Semele, mother of the second Dionysus, in the Greek legend. In order that He might incarnate, an adult body was necessary, a body evolved by a strong race to such a degree of perfection and purity that it was worthy to contain the human Archetype, the primeval Adam, moulded by the Elohim in the uncreated light at the beginning of the world.

This body, chosen from all others, was provided by the Jewish people in the person of the Master Jesus, son of Mary. But it was still necessary that from birth up to the age of thirty, when the Christ would take possession of His human habitation, the body of Jesus should be refined and harmonised by an initiate of the highest rank, so that a man almost divine should offer himself up as a sacrifice, a consecrated vessel, to receive the God made man. Who was the great prophet, famous in the religious records of humanity, who undertook this difficult task? The Evangelists do not say, but the Gospel of St. Matthew gives us an inkling, and even clearly indicates the truth in one of its most suggestive passages.

The divine Child is born in the balmy and peaceful night at Bethlehem. Silence hangs upon the dark hills of Judea. Only the shepherds hear the angelic voices pealing across the starry sky. The Child sleeps in his crib, his mother brooding over him in ecstasy. When he opens his eyes, Mary is pierced to the heart as by a sword, by that Solar Ray that questions her in amazement. The astonished soul, drawn from the Beyond, casts an affrighted glance at its surroundings; but, having found his lost heaven in his mother's tender eyes, the Child again falls into a deep slumber. The Evangelist who describes this scene sees something more besides. He sees the spiritual forces from the depths of space and time that are concentrated upon this group, and that form themselves for him into a picture of great sweetness and dignity. Three Wise Men from the far East are crossing the desert and approaching Bethlehem. The star stands still above the stable where the infant Jesus is sleeping, and the priest-kings, full of joy, prostrate themselves before the new-born child, adoring him, and offering him in homage myrrh, frankincense and gold, which signify will-power, holiness and wisdom.

What is the meaning of this vision? The Wise Men were disciples of Zoroaster, and looked upon him as their king. They were called kings themselves, because they could read the heavens and influence men. Among them there had long been current an old tradition that their master would reappear in the world under the name of Saviour (*Sosiosh*) and re-establish the rule of Ormuzd. For centuries this prediction of a Messiah had haunted the initiates of the East [1]—and at last it was realised. The Evangelist who describes this scene is telling us, in the language of the adepts, that the Eastern magi came to salute in the Child of Bethlehem *a reincarnation of their Master, Zoroaster*. Such are the laws of divine evolution and of spiritual psychology. Such is the affiliation of the loftiest individualities. Such is the force that draws, with great souls, great strokes upon the map of history. The same prophet who had proclaimed the Solar Word to the world under the name of Ahura-Mazda, from the heights of Mount Alborj and in the plains of Iran, was to be reborn in Palestine that the Word might be incarnated in all Its glory!

However great an initiate may be, when he reincarnates his consciousness is darkened; he must suffer the veil of the flesh. He is, in a sense, obliged to reconquer his higher self in this earthly life, and to expand it by a fresh effort. The infancy and adolescence of Jesus were protected by his simple and pious family. His thoughtful and reflective mind could expand without hindrance, like the wild lilies in the long grass of Galilee. He turned a clear and open gaze upon the world, but his inner life remained deeply hidden. He did not yet know what he was, or what he expected. But as a mountainous country, under a stormy sky, is sometimes lit up by sudden calms, so was his soul illuminated by intermittent visions. "One day, in ecstasy, upon the blue mountains of Galilee, among the white lilies with violet hearts that grow in the tall grasses, he had seen a marvellous star approaching him from the far distances of space. As it drew nearer it became an immense sun, and in its centre was enthroned a human figure, radiant and colossal. It had the majesty of the King of kings, and the gentleness of the Eternal Woman, so that it was Man without and Woman within." [2] And the youth lying in the long grass felt himself lifted up into space by this star that drew him towards it. When

---

[1] See the chapter entitled *A Chaldean Priest in the Time of the Prophet Daniel*.

[2] *Sanctuaires d'Orient* by Edouard Schuré.

he awoke from his dream he seemed to have become lighter than a feather.

This stupendous vision that haunted him at times was like those described by other prophets, and yet quite different. He spoke of it to no one, but he felt that it contained his past and future destiny. Jesus of Nazareth was one of those who develop entirely from within, without anyone's being aware of it. The interior working of the spirit is suddenly revealed one day through some outward circumstance, and fills everyone with astonishment. This phase of psychic development has been described by St. Luke. Joseph and Mary have lost the Child Jesus whom they had taken with them to Jerusalem for the feast-days, and, turning back again, they find him seated in the midst of the doctors of the temple, " both hearing them, and asking them questions." To the complaint of his distressed parents he answers, " How is it that ye sought me? Wist ye not that I must be about my Father's business?" But they did not understand their son's words, adds the Evangelist. Nevertheless, this young boy who lived a double life was " subject unto his parents . . . and increased in wisdom and stature, and in favour with God and man."

CHAPTER III

WHAT was Jesus doing from the age of thirteen to thirty? The Evangelists tell us nothing; it is a deliberate omission and a profound mystery. For every prophet, however great, must be initiated. His higher self must be awakened and made conscious of its own strength, that the new mission may be fulfilled. The esoteric teachings of Theosophy, both ancient and modern, unite in declaring that Jesus could only have been initiated by the Essenes, the last fraternity to keep alive the ancient tradition of the prophets. They dwelt on the borders of the Dead Sea, and were chiefly known as spiritual healers, *asaya* meaning doctor. They were the doctors of the soul, and Philo of Alexandria has told us something of their customs and secret doctrines.[1]

It was necessary that, as far as ordinary humanity was concerned, the Evangelists should let absolute silence, as deep as that of the Dead Sea, cover the initiation of the Master Jesus. They have shown us only its final stage in the Baptism. But having recognised his exalted individuality, identical with that of the prophet of Ahura-Mazda, and knowing that the Baptism signifies the great mystery of the incarnation of the Christ—secretly indicated by the occult language and symbols used in the Gospel story—we can reconstruct, in all its essentials, this unique preparation for the most extraordinary event in history.

The valley of the Jordan, where it opens upon the Dead Sea, provides the most impressive landscape of all Palestine. Coming upon it as one descends from the sterile hills of Jerusalem, it affords a spectacle of magnificent desolation, with an atmosphere of holiness that grips the heart. At the first glance one realises that the greatest religious events the world has known could have taken place here. Across the horizon stretches a high barrier of vaporous blue—the mountains of Moab. Their bare summits

---

[1] A short sketch of the Essenes will be found in *The Great Initiates*.

rise in domes and cupolas, but the ocean-like mass of them, veiled in delicate mist and light, is dominated by the great horizontal line, as time by eternity. More barren than the rest, one can distinguish Mount Nebo, where Moses yielded up his soul to Jahveh. Between the steep hills of Judea and the immense chain of Moab stretches the wide valley of the Jordan, a tawny desert bordered by fields and groups of trees.

Before us lies the oasis of Jericho, with its palms and its vines as large as plane-trees, and its grassy carpets which in spring are enamelled with red anemones. Two or three miles away the Jordan flows across white sands to lose itself in the Dead Sea, which gleams like a blue triangle between the promontories of Judea and Moab, closing around it as though protectingly. Upon the accursed lake—beneath which lie, according to Biblical tradition, the cities of Sodom and Gomorrah that were destroyed by fire—broods a stillness as of death. Its salt and oily waters are charged with asphalt, and kill everything they touch. No sail is spread upon them; no bird is seen to fly. On its stormy, arid shores only dead fishes are found, and the whitened skeletons of aloes and sycamores. Nevertheless its surface is a magic mirror, the colour of lapis lazuli, ever changing like a chameleon. Sinister and leaden in time of storm, it reveals to the sun's touch depths of limpid blue, and reflects fantastically the colossal architecture of the mountains and the clouds. The lake of death is also a lake of apocalyptic visions.

This valley of the Jordan, formerly so fertile, but now devastated, ending in the Dead Sea as in a hell without exit, seems like a place separated from the rest of the world, and full of terrifying contrasts. Here is volcanic nature, ravaged by the forces of production and destruction. The rich oasis of Jericho, watered by sulphurous springs, seems, with its warm airs, to defy the demoniacally convulsed mountain-shapes. Here King Herod maintained his harem in sumptuous palaces; there, in the caves of Moab, thundered the voices of the prophets. The footsteps of Jesus imprinted on this soil have silenced the last echoes of those infamous cities. It is a land stamped with the Seal of the Spirit. Everything in it is sublime; its sadness, its silence, its immensity. Human speech dies away; it is made for the speech of God.

We can easily understand why the Essenes should have chosen for their retreat the most retired part of the lake, called in the Bible "the sea of solitude." En-gedi is a narrow, half-moon-shaped terrace, lying at the base of a high cliff on the western side, below the mountains of Judea. In the first century of our era the houses of the last healers, built of dried earth, could still be seen. In a narrow ravine they cultivated sesame, wheat and the vine, but passed the greater part of their time in reading and meditation. It was there that the Master Jesus was initiated into the prophetic tradition of Israel, and into the concordant traditions of Babylon and Egypt, concerning the Solar Word. Night and day, the pre-destined Essene read the histories of Moses and the prophets, but only through meditation and the inward light which ever increased within him did he become conscious of his mission. Now, when he read the verses of Genesis, they resounded in his ears like the harmonious thunder of the circling stars, and created visions of the things of which they spoke. " Elohim said, Let there be light ! And there was light. . . . Elohim divided the light from the darkness." And Jesus saw the birth of worlds, of the sun and the planets. But what was his amazement when, towards his thirtieth year, sleeping one night in a cave near the top of the cliff, he was again visited by the vision of Adonaï that he had not had since his childhood. In a flash he remembered that he had been His prophet a thousand years before. As a torrent of fire swept through him he knew that he, Jesus of Nazareth, had been Zoroaster, the prophet of Ahura-Mazda, on the heights of Mount Alborj and among the Aryan peoples ! Had he then come back to earth to proclaim Him anew ? Joy and glory ineffable ! He lived and breathed in light. . . . But what new service did the Supreme God require of him ?

Weeks of silent and concentrated ecstasy followed, during which the Galilean relived his former life. Then it was once more effaced, like a cloud from the sky, and it seemed to him as though he watched, through the eyes of Ormuzd-Adonaï, all the centuries that had passed since his death. This caused him bitter pain. As on the canvas of an immense painting, the decadence of the Aryan, Jewish and Greco-Roman races was unrolled before him. He saw their vices, crimes and sufferings. He saw the earth deserted by the gods—for most of the ancient gods withdrew from perverted humanity, and God the Father, the Incompre-hensible, was too far removed from poor human consciousness. Degenerate and sinful man was dying, without knowing it, of thirst for these absent gods. Woman, who needs the vision of God in man, was dying for want of the Hero, the Master, the Living God. She became either courtesan or victim, like the tragic Mariamne, daughter of the Maccabees, who loved Herod the Tyrant greatly and met only with jealousy, defiance and the assassin's dagger.

The Master Jesus, wandering on the cliffs of En-gedi, heard afar off the rhythmic pulsation of the lake. This deep voice, amplified by the echoes among the piled-up rocks, seemed like a tremendous moaning, the cry of a human flood reaching up towards Adonaï, and demanding of Him a prophet—a Saviour—a God !

And the ancient Zoroaster, become the humble Essene, also cried upon the Lord, that the King of the Solar Archangels might instruct him concerning his mission. But He came not. In place of the former dazzling vision, a black cross now haunted him, sleeping and waking. Within and without, it seemed to hover before his eyes. On the shore and on the cliffs it was with him, and at night it rose like a gigantic shadow between the Dead Sea and the starry sky. When he questioned this immovable phantom, a voice replied from the depths of his own being : "Thou hast laid thy body upon the altar of Adonaï like a lyre of ivory and gold. Now thy God claims thee that He may manifest Himself to men. He seeks thee, and thou canst not escape Him ! Offer thyself as sacrifice ! Embrace the cross ! "

And Jesus shuddered from head to foot.

About this time strange rumours were heard by the solitary monks of En-gedi. Two Essenes returning from the Jordan, announced that John the Baptist was preaching the repentance of sins on the banks of the river, amid a great multitude. He proclaimed the Messiah, saying : " I baptize you with water, but He that cometh shall baptize you with fire." The movement was spreading throughout all Judea.

So one morning when Jesus walked upon the beach at En-gedi with the patriarch of the Essenes, he asked the centenarian head of the community :

" John the Baptist is foretelling the Messiah—who will this be? "

The old man looked long at the young disciple.

" Why dost thou ask, since thou knowest ? "

" I would hear it from thy lips."

" Then it will be thou, thyself. For ten years now we have prepared thee. The light burns in thy soul, but the will is yet lacking. Art thou ready ? "

In reply Jesus stretched wide his arms in the form of a cross, and bowed his head. The patriarch knelt before him and kissed his feet, bathing them with tears, and saying, " Into thee shall descend the Saviour of the World."

Lost in terrible thought, the Essene dedicated to so great a sacrifice stood without moving. When the old man rose, Jesus said, " I am ready."

They looked at one another again. The same light and the same resolution shone in the moistened eyes of the Master and the blazing eyes of the disciple.

"Go then to Jordan," said the old man. "John is waiting to baptise thee. Go in the name of Adonaï."

So Jesus went, accompanied by two young Essenes.

John the Baptist, in whom the Christ later recognised the prophet Elijah, was the last of the old inspired prophets—the last incarnation of one of those wild ascetics who, when the spirit moved them, preached the vengeance of God and the reign of Justice to peoples and kings. Around him there gathered ever increasing crowds, attracted by his authoritative words, and composed of every element of society. There were hostile Pharisees, enthusiastic Samaritans, simple tax-gatherers, soldiers of Herod, bearded shepherds with their flocks of goats, Arabs with their camels, and even Greek courtesans from Sepphoris who had come out of curiosity, in sumptuous litters with escorts of slaves. Everyone flocked, with diverse feelings, to hear "the voice of one crying in the wilderness." Those who wished it were baptised, but this was no light matter. The imperious voice and strong hand of the prophet impelled them to plunge into the river and remain submerged for several seconds, after which they came out purified and as though transformed. But it needed courage and endurance, for during the long immersion they risked suffocation, and many thought they were dying and lost consciousness. It was even said that some were drowned, but this seemed to add an even greater attraction to the ceremony.

On this particular day the crowd encamped round the bend of the river where John preached and baptised was in a state of revolt. A malicious scribe from Jerusalem, incited by the Pharisees, had stirred it up, saying to the prophet in his camel's hair raiment, "It is now a year since thou hast begun to proclaim the Messiah, who is to overthrow the great ones of the earth and re-establish the kingdom of David. When will he come? Where is he? Who is he? Show us this Maccabean, this king of the Jews. We are armed, and in great numbers. If thou art he, tell us, and lead us to attack Machærus, or the palace of Herod, or the tower of Sion occupied by the Romans. Men say that thou art Elijah. If so, produce the fire from heaven!"

Cries broke out, and lances gleamed. A menacing wave of anger swept the crowd towards the prophet.

John turned upon the excited people, with his ascetic, bearded face and lion-like brow, and cried: "Back, race of vipers and jackals! The thunderbolts of Jehovah are being prepared for you!"

Ever since the early morning, sulphurous vapours had been drifting across the Dead Sea. A black cloud hung over the whole valley of the Jordan, and distant thunder was rumbling. This voice from heaven seemed to reply to the voice of the prophet, and the crowd, seized with superstitious fear, fell back and dispersed. Very soon the Baptist was left alone on the shores of the bay formed by the Jordan where it curves around a thicket of tamarisk, mastic-trees and arborescent reeds.

Shortly afterwards the sky cleared at the zenith. A soft mist, almost like diffused light, filled the valley, hiding the mountain-tops and leaving only their copper-coloured bases to be seen.

John saw three Essenes approaching him. He knew none of them, but their white robes told him to what order they belonged. The youngest one addressed him.

" The patriarch of the Essenes prays the prophet John to accord baptism to our chosen brother, Jesus the Nazarene, whose head has never been shaven."

" Let him receive blessing from the Eternal, and enter the sacred waters," said John, filled with respect at the sight of the tall, dignified figure, beautiful as an angel and pale as death, advancing towards him with downcast eyes. But the Baptist had as yet no suspicion of the sublime mystery in which he was to officiate.

The Master Jesus hesitated for an instant before entering the deep pool where the Jordan formed an eddy ; then he plunged resolutely into it and disappeared beneath the surface. John stretched out his hand over the turbid water, and pronounced the sacramental words. On the bank the two Essenes stood motion-less, rooted to the soil, in deep anxiety. It was forbidden to help the one who was being baptised to leave the water ; for the belief was that a breath of the Divine Spirit entered into him through the hand of the prophet and the waters of the river. The majority emerged from the test revivified ; some died ; and others became insane and as though possessed. These were called demoniacs.

Why was the Master Jesus so long in leaving the Jordan, whose sinister eddies continued to swirl above the fatal spot ?

In the solemn silence of this moment, an event of incalculable significance for our earth was taking place. Though there were thousands of invisible witnesses, there were only four earthly ones—the two Essenes, the Baptist, and Jesus himself. This event flamed through the three worlds like a lightning-flash, coming from the spiritual world, through the astral atmosphere of the earth, down to the human physical plane. The earthly actors in the cosmic drama were affected by it in different ways, all equally overwhelming.

First of all, what is taking place in the consciousness of the Master Jesus ?—He is aware of a sensation of drowning, followed by a terrible convulsion. The etheric body is violently torn from its physical envelope, and for some seconds he sees a chaotic picture of his whole past life. Then an immense relief, and the darkness of unconsciousness. The transcendent Self, the immortal Soul, of the Master Jesus has left his physical body for ever, and is received back into the aura of the sun. At the same moment, by an inverse movement, the Solar Genius, the sublime Being whom we call the Christ, entered the abandoned body and took possession of it, animating with new fire this human lyre that had been prepared through hundreds of generations and by the sacrifice of the Master.

Was it this that caused the two Essenes to see a streak of lightning dart from the blue sky and illumine the whole valley of the Jordan ? They closed their eyes under its piercing brilliance, as though they had seen a glorious Archangel plunge head first into the river, leaving behind him a flaming trail composed of myriads of spirits.

The Baptist saw nothing of all this. He awaited the reappearance of the submerged one with great anxiety. When the Master stepped at last from the water, John trembled, for the Essene's whole body seemed to be bathed in light, and the shadow that before had veiled his face was replaced by a serene majesty. Such glory, such sweetness, were in his look that in that instant the dweller in the wilderness felt all the bitterness of his heart melted within him. When the Master Jesus, helped by his disciples, had replaced his long robe, he turned towards the prophet with a gesture of blessing and of farewell. Then John, suddenly seized with ecstasy, beheld the vast aureole that surrounded the body of Jesus. Above his head he saw floating miraculously a great luminous dove, bright as molten silver poured from the crucible ; and he knew that this dove, Iona, meant, in the astral world, the mystery of the Eternal-Feminine, the spirit of Divine Love, transformer and vivifier of souls, to be called later by Christians the Holy Spirit. Simultaneously he heard, for the second time in his life, the primordial Word that echoes in the secret places of the soul, and that had before driven him into the desert like a trumpet-call. It resounded now in melodious thunderings, and its meaning was : " This is my beloved Son ; to-day have I begotten him."[1] Only then did John understand that Jesus was the predestined Messiah.

He saw him depart with regret. Jesus passed through the encampment, where camels, asses, women's litters and flocks of

---

[1] These last words are found in the early Hebrew Gospel, and in the first text of the Synoptics. Later the version that we have to-day was substituted : " This is my beloved Son, in whom I am well pleased "—which seems a useless repetition. It must be added that in sacred symbolism, which is *occult writing* drawn from the archetypes of the spiritual world, the presence of the mystical Dove at the Baptism indicates the incarnation of a Son of God.

goats were all huddled together ; elegant Sepphorians, and uncouth Moabites, and crowds of people of every kind. When he had disappeared, the Baptist thought he still saw the subtle rays of his aureole illumining the air and stretching to a vast distance. Then the prophet seated himself sadly upon a heap of sand, and leaned his forehead on his hands.

Evening had come, and the sky was clear once more. Emboldened by the humble attitude of the fierce prophet, some soldiers and tax-gatherers, led by the emissary of the synagogue, approached him. The mocking scribe leaned over him, and sneered, " Well, when art thou going to show us the Messiah ? "

Without rising, John looked at him gravely, and said, " Madmen ! He has just walked among you, and you did not know him ! "

" What ? Is that Essene to be the Messiah ? Why is it not thyself ? "

" That is forbidden. He shall grow greater, and I less. My task is finished. I shall preach no more . . . Go to Galilee ! "

A soldier of Herod, a Goliath with the face of a hangman, who respected the Baptist, and had liked to hear him, said pityingly, " Poor man ! His Messiah has made him ill."

But the scribe from Jerusalem burst into loud laughter, crying, " How foolish you are ! He is mad. Now you see that I have been able to silence your prophet ! "

Such was the descent of the Solar Word into the Master Jesus. Solemn hour, supreme moment of history ! Mysteriously—and with what great love !—the divine powers have been working from above, throughout untold æons, secretly preparing the Christ and letting Him shine upon humanity through other gods. Tempestuously—and with what great desire !—the human ocean has uplifted itself from below, with the Jewish people forming, at its summit, a body worthy to receive the Messiah. At last the hope of the angels, the dream of the magi, the cry of the prophets, is fulfilled. The two spirals have met. The whirlpool of divine love is joined to the whirlpool of human suffering—the waterspout is formed. And for three years the Solar Word shall tread the earth in a body full of grace and strength, to prove to all men that God exists, that Immortality is not an empty word, that those who love, believe, and will, can attain to heaven through death and resurrection.

CHAPTER IV

RENEWAL OF THE ANCIENT MYSTERIES THROUGH THE LIFE OF CHRIST, FROM THE TEMPTATION TO THE TRANSFIGURATION

LET us try to define the nature of this unique Divine Being who emerged from the Baptism in Jordan.

The Master Jesus, the Essene initiate, son of Mary, who offered his physical body to the Christ, also gave up at the same time his etheric and astral bodies—a triple envelope carefully evolved and perfectly harmonised. By using it, the Solar Word, Who appeared to Zoroaster in an astral vision and to Moses in etheric form as an Elohim, was enabled to speak to men as a Man of flesh and blood. This was necessary in order to arouse and convince them, so blind had they become to the Light, so deaf to the voice of the Spirit. Innumerable times, and in how many diverse forms, the Gods had manifested !—from the Atlantean epoch down to the heroic ages of Greece and Judea. They had overshadowed the Rishis, illumined the Prophets, inspired the Heroes. But in the Christ there appeared for the first time a God completely incarnated in humanity. This phenomenon could only happen once in history, at the critical moment of human evolution—that is, at the lowest point of its descent into matter. How was it to rise again from this darkness to the heights of the Spirit ? Only through the great impetus given by a God who was made man—and, this impetus once given, the Word would still continue to act upon and influence humanity, though actual incarnation would not again be necessary.

Hence the marvellous organism of the Being called Jesus Christ. Through His sensations, He is in and of matter ; through His thoughts He soars to the world of Archetypes. He breathes divinity. His whole consciousness is expressed in the words so often on His lips : " I and my father are one." At the same time He is one with suffering humanity through the all-embracing tenderness, the great Love, which caused Him voluntarily to accept His mission. His soul is as a living fire arising from the perpetual combustion of the human by the Divine. We can dimly imagine the radiant power of attraction of such a Being. His human aura is surrounded by an immense spiritual aura, which puts Him into touch with all the spiritual Powers. His thoughts do not stumble through the slippery lanes of reason; they flash forth from the central Truth that embraces all things. Drawn by this primordial force, souls crowd around Him, and are stirred and made new by His influence. The object of His mission is the spiritualisation of the world and of man, the raising of them to a higher level of evolution. The means used are both moral and intellectual—moral, through love and the feeling of universal brotherhood which flow from Him as from an inexhaustible spring; intellectual and spiritual through the opening of the Mysteries to all souls who are athirst for truth.

Thus, during His three years' ministry, the Christ initiates the community into His moral teachings and the apostles into those ancient Mysteries which He revives and expands. But, in contrast to what happened formerly in Persia, Egypt, Greece and Judea, this initiation, then reserved for a chosen few only, now took place publicly and in broad daylight, that the whole of humanity might participate. " The true life of Jesus," Rudolf Steiner says, " was the actual happening, historically, of what before Him had only happened in initiation. All that up till then had been shrouded in the secrecy of the temple, was through Him to be displayed to the world in poignant reality. The life of Jesus is thus a public confirmation of the Mysteries."

The Temptation

Although He was essentially God, the Christ had to pass through the first stage of initiation before He could begin His ministry. Ordinary man can only acquire vision in the spiritual worlds by perceiving his own lower self that conceals them from him. This is what occult tradition calls *the Guardian of the Threshold*, and what is symbolised in legend by the Dragon.[1] It is an astral condensation of all his previous incarnations in an impressive and sometimes terrifying form. He can only destroy this phantom that bars his way to the spiritual world by expelling from his soul the last vestiges of the baser passions. The Christ, the pure Solar Spirit, has no lower self, and no *Karma*. He is free from every stain, never having been separated from God. But humanity, into which the Christ must enter, has its *Guardian of the Threshold* in the Cosmic Power which has watched over its precedent evolution, and enabled it to attain self-consciousness by driving it down into the material realm. It is this Power that now hides the spiritual worlds from

---

[1] See the description on p. 207, in the chapter on *Dionysus of the Mysteries*; and on p. 107 in the chapter on *The Life of Buddha*.

the great majority of mankind. In the Bible it is called Satan, corresponding to the Persian Ahriman. Ahriman, as I have said when writing of Zoroaster, is the lower side of Lucifer, his shadow and projection in the lower world, the *dæmon* that has lost its divine consciousness. So Satan—or Ahriman—has come to be the King of Shadows, while Lucifer is still, despite his fall, the potential Light-Bearer, and will yet be so again in actuality.

This is why the Christ had to meet and conquer Ahriman in the magnetic aura of the earth before He could begin His mission. Hence His forty days' fast, and the three tests described symbolically in the Gospel of St. Matthew. The prince of this world puts Him, in succession, through the temptation of the senses (by hunger), the temptation of fear (by placing him on the pinnacle of the temple), and the temptation of absolute power (by offering Him all the kingdoms of the world) ; and each time the Christ repulses him in the name of that voice of truth that resounds within Him like the harmony of the spheres. By this unconquerable resistance Ahriman is vanquished, and falls back with his innumerable legions before the Solar Genius. A rent has been made in the shadowy webs in which they had enshrouded the earth ; the doorway of the human soul is once more opened ; and the Christ can enter in.

In the teaching given by the Christ to His followers we shall now trace the four stages of ancient initiation, formulated as follows by Pythagoras :—1. Preparation or instruction, παρασχειή ; 2. Purification, χάθαρσις ; 3. Achievement or illumination, τελείωτης ; 4. Higher vision or synthesis, επιφάνια.[1] The first two degrees of this initiation, being meant for the people, that is to say, for all, are combined and simultaneous. The two last degrees, reserved for the apostles, and especially for three among them, are stages towards the close of His life. This revival of the ancient Mysteries is, in one sense, a popularisation and a widening; in another, a deepening, and an approach to synthetic vision through higher spiritualisation.

First Degree : Preparation.—The Sermon on the Mount and the Kingdom of Heaven.

The work of the Christ begins with the Galilean idyll and the proclamation of " the kingdom of heaven." This is His popular teaching, and also a preparation for the more sublime Mysteries that He will gradually reveal to His apostles, that is, His

---

[1] See *Pythagoras* in *The Great Initiates*, by E. Schuré.

intimate disciples. It thus corresponds to the mental preparation that was a part of the ancient Mysteries. But we are no longer in crypts and temples ; the Galilean initiation has for setting the Lake of Gennesareth. Its clear waters, swarming with fish, its banks covered with flowers and trees, its undulating blue and violet hills, enclosing it as in a golden cup—this whole paradise, fragrant with sweet herbs, forms the most complete contrast to the infernal landscape of the Dead Sea. Such a frame, and the frank and simple people that dwelt within it, is necessary for the first steps of the Messiah. The God Who is incarnated in the body of Jesus of Nazareth carries within Him the divine Plan that He has been preparing throughout the centuries, in strokes vast as the rays of the sun. Now that He is man, captive upon earth, in the world of appearances and shadows, He must work out the application of this Plan, step by step, stage by stage, along His rock-strewn path.

He is equipped for that. He reads men's minds ; He draws their hearts. By a single look He can penetrate into souls and destinies. When He says to Peter the fisherman, mending his nets on the shore, " Follow me, I will make thee a fisher of men "— Peter rises and follows Him. When He appears in the twilight to James and John, in his white Essene robe, with an aureole of light around Him, they ask Him, " Who art thou ! " He replies simply, " Come into my kingdom "—and they go with him. Already a crowd of fishermen, tax-gatherers and women, young and old, follow Him from village to village, across the countryside. And now He preaches on the mountain, in the shade of a large fig-tree. What does He say ?—" Blessed are the poor in spirit, for theirs is the kingdom of heaven. Blessed are they that mourn ; for they shall be comforted . . . Blessed are they which do hunger and thirst after righteousness ; for they shall be filled . . . Blessed are the pure in heart ; for they shall see God." These truths, impregnated with the powerful voice and look of the Master, appeal not to the reason but to the heart. They sink into the souls of the hearers like heavenly dew ; and whole worlds are contained in them. All the mystery of the spiritual life—the law of compensation which acts from one existence to another—is there. Those who hear them cannot gauge their import, but grasp their meaning intuitively. They drink them in like life-giving wine, and when the Master adds, " The kingdom of heaven is within you," a flower of joy expands in the women's hearts, like a rose that sheds its perfume when shaken by the wind.

The word ' brotherhood ' which is often used to define the moral teaching of Christ, is inadequate to express its true essence Two of its chief characteristics are the *enthusiasm* that it arouse and the *faith* that it demands. " With the Christ something quit new enters into the human *self*, something that enables it to perceive in the depths of the soul that spiritual world that it had only perceived before in its astral and etheric bodies. Formerly, in spontaneous vision as in the Mysteries, there was always a part that remained unconscious. The decalogue of Moses, for instance, was presented as *Law*, not as *Life*, and spoke only to the astral consciousness. The *Life of Love* did not enter into humanity until the coming of the Christ. The Buddha had, it is true, given the world a teaching of Love and Compassion, but it was his mission to inculcate these through the reason. The Christ, being Love personified, brought Love itself, acting solely through its own presence, with the irresistible force of a radiant sun. There is a difference between a *thought* that you can understand and a *force* that enters into you like a torrent of life. It was the *Substance of Love* and not only the *Knowledge of Love* that the Christ brought to the world when He gave Himself to it by merging Himself in humanity."[1]

This is the reason for the special *faith* that Christ demands from His followers. "Faith, in the New Testament sense, does not mean—as the so-called 'orthodox' Christian would often have us think—a blind submission and adherence of the intelligence to abstract and unchangeable doctrines, but a conviction of the soul and a fulness of love that overflows from one soul to another. It is a communicative perfection. Christ said, 'If ye lend to them of whom ye hope to receive, what thank have ye? for sinners also lend to sinners, to receive as much again. But love ye your enemies and do good, and lend, hoping for nothing again.' The love of Christ is an overflowing and submerging love."[2]

Such was the preaching of the "kingdom of heaven" that is within man, and that the divine Master often compared to a grain of mustard seed, which when sown in the earth grows into a tall plant and produces thousands of seeds. This kingdom that is within us contains the germs of all other things. It suffices the simple-minded, of whom Jesus said—"Blessed are they who have not seen and yet have believed." The inner life is in itself a force and a blessedness, but in the thought of Christ it is only a preparation for a wider kingdom, for the spheres of infinity, the kingdom of His Father—that divine world, the dazzling vision of which He would reveal to His chosen ones, the way towards which He would throw open to all humanity.

In the meantime the community which surrounds the Master is increasing, and follows Him everywhere—from one shore of the

---

[1] Lecture given at Basle by Rudolf Steiner on the Gospel of St. Luke (1910).
[2] Rudolf Steiner. *Ibid.*

lake to another, from the orange-trees of the plain to the almond-trees of the hills, through the ripe cornfields and the white lilies that grow among the tall mountain-grasses. He preaches the kingdom of God to the crowds from boats drawn up on the shore, in the small synagogues, and under the great sycamores by the roadside. These crowds already call Him the Messiah, without knowing what the word signifies, or where it will lead them. He is there, and that is enough. Only the women, perhaps, divine His superhuman nature, and strew flowers before His feet. He Himself rejoices silently, as befits a God, in this earthly spring-time of the Kingdom. His divinity is humanised and softened at the sight of all these eager souls who expect salvation from Him, whose entangled destinies He can unravel, whose future He can foresee. He rejoices in this flowering of the spirit, as the bridegroom at the wedding in Cana rejoices in the silent, perfumed bride amid the paranymphs.

The Evangelists tell us of a dramatic episode that casts its shadow amid the sunbeams that play upon this Galilean spring-tide. Is it the first attack of the hostile forces that are already gathering invisibly against the Christ? During a crossing of the lake, one of the fierce squalls, so frequent on the sea of Tiberias, rises up. Jesus was asleep in the stern. Was the tossing boat going to sink? The Master was awakened, and with outstretched hand calmed the waves, while the ship, driven by a favourable wind, safely gained the farther shore. That, at least, is what St. Matthew tells us—and why should it be impossible? The Solar Archangel, in close communion with the powers that rule the terrestrial atmosphere, might well project His will like a magic circle into the fury of Æolus. He can pierce the darkness of the sky with a blue centre, and create for an instant *the eye of the tempest* with the heart of a God. Reality or symbol? In either case, divine truth. Christ sleeping in the fishing-boat amid the angry waves—what a marvellous image of the peace of the soul conscious of its divine home, in the midst of wild elements and unchained passions!

Second Degree: Purification.—Miraculous Healings—Christian Therapeutics.

In all the ancient Mysteries, moral and mental preparation was followed by a purification of the soul which was to awaken new faculties in it, and consequently to render it capable of seeing the divine world. This was essentially a purification of the etheric and astral bodies. With the Christ, as we have said, divinity had descended through the astral and etheric planes to the physical plane, so that it could affect the physical bodies of the faithful through the two others. Their whole beings could thus be transformed, for this influence, having passed through the three life-spheres, could rise upwards from the blood in the veins to the highest point of the self. Christ was the healer of both the soul and the body, hence this new therapeutics that had such immediate and startling effects. It was a magnificent example, never to be equalled, but in whose footsteps the faithful could walk.

In esoteric teaching a miracle is not looked upon as an interruption or overturning of natural law, but as a concentration of the scattered forces of the universe upon a given point, and a hastening of the vital processes of nature. Miracles similar to those of the Christ had been worked before Him in the sanctuaries of Asia, Egypt and Greece ; by Æsculapius, among others, at Epidaurus, a fact to which numerous inscriptions bear witness. Those of the Christ are distinguished by their intensity, and by their moral effects. Lepers, paralytics, the blind, and the ' possessed '—all, when once cured of their ills, feel that their souls have been changed. The equilibrium of their bodily forces has been restored by the Master's influence, and at the same time His love has given them the light of faith, and His divine beauty the radiance of hope. They will be aware of this contact in all their future existences.

" Love in action—that is the gift of the Christ. Luke recognised in Him the Healer of body and soul. Because he was himself a physician and had practised the art of spiritual healing, he could understand the therapeutics of Jesus. This is why the lofty teachings of Buddhism reappear in St. Luke's Gospel as though renewed in a fountain of youth."[1]

Third Degree : Illumination.—The Raising of Lazarus.

An opinion widely held to-day is that Jesus meant to bring the kingdom of God only to the masses, that he had only one and the same teaching for all, and that in consequence His doctrines put an end to mystery in religion. Our present age, which crudely believes that it has found a new religion in democracy, has sought to relate the greatest of the Sons of God to this grotesque and paltry ideal of the overwhelming of the few by the many. Has not the most famous of His biographers thought that he was giving him an irresistible recommendation in the eyes of the modern world in calling Him " a lovable democrat " ?

Certainly the Christ wished to open the way of truth to all souls of goodwill ; but He knew well that it must be done in proportion to their various degrees of intelligence. Simple commonsense

[1] Rudolf Steiner. *Ibid.*

forbids us to believe that so great a Spirit could have been unaware of the hierarchical law that governs the universe, nature and humanity. The idea that the teaching of Christ had neither degrees nor mysteries is refuted by all four Evangelists. The disciples having asked Him why He spoke to the people in parables, He replies, " Because it is given to you to know the mysteries of the kingdom of heaven, but to them it is not given. For whosoever hath, to him shall be given, and he shall have more abundance ; but whosoever hath not, from him shall be taken away even that he hath." (Matt. xiii. 11-12). This means that conscious truth—that is, truth *crystallised by thought*—is indestructible, and becomes a centre of attraction for new truths ; while vague, instinctive truth becomes scattered and exhausted in the multiplicity of impressions. Therefore the Christ had a secret teaching, reserved for His apostles, a teaching that He called " the mysteries of the kingdom of heaven." And further, when we look more closely, the hierarchy can be discerned in four stages corresponding to the four degrees of classical initiation :—1. The *multitude*, to whom He gives moral teaching in the form of metaphors and parables. 2. The *seventy*, who heard the explanation of these parables. 3. The *twelve apostles*, initiated into the mysteries of the kingdom of heaven. 4. Finally, among these, the *chosen ones*, Peter, James and John, initiated into the deeper mysteries of the Christ Himself, the only three who were present at the Transfiguration. It may be added that, among these three,' John was the only *epopt* in the sense of the Mysteries of Eleusis and of Pythagoras—that is, *a seer who understands what he sees.*

And indeed the Gospel of John, from beginning to end, expresses the highest stage of initiation. The Creative Word, the Word that " was in the beginning with God," and that *was God*, resounds through it from the opening verses, like the harmony of the spheres— the Word that is the eternal moulder of worlds. And together with this metaphysical conception of the Father, Son and Holy Ghost, which is the *leitmotiv* of the whole Gospel—and in the form chosen to express this conception the Alexandrian influence has justly been recognised—we find a familiarity, a touching realism in exact and striking points of detail, that suggests a special intimacy between this disciple and the Master. This applies to the whole account of the Passion and especially to all the scenes at Bethany, of which the raising of Lazarus is the most important.

Lazarus, whom John simply describes as the brother of Martha and Mary of Bethany, is the most singular and puzzling figure in the Gospels. Only John mentions him ; the Synoptists know him not. He appears only for this one scene of the raising from the dead. The miracle accomplished, he vanishes, as through a trap-door. Nevertheless he belongs to the group of those who were nearest to Jesus, and who accompanied Him almost to the tomb. From this two questions arise. What is this dim figure of Lazarus that moves like a phantom amid the other characters so vividly and clearly drawn by the Evangelist? And what does his resurrection mean? According to the general belief, Jesus brought Lazarus back to life in order to prove to the Jews that He was the Messiah. But this reduces Him to the level of a common miracle-worker. Modern criticism, always ready to deny wholesale anything that it cannot explain, settles the question by declaring that this miracle, like all the others, was a delusion of the popular imagination. We might as well say, as some do, that the whole story of Jesus is a fabrication, and that the Christ never existed. Let us add that the idea of resurrection is the centre and mainspring of Christian thought. To interpret it, to understand it, to bring it into line with the laws of the universe, is necessary, but merely to suppress it robs Christianity of its light and strength. In losing the immortality of the soul it would lose its chief lever.

Now the Rosicrucian tradition offers us a solution of this disturbing problem as bold as it is illuminating.[1] It causes Lazarus to emerge from the shadows, and gives to his resurrection its esoteric meaning, its sublime reality. For those who can see through the veil of appearances, Lazarus is none other than the disciple John himself. If he has not said so, it is because of a kind of spiritual modesty, and because of the admirable self-effacement practised by the followers of Jesus. The fear of seeming to place himself above his brethren prevented him from describing, under his own name, the greatest event of his life, which made him an initiate of the first rank. Hence the mask of Lazarus worn in this instance by the apostle John; while his resurrection takes on a new character and is revealed to us as the highest stage of ancient initiation, that of the third degree.

In Egypt the initiate, after lengthy tests, was thrown by the hierophant into a deep sleep, and passed three days in a sarcophagus placed in the temple. During this time the physical body became icy-cold, and had all the appearance of death, while the astral body, completely freed, could roam about the Cosmos. As to the etheric body, the seat of life and memory, it also freed itself and followed the other, leaving in the physical body just enough of its substance to prevent death. When he awoke from this cataleptic sleep, induced by the hierophant, the man who stepped from the sarcophagus was no longer the same. His soul had travelled through other worlds, and retained the memory thereof. He had become a true

---

[1] See *The Christian Mystery and the Ancient Mysteries* by Rudolf Steiner.

initiate, a member of the magical chain associated, according to an old inscription, "with the army of the higher gods." The Christ, Whose mission it was to reveal the Mysteries to the world, and to widen their doorway, wished His favourite disciple to pass through the supreme test that leads to a direct apprehension of truth. Even in the text of the Gospel we can see that all was willed by Him and prepared in advance. Mary sends a message from Bethany to Jesus Who is preaching in Galilee, saying, "Lord, *he whom thou lovest* is sick." ('Does not this clearly indicate the apostle John, *the disciple whom Jesus loved*'?) But Jesus, instead of hastening, waits two days, and says to His disciples, "This sickness is not unto death, but for the glory of God, that the Son of God might be glorified thereby . . . Our friend Lazarus sleepeth, but I go that I may awake him out of sleep." Thus Jesus knows beforehand what He wishes, and what He is going to do. He arrives in the nick of time for the phenomenon that He has foreseen and prepared. So, in the presence of the weeping sisters and the assembled Jews, before the tomb cut in the rock, from which the stone has been rolled away, and where the one believed dead lies in a heavy sleep, the Master cries : " Lazarus, come forth ! " And he who appears before the astonished crowd is not the legendary Lazarus, a pale ghost still shadowed by the darkness of the grave, but a man radiant and transfigured. It is the apostle John, and the splendours of Patmos shine already in his eyes. For he has seen the light divine ; during his sleep he has known eternity. His supposed shroud becomes the linen robe of the initiate. Now he knows the meaning of the Master's words, " I am the resurrection and the life." The Creative Word, " Lazarus, come forth ! " has penetrated to the marrow of his bones, and brought about a resurrection of both body and soul. John knows now why he is the disciple loved more than the others by Jesus, for only he can fully understand Him. Peter remains the man of the people, the simple and impetuous believer, who weakens at the last moment. John becomes the Initiate and Seer, who follows the Master to the foot of the cross, to the darkness of the tomb, and to the glory of the Father.

Fourth Degree : Spiritual Vision.—The Transfiguration.

The Epiphany, or vision from on high, signified, in the Pythagorean initiation, the vision of the Whole which should follow spiritual contemplation. It was the intimate comprehension and deep assimilation of things seen in the spirit, and should lead to a *synthesis of the Cosmos*. This was the crown of initiation, and to this phase corresponds, in the teaching given by Christ to His apostles, the phenomenon of the *Transfiguration*.

Let us recall the circumstances in which this event took place. The spring-like dawn of the Galilean idyll had paled. Darkness was gathering around the Christ. The Pharisees and Sadducees, His mortal enemies, were lying in wait for His return to Jerusalem that they might seize and arraign Him. In the Galilean towns and villages many were deserting Him because of the calumnies of the Synagogue, which accused Him of blasphemy and sacrilege. Soon Jesus, preparing for His last journey, climbed a hill to make His sad farewells to the towns and the lake that He had loved. " Woe unto thee, Chorazin ! Woe unto thee, Bethsaida ! . . . And thou, Capernaum . . ." The attacks of hatred were gradually obscuring the aureole of the Solar Archangel. The news of the death of John the Baptist, beheaded by Herod Antipas, was a warning that His hour was drawing near. He knew His destiny, and did not recoil from it. But the question must have arisen within Him— " Have my disciples understood my teaching and its mission in the world ? " Most of the twelve, imbued with Jewish ideas, imagined the Messiah as One who would rule the nations by the sword. They were still incapable of understanding the work the Christ was to accomplish in history. Jesus wished, however, to prepare His three chosen ones—and here the account of St. Matthew stands out in strong relief and with a peculiar significance.

" And after six days Jesus taketh Peter, James and John his brother, and bringeth them up into an high mountain apart, and was transfigured before them : and his face did shine as the sun, and his raiment was white as the light. And behold, there appeared unto them Moses and Elias talking with him. Then answered Peter and said unto Jesus, ' Lord, it is good for us to be here : if thou wilt, let us make here three tabernacles ; one for thee, and one for Moses, and one for Elias.' While he yet spake, behold, a bright cloud overshadowed them : and behold a voice out of the cloud, which said, ' This is my beloved Son, in whom I am well pleased ; hear ye him.' And when the disciples heard it, they fell on their face, and were sore afraid. And Jesus came and touched them, and said, ' Arise, and be not afraid.' And when they had lifted up their eyes, they saw no man, save Jesus only." (Matt. xvii, 1—8.)

In his picture of the Transfiguration, Raphael, with his angelic and Platonic genius, has marvellously interpreted the spiritual meaning of this vision. The three worlds—physical, astral and spiritual ; the last dominating and permeating the others with its brightness—are clearly defined, and are represented by three groups that form the three sections of the picture. At the foot of the mountain we see the uninitiated disciples and the crowd. They are violently arguing and disputing about some miracle, but they do not see the Christ. The demoniac who had been healed alone among them perceives the vision, and cries out ; the spiritual eyes of the others are not yet opened. On the mountain-summit, Peter, James and John lie wrapped in heavy slumber. They are not yet capable of spiritual vision in the waking state. The Christ, Who appears to be raised above the earth in a shining cloud between Moses and Elijah, represents the vision of the three chosen ones. In contemplating and striving to interpret this vision, we see that the three initiated apostles have before them in these three figures a symbol of the whole of divine evolution. For Moses, the prophet of Sinai, the mighty scribe of *Genesis*, represents earthly history from the beginning of the world. This is the whole past. Elijah represents Israel and all its prophets, the foretellers of the Christ. This is the present. The Christ Himself is the translucent, radiant incarnation of the Solar Logos, the Creative Word, which has sustained our world from the beginning, and which now speaks through a Man. This is the whole future.[1] The voice that the apostles hear is the universal Voice of the Father, the Pure Spirit whence all Words emanate. It is like the spheral music that flows around the worlds and orders their rhythmic movements, and that can be heard only by those whose ears are opened. In this unique and solemn hour the apostles hear it translated into human language.

Thus the vision of Mount Tabor gathers up into a picture of sublime simplicity the whole of evolution, human and divine. The *Transfiguration* was the starting-point of a new mode of spiritual ecstasy and a clearer spiritual vision.

---

[1] In *The Great Initiates* I have sought to describe what took place in the soul of the Christ during the Transfiguration.

CHAPTER V

THE NEW MYSTERIES: THE PASSION, DEATH, AND RESURRECTION OF THE CHRIST

SMILING and sunlit were the three years of the ministry of Jesus. The wandering life amid the fields and on the shores of the lake was combined with serious teaching ; the bodily and spiritual healings were alternated with the practice of prophecy and seership. Sometimes there seemed to be a sudden ascent of the Master, that He might draw His own to the spiritual heights where they belonged. But in proportion as He rose, numbers fell by the wayside. Only three accompanied Him to the summit, where they were overwhelmed by the revelation as by a lightning-stroke. Such was the manifestation, ever increasing in strength and beauty, of the Christ through the Master Jesus. And then He abruptly descends from this glory to a gulf of ignominy. Voluntarily, in the sight of His disciples, He allows Himself to be taken by His enemies, and delivers Himself up unresistingly to the last outrages, to torture and to death. What was the reason for this appalling downfall ?

Plato, that great and modest initiate who marks the transition stage between Hellenism and Christianity, has said somewhere that " the soul of the world is crucified in all the creatures of the universe and awaits its deliverance." Strange words, in which the author of the *Timæus* seems to have foreseen the mission of the Christ in its deepest and most transcendent meaning. For these words enfold both the problem of planetary evolution and its solution through the mystery of the cross. After the long entanglement of the human soul in the bonds of matter, nothing less than the sacrifice of a God was needed to free it from them and show it the Way of the Spirit.

In other words, the Christ, after initiating His disciples, had to undergo a personal initiation, in order to complete their education and accomplish His mission. The Divinity had to descend to the depths of suffering and death, to identify Himself with the heart and blood of humanity, and to give the world a new impulsion. Spiritual power is in direct proportion to the gift of self ; so that it was for the Christ Himself an exaltation to give Himself to humanity by entering a human body and accepting martyrdom.

Here we have the new Mysteries, unique, and of a kind that had never before been seen; that, doubtless, will never again be seen in all the metamorphoses that earth may undergo in the course of future evolution. For in these Mysteries, a God, the Solar Archangel, has been initiated—and the Hierophant is the Pure Spirit, the Father. The resurrected Christ arises as Saviour of humanity, and the result is, for man, an immense widening of his sphere of spiritual perception, and an incalculable expansion of his earthly and heavenly destiny.

For more than a year the Pharisees lay in wait for Jesus, but he would not give Himself up until His hour had come. Many times He had disputed with them on the threshold of the synagogues, or under the portico of the temple at Jerusalem, where the highest dignitaries of the religious power walked in their gorgeous vestments. Many times He had reduced them to silence by His closely reasoned dialectic, replying to their snares with snares more subtle. Many times, too, He had alarmed them with sayings that seemed to fall from the sky like thunderbolts. " In three days I will overthrow the temple . . . in three days I will rebuild it." Often He had defied them openly, and certain of His epithets remained like barbs in their flesh. " Hypocrites ! Race of vipers ! Whited sepulchres ! " And when in their fury they would have had him seized in the temple itself, Jesus more than once had made use of the same means employed later by Apollonius of Tyana at the tribunal of the Emperor Domitian—He had thrown a veil over their eyes and rendered Himself invisible. " He passing through the midst of them went his way," says the Gospel of St. Luke.

However, at the chief synagogue all is ready for the judgment of the dangerous prophet who has threatened to destroy the temple, and who calls himself the Messiah. In the eyes of the Jewish law these two accusations are sufficient to ensure his condemnation to death. Caiaphas has said in the sanhedrim that it was expedient " that one man should die for the people "—and when heaven speaks through the mouth of hell catastrophe is imminent. Also a conjunction of the stars in the sign of the Virgin has marked the fatal hour on the dial of the sky as on the dial of history, shooting its black arrow into the solar heart of the Christ. He gathers His apostles together in His habitual retreat, a cave on the Mount of Olives, and announces to them His approaching death. Filled with consternation, they do not understand ; they will not understand until afterwards. It is the day of the Passover. Jesus orders the farewell repast in a house in Jerusalem.

And behold the twelve seated in a vaulted room, towards the fall of night. On the table is the Paschal-lamb, commemorative of the flight from Egypt, which is to become a symbol of the supreme Victim. Through the windows of the arcade can be seen the dark citadel of David, the golden roof of Herod's temple, the sinister tower of Antony where the Roman sword holds sway—and over all, the pallid twilight. An oppressive silence reigns, and a ruddy vapour seems to float in the air. John, who sees and suspects more than the others, asks himself why, in the growing darkness, a dim halo should appear round the head of the Christ. It emits faint rays that are quickly extinguished, as though the soul of Jesus were stirred to its depths and trembling before a final resolve. Without speaking, the loved disciple leans his head upon the Master's breast. At last the silence is broken : " Verily I say unto you, that one of you shall betray me this night." Spoken in a grave voice, these words sound to the twelve like the alarm-signal of a ship in distress. " Who ? Who ? "—and Jesus, having indicated Judas, who is convulsively clutching his purse, adds calmly, " That thou doest, do quickly." Then the traitor, seeing himself discovered, goes forth in anger.

Then Jesus, breaking the bread and offering the cup, solemnly speaks the words that consecrate His mission and echo through the centuries. " Take, eat ; this is my body . . . drink, this is my blood." Less than ever do the amazed disciples understand. Only the Christ knows that in this moment He is accomplishing the greatest action of His life. In these words, which inscribe themselves in the invisible records, He delivers Himself up to humanity, He sacrifices Himself in advance. Before this, the Word, the Son of God, freer than all the Elohim, could have turned back—could have refused the agony ; but now He can no longer do so. The Powers have heard His vow. Like a vast aureole the divine part of Jesus Christ, His Solar Spirit with all its forces, rises towards the Elohim, who receive it into their waiting circle—a dazzling token of the divine sacrifice. They do not render it back to Him until after His death. On the earth there remains only the Son of Man, a victim advancing to the sacrifice.

It is He alone, also, who knows what is meant by " the body and blood of Christ." Long ago the Thrones had given their bodies for the creation of the nebula ; the Archaï had given their last breath to cause the sun to shine forth in the Saturnian night ; the Archangels, their fiery souls to create the Angels, the prototypes of Man. Now the Christ is to give His body for the salvation of humanity. From His blood is to arise the human brotherhood, the regeneration of the species, the resurrection of the soul. And while His disciples drink the sour wine of Judea that reddens in the cup, Jesus thinks of His heavenly dream, His cosmic dream before His incarnation—when He still breathed in the solar sphere—when the twelve great Prophets offered to Him, the thirteenth, the dreaded cup—and He accepted it.

But the apostles—except John, who divines the ineffable—cannot understand. They feel that something terrible is going to happen. They tremble, they grow pale. They are seized by uncertainty and doubt, father of cowardly fear. When the Christ rises and says, " Let us go to pray in Gethsemane," they follow Him in couples. The sad procession passes through the low postern of the golden gate, and descends into the dark valley of Hinnom, the Jewish cemetery and the " valley of the shadow of death." They cross the bridge over the Cedron, and enter the cave on the Mount of Olives. The apostles are silent, powerless, overwhelmed.

Under the great trees of the Mount of Olives, with their angular outlines and thick foliage, the circle of the infernal powers closes around the Son of Man as though to strangle him with an iron band.

The disciples fall asleep. Jesus is praying, and His brow is covered with a bloody sweat. It is necessary for Him to endure this suffocating anguish, to drink the cup to the dregs, savouring the full bitterness of desertion and despair. At last torches and weapons gleam among the trees. It is Judas with the soldiers. He gives Jesus the treacherous kiss, and so betrays Him to them. There is an infinite tenderness in the Christ's question : " Friend, wherefore art thou come ? "—a tenderness so penetrating that it will drive the traitor to suicide, despite the blackness of his soul. After these words of perfect love, Jesus remains unmoved till the end. He has armed Himself against all tortures.

We see Him before the high priest Caiaphas, a hardened Sadducee, and a type of sacerdotal pride without faith. Jesus declares Himself to be the Messiah, and the pontiff rends his clothes, as a sign of condemnation to death. At the Roman pretorium Pilate tries to save the Galilean, whom he looks upon as a harmless dreamer. For this supposed " King of the Jews " who calls himself " Son of God " adds that " his kingdom is not of this world." But the Jewish priests appeal to the jealous shade of Cæsar, and the crowd shouts, " Crucify him ! " so that the proconsul, having washed his hands of the crime, delivers the Messiah into the brutal hands of the Roman legionaries. He has been dressed in a purple robe ; His brow is wounded by the crown of thorns ; in His hands they have placed a reed for a mock sceptre. Blows and insults are rained upon Him. To show his contempt for the Jews, Pilate says to them, " Behold your king ! "—and adds, with bitter irony, " Ecce Homo ! " as though all human misery and degradation were summed up in this fallen prophet.

Expiring antiquity, and even the Stoics, did not understand the

Christ of the Passion any better than Pilate. They only saw the distressing exterior, and His apparent inertia filled them with indignation. But every act in the life of Jesus had both a symbolical meaning and a mystical effect upon future humanity. The Stations of the Cross, perceived by the saints of the Middle Ages in astral symbolism, became for them a way of initiation and a means of perfection. The Order of St. John, the Templars, the Crusaders who desired to conquer Jerusalem that they might make it the capital of the world, the mysterious Rosicrucians of the fourteenth century who sought to reconcile Science and Faith, the East and the West, through the higher wisdom—all these spiritual men of action, in the most intense meaning of the words, were to find in the Passion of Christ an incalculable source of strength. When they visualised the *Scourging*, the bruised figure of Jesus said to them : " Learn from Me to remain unmoved under the blows of destiny, to endure all suffering, and thou shalt acquire a new faculty : the comprehension of all sorrow, the sense of unity with all beings. For I have consented to suffer for men that I may reach the depths of their souls." The *Crown of Thorns* taught them to defy the world morally and intellectually, to endure contempt, and attacks upon all that they held most dear. It said to them : " Stand up, when all the world strikes thee. Know how to say *Yes*, when all the world says *No*. Only thus wilt thou come to be *thyself*." The scene of the *Carrying of the Cross* taught them another virtue, saying : " Learn to carry the world in thy consciousness as Christ carried the Cross to identify Himself with the earth. Learn to carry thy body as an external thing. The spirit must hold the body in its will as the hand holds the hammer ! " Thus it was not at all *passivity* that the Mysteries of the Passion taught to the peoples of the west and north, but a new energy through Love and Sacrifice.

The scene on Golgotha was the final stage of the life of Christ, the seal of His mission, and consequently the most sacred mystery of Christianity. In this connection Goethe has truly said : " The supreme mystery of suffering is so sacred a thing that to display the image of it to the eyes of the crowd seems almost a sacrilegious profanation." Why the mournful scene of the Crucifixion ? asked the pagans of the first century. Is the world to find salvation through this cruel horror ? And many a modern thinker has repeated : Can humanity be saved only through the death of a righteous man ? If so, the universe is an instrument of torture and God the torturer ! The most philosophical solution of this poignant problem has been given by Rudolf Steiner, as follows: " The proof that the spiritual always triumphs over the material had to be given to the world. *An initiation transferred to the plane of universal history*—that is the meaning of Golgotha. Torrents of spiritual life are poured from the drops of blood spilt upon the Cross. The blood is the substantialisation of the self. Through the blood spilt on Golgotha the love of Christ penetrates human egoism like a vivifying fluid."

Slowly the cross is raised upon the fatal hill that overlooks Sion. The tortured victim upon it is animated by a superhuman soul—but the Christ has abandoned His powers to the Elohim. He feels Himself cut off from His solar aura, in a frightful solitude, a pit of darkness where soldiers shout and enemies vociferate. A black cloud hangs above Jerusalem, for the earthly atmosphere is like a prism reflecting the life of the universe. Its waters, winds, and elemental spirits gorge themselves upon human passions, and respond also to the cosmic influences, in tempest and convulsions. And these are for Jesus the hours of agony, long as eternity. In spite of the rending torture, He remains the Messiah. He pardons His tormentors, and comforts the penitent thief. At the approach of death, He has felt the devouring thirst that is the presage of relief, but to empty His cup He must experience that sense of total abandonment that causes Him to cry, " My Father, why hast thou forsaken me ?—followed by the supreme words, " All is accomplished," which place the seal of Eternity upon the brow of the astonished centuries.

One last cry issues from the lips of the Crucified, loud as a clarion, or as the sound of a harp whose strings are all snapped simultaneously. So terrible, so powerful, is this cry that the Roman legionaries fall back, murmuring, " Can this be the Son of God ? "

Jesus is dead—but Christ is living—more living than ever ! In the sight of men nothing of Him remains save a corpse hanging on a cross, beneath a sky that is darker than hell ; but in the astral and spiritual worlds a great light blazes forth, followed by a thunder-clap that has a million echoes. The soul of the Christ has rejoined His solar aura, attended by myriads of souls and greeted by the hosannas of the heavenly legions. Henceforth the Elohim and the seers beyond the tomb know that the victory is won, that death has lost its sting, that the walls of the sepulchres are broken down, and that souls in glory will be seen floating above their empty depths. The Christ has reintegrated His Kingdom with powers increased a hundredfold by His sacrifice. He is indeed ready to re-enter the heart of the Infinite, the living Centre of Light, Love and Beauty, that He calls His Father. But His compassion draws Him back to earth, whose Master He has become through His martyrdom.

A sinister haze, a mournful silence, still envelops Jerusalem.

The holy women weep over the body of the Master; Joseph of Arimathæa wraps it in fine linen. The disciples are hiding in the caverns of the valley of Hinnom. Their Master dead, they have lost all hope. Apparently nothing is changed in the opaque world of matter. But in the temple of Herod a strange thing has happened. At the moment when Jesus gave up the ghost, the magnificent blue and purple veil, woven of linen, that concealed the tabernacle, was rent from top to bottom. A Levite who was passing by saw, in the sanctuary, the golden ark flanked by two massive golden Cherubim, whose wings soared towards the vaulted roof. Unheard-of thing, that profane eyes should have beheld the mystery of the Holy of Holies, which the High Priest himself was allowed to enter only once a year! The horrified priests sent the people out of the temple, that they should not witness the sacrilege. This sign had a special meaning. The form of the Cherubim, with lion's body, eagle's wings, and angel's head, is similar to that of the Sphinx. It symbolises the whole evolution of the human soul, its descent into matter and its return to spirit. Thanks to the Christ, the veil of the sanctuary is torn, the enigma of the Sphinx is solved. Henceforward the mystery of life and evolution will be open to all those who *dare* and who *will*.

To explain the task accomplished by the Christ while His followers watched over the entombment of His body, we must once again recall the chief feature of Egyptian initiation. The initiate passed three days and three nights in a tomb, watched over by the hierophant who had thrown him into a deep sleep. During this time he travelled through the other worlds, according to his degree of advancement. When he remembered this on awaking, and knew that he had visited, in advance, the kingdom of the dead, he was as though revivified, and *twice-born*, in the language of the temples. So the Christ accomplished His cosmic voyage, during the entombment, before His resurrection. Here also there is a parallel between ancient initiation and the new mysteries brought to the world by Christ—a parallel, but also an immense expansion. For the astral voyage of a God who has passed through the test of physical death must be of a different kind and vaster range than the timid adventuring of a mortal into the country of the dead, upon the Barque of Isis.[1]

There are two psychic currents that envelop the earth with their multiple rings, like ever-moving serpents of electricity. The one that Moses named *Horeb*, and Orpheus *Erebus*, can also be called *the centripetal force*. It has its centre in the earth, and draws

---

[1] This barque was in reality the initiate's own etheric body, separated by the hierophant from his physical body and borne away on the astral currents.

back to her everything that falls into its torrential flood. It is the abyss of generation, desire and death, the sphere of ordeals, also called purgatory. All souls that are still dominated by earthly passion are swept along in its eddies and whirlpools. The other current is named *Iona* by Moses, and can also be called *the centrifugal force*. It contains the forces of expansion, as the other contains those of contraction ; and it is linked up with the whole Cosmos. It enables souls to rise again to the sun and to heaven ; it is the vehicle for divine influences ; and by means of it the Christ descended in the symbol of the Dove. But although initiates, prepared through a long evolution for their cosmic voyage, knew in all ages how to enter the current of Iona after their death, the great mass of souls, still blinded by the darkness of matter, could accomplish this only with difficulty, and often scarcely emerged from the current of Horeb between their incarnations. The passage of the Christ through these shadowy regions left luminous trails there, and re-opened to these straying souls, as to those of the second sphere of Dante's Inferno, the way to the heavenly world. Thus the Christ widened and illuminated the life after death as He had widened and illuminated life upon earth.

But the essence of His mission was to instil the certainty of spiritual resurrection into the hearts of His apostles, who were to spread His teaching through the world. After being Himself resurrected, He must be resurrected in and through them, that this fact might dominate future history. The Resurrection of the Christ was to be the pledge of the resurrection of souls after this life, and of their faith in the future life. And for this it would not suffice for the Christ to show Himself to His followers astrally, during sleep. He must appear to them when awake, on the physical plane, that His resurrection might seem a material fact. Such a manifestation, though difficult for others, was easy for the Christ ; for the etheric bodies of all great Adepts—and His must have possessed a particularly intense and subtle vitality—continue to exist long after death, and retain a certain amount of power over matter. When reanimated by the Spirit, they can under certain conditions become visible.

Faith in the resurrection did not seize hold of the disciples all at once. It had to penetrate them gradually like a communicating breath of life, like a voice that speaks in the accents of the heart. It entered into their souls as the day dawns gradually after the dark night. It was as a clear morning rising over darkened Palestine. The appearances of the Christ are progressive, producing ever greater effects. At first vague and fugitive as shadows, they increase in strength and brilliance. But how did the body of Jesus disappear ? Was it consumed by the breath of the Fire-

Principle, like those of Moses, Zoroaster and Elijah, and did the earth tremble like the keepers of the tomb, as the Evangelist says? Or was it so refined and spiritualised as scarcely to be material, and so was dissolved into the elements like an aroma in a liquid, like a perfume in the air? However this may be, its exquisite quintessence was, by some marvellous alchemy, drawn up into the atmosphere.

Here comes Mary Magdalene, carrying balms and spices, and sees in the empty sepulchre "two angels in white, sitting . . . where the body of Jesus had lain." She turns round and sees another figure which in her fear she does not recognise; but at the voice that pronounces her name, "Mary!" she is moved to the depths of her soul, knows the Master, and falls at His feet, seeking to touch the hem of His garment. But He, as though He feared the too material contact of the one from whom He had cast out seven devils, says: "Touch Me not, but go to My brethren." Here the Saviour speaks directly to passionate woman, to the sinner who has become a worshipper of the Lord. With one word He pours the balm of Eternal Love into the depths of her heart, knowing that through Woman He can reach the soul of humanity. When He appears again to the eleven behind closed doors in a house in Jerusalem, and tells them to meet Him in Galilee, it is the Master gathering together the chosen ones of His flock for the work of the future. In the sad twilight of Emmaus, it is the divine Healer of souls who rekindles the light of faith in the burning hearts of the despairing disciples. On the shores of the Lake of Tiberias He appears to Peter and John to prepare them for their dark destinies. When, finally, He shows Himself to His own for the last time, on a mountain in Galilee, it is to speak these supreme words: "Go ye therefore and teach all nations . . . and lo, I am with you alway, even unto the end of the world." This is the solemn farewell of the Master, and the testament of the King of the Solar Archangels.

Thus the mystical truth of the Resurrection, which first dawns but faintly upon the apostles, grows ever clearer, and finally culminates in a glorious sunset whose prophetic crimsons and purples will colour their thought for ever.

Once again, several years later, the Christ appears to His adversary, Paul, upon the road to Damascus, in such a manner that the latter becomes His most ardent defender. If the former appearances are as though bathed in a dream-like light, this one is of an incontestably historical character. More unexpected than the others, it is also more vivid, and here again the amount of force displayed is in proportion to the effect desired. For this vision, and these electrifying words, brought about the mission of the apostle to the Gentiles, the conversion of the Greco-Roman world, and through it that of the whole West.

As a brilliant star, the promise of a future world, shines above the mists on the horizon, so does the fact of the Resurrection shine above the whole life-work of the Christ—its necessary conclusion and its consummation.

Neither hatred, nor doubt, nor evil have been overthrown. They cannot yet be, for they are the leaven of the evolutionary process. But henceforward the heart of man can never be robbed of its Immortal Hope. Beyond all defeat, beyond all death, an everlasting chorus shall ring throughout the ages—" Christ is risen ! . . . The way from earth to heaven is once more open ! "

CONCLUSION

THE FUTURE

Christus Luciferus verus.
(Rosicrucian Saying.)

CONCLUSION

THE FUTURE

WE have now surveyed, from one stage to another, planetary evolution and human development up to their central point—the Coming of the Christ. I am conscious of all the omissions in this broad outline, but I hope that it will prove at least one thing ; namely, that there is a Western esoteric tradition which rests on the Christ as the axis of humanity. In it He appears as the consummation of the whole past of mankind, and as the guerdon of its future.

History would be but an exercise of pedants or a diversion of futile story-tellers, if she merely strung together the sparse facts found in human records. But no—she is not a morose jailor who imprisons us in her dungeons ; rather is she a serene Muse who sets us free by transporting us to the heights whence we can see all things unrolled in the immensity of space. She should play the part, not of an immovable Fate always ready to cut the thread of life, but of an intelligent Ariadne, guiding us through the labyrinth. While unveiling Eternal Laws and First Causes, she presents us with a torch to lighten the darkness that surrounds us. Thus armed, let us seek to *see* and to *will*. For humanity, as for individual man, to recover possession of the past is to gather up all its accumulated forces in order to advance into the future, moved by the deep impulses that spring from the soul and from the mystery of Infinity.

Two great currents have marked the course of history for a thousand years. They can be distinguished everywhere upon the surface of the great sea formed by evolving humanity. Sometimes they collide with violent shocks ; sometimes they are at peace, and seem gently to caress one another, as though in these deceptive calms they would unite. Sometimes, even, they intermingle, and strive to be merged in one another ; but without success. The struggle between their conflicting waves ever begins anew. It is the struggle between the religious world and the lay world, between Faith and Science, between Christianity and Paganism, between the Eternal and the Present—a desperate,

271

bitter and obsessing struggle from which none can escape. It is the misfortune and the greatness, the scourge and the honour, of our age ; for all history leads up to it as to an inevitable crisis.

In the pages of this book we have sought to trace the occult causes of this struggle, which is called in esoteric tradition *the War in Heaven ;* and we have found it echoing from planet to planet, from age to age, from race to race, and from nation to nation.

Considering synthetically the initial causes of these two currents and their effects through an indeterminate length of time, we may venture to call them : *the Current of Christ and the Current of Lucifer.*

Let us first note their effects upon the surface of history.

What the Christ brought to the world and taught to His apostles was not an abstract dogma, but a new life, a sovereign impulsion, an immense faith in earth made new and heaven reopened, by means of the Divine Presence that radiated from His Person. This radiation, prolonged for a time by the phenomenon of spiritual resurrection, created the first Christian communities and was sufficient for them. In their eyes, the whole past of humanity, all religions, all ancient initiation, all the knowledge acquired by Asia, Egypt and Greece, were identified with Greco-Roman decadence, and were the work of the devil. Only the Christ existed. Had He not walked the earth as Very God ? But in spite of this, during the first two centuries a number of Christian communities maintained the ancient hierarchical tradition of graduated initiation. This was called the *Gnosis,* and looked upon union with the Christ as a mystical phenomenon greater than any other, a reality that was both individual and collective. But after Saint Augustine's pronouncement that faith in the Established Church should take the place of everything else, the principle of initiation was suppressed, and blind faith superseded true knowledge. Submission to the Church and to her ordinances replaced union with the living Christ. While saints and martyrs were converting the Northern peoples by their sublime exaltation and the shedding of their blood, the Church was becoming more and more romanised, until, confined within narrow dogmas, she thought only of temporal power and of bringing souls into subjection. It is true that some of the later doctors of the Church—such as Albertus Magnus, John Scotus Erigena and Thomas Aquinas—built up a remarkable system of metaphysics by combining the teachings of Plato and Aristotle with Christianity ; but their doctrines lacked what the modern spirit demands—a knowledge of nature, such as was contained synthetically in ancient initiation, and the idea of spiritual evolution through reincarnation and the plurality of existences. The

Church's intellectual narrowness, already marked since Saint Augustine, reached its climax with the two parallel phenomena of the Reformation and the Renaissance, the first of which proclaimed freedom of thought, and the second freedom of scientific investigation. The Church burned John Huss for his independent faith ; she condemned Galileo for asserting that the earth moved round the sun ; she burned Giordano Bruno, the Dominican, because he saw God in the Cosmos and worshipped Him in Infinity.

The proclamation of the dogma of papal infallibility may be considered the last stage of religious agnosticism, spiritual tyranny, and materialism. It despoiled the Church, militant and contemplative, of her weapons and her dignity.

No more need of Jesus Christ, since we have the Pope ! Let darkness reign in the mind, so long as the body of the Church survives ! Can thisb e what poor Brunetière called "*le fait pontifical*," and adopted as sole article of faith for lack of finding one within himself?

Such was the retrogression of Christianity, seen from without, after its magnificent expansion in the twelfth and thirteenth centuries, due to its esoteric reserves and to a mysterious influx of divine forces. Its movement from the fourteenth to the fifteenth century was a contraction rather than a development. When Jesus said to His followers : " The kingdom of heaven is within you," He was promising the conquest of heaven through the inner life. We have seen how the Church succeeded in veiling the heaven of the Cosmos and the heaven of the soul by intellectual narrowness and the idea of spiritual domination.

Let us now see what results have been attained by the *Luciferian current of Science*, which has never ceased to move beside the *Christian current of the Church* and to conflict with it, and which at the present time is growing so wide and powerful as almost to overwhelm it altogether.

It has its source in the Greek world. When Socrates put forward the axiom that truth can be attained by reason alone, and that dialectic is the infallible road to moral perfection and to supreme happiness, he formulated, in a way, the principle of all contemporary science, whose last phase was seen in Positivist philosophy. In parallel fashion, Aristotle, in basing all the sciences upon the observation of natural phenomena, inaugurated the new method of scientific investigation. *Observation, analysis* and *reason*, the three faculties that were set up as sole mistresses of truth, were soon to displace, little by little, from the scientific domain, *contemplation, intuition* and *vision*. Yet these alone can reach the inner principles of things, and had up till then governed the higher races of humanity through the centres of initiation and the temple schools. Repressed by the Church, and overlaid by the warlike activities of the Northern races, scientific inquiry slept during the early Middle Ages and was only awakened by the world-explorations and discoveries of the fifteenth and sixteenth centuries. Christopher Columbus having proved that the earth was round, and Galileo that it moved round the sun, Copernicus and Kepler having measured the stars and their distances, the human mind, entering into possession of the entire universe, underwent a radical change. It should be remembered that these great astronomers were still, in a large measure, believers and seers of the old order. They conceived the universe as a living being, animated by a divine principle, and held this to be proved by its unity and harmony. Just as the last great scholars of the Church—Albertus Magnus, John Scotus Erigena and Thomas Aquinas—rendered homage to human reason, which they strove to reconcile with theology, so did these pioneers of the stellar spaces find and worship God in Nature. We may even declare that, without this faith based on intuition, they would never have discovered the laws that rule the stars. But it was not thus in later times, for while the Church gradually contracted by banishing Nature from Religion, the scientists darkened the understanding by banishing the conceptions of God and the soul from Science. In our own days it has come about that man, having subjected the material elements of Nature to his will—chemicals, steam, light, electricity—and having forced them to subserve his needs, believes himself to be their sole master, ignoring the divine powers of which they are but the vestments. He has treated them like an egoistic and tyrannous child, and has abused them until, through an occult reaction, these forces have become hostile and have turned against him, driving him to frenzied cupidity and heartless materialism. Thus the new apostles of Science, misinterpreting their own admirable discoveries, have come to believe in nothing but their instruments and the decomposed matter that they study in their experiments, and to deny the existence of Spirit, which is dynamic throughout all the vast kingdoms of Nature, but is revealed only to the intuition on the serene heights of contemplation. This exclusive method has resulted in intellectual and social anarchy. It disaggregates the human being, sterilises its creative powers, and tends to kill its immortal principle, and even its vital principle. With machines, instruments and theories, it has already succeeded in destroying the external beauty of life.

Thanks to this mentality, when man now removes his gaze

from the earth that he has laboriously conquered and turns it upon himself, he finds nothing but the chaotic anarchy of his ungoverned passions; and if he raises it to the sky he is lost in a glacial and terrifying void.

Here we see the deadlock reached by a Christianity mutilated by the suppression of initiation, and a Science robbed of belief in God; on the one hand, ossification in abstract dogma, on the other, asphyxiation in dead matter.

There has always existed, since the beginning of our era, a minority, misunderstood and persecuted, but powerful and not to be destroyed, whose ceaseless effort and aim has been *to reconcile the Christian current with the Luciferian current*, binding them into one sheaf, uniting into one organic whole Faith and Reason, Religion and Science, and thus raising ancient initiation to the level of the Christian revelation. It is difficult to distinguish clearly the members of this minority in the mutilated and travestied documents which are all that remain to tell us of their earthly existence. Usually they were forced to hide themselves, to be disguised, and to slip like phantoms through the outskirts of history; for they were equally suspect to established religion and to official science.

These outcasts are nearly always accused of heresy and sorcery. We find them more or less everywhere, far apart, but scattered through all countries, all professions, all ranks of society. Solitary philosophers, clever physicians, learned rabbis, silent monks hiding their wide knowledge under the narrow scapular, alchemists who seek the arcana of the elements at the bottom of their athanors, astrologers who scrutinise the movements of the stars to discover the laws of destiny. Sometimes they are inquiring princes or thoughtful kings within their palaces; sometimes dreaming shepherds in their fields, or women who relate old legends in their humble cottages. A secret sympathy unites this great brotherhood. They recognise one another by a sign, by a look; by the magnetic atmosphere that each one emanates; by their silences more than by their words.

Like the *Brothers of Christ* they feel the need to love and to believe; like the *Children of Lucifer* they have the desire to know and to understand. These powers unite in them to form one single force, one mind, one will. The countenances of the greatest among them are veiled by a strange melancholy; for the tragedy of the universe weighs heavily upon their heart and brain. They feel themselves responsible for it, as portions of the earthly providence that watches over human destiny. But through this veil there shines like an aureole of light the inward joy of those who behold Divinity. They know that the sorrows of the world are the sorrows of God, as the colours of the prism are the sufferings of Light. They are conscious of being united to all living creatures by an invisible thread. They remember their past lives more or less clearly, and are preparing their future lives, but they do not speak to the masses of these mysteries, and seldom even to their own disciples. To spread them abroad would be to profane them, and to encourage superstition and charlatanism. Such things are of value only to those who have seen and lived them ; then they become the diamond citadel of the strong and the pure-hearted.

The essential feature of western esotericism is that it is both intellectual and mystical. It is the son of Lucifer and the servant of Christ. I have now sketched its general characteristics, but its history would be far more dramatic and colourful if one could call to life again all its heroes, famous or obscure, who suffered ostracism and whose brows were marked with the fatal *signum reprobationis* of the heretic and the accursed.

Here I can only show its affiliation and briefly enumerate its stages.

We find it beginning with the Gnostics. From their confused and involved expositions we can infer that they had a deep apprehension of the presence of the Divine Word in the universe, and of its hypostases, of which the last and greatest was the Christ. But Christian esotericism only became consolidated in the fourteenth century with the indomitable and mysterious Mani, father of Manicheism. This was the first attempt to bring the Luciferian current into the Christian current. No other religious personage has been more outrageously misrepresented, one might say more radically extirpated from the official tradition, than was Mani by the Church, which saw a dangerous rival in him. All his writings were ruthlessly destroyed, and are only known to us through the refutations and calumnies of his adversaries ; but his great personality has nevertheless left its mark in the controversies that he aroused and in the fraternities that were inspired by his teachings. Pupil of the Persian magi, he had a personal revelation of the Christ. Having attracted numerous disciples, among them the king's son, he was called up before a council of the Byzantine Church, to defend himself against his accusers. Condemned and excommunicated, he died soon afterwards in a mountain fortress, some said by the order of the king ; others, at the instigation of Christian fanatics. The originality of his thought lay in his conception of evil as a necessary counter-weight to good in the world-system, and in the introduction of the idea of reincarnation into Christianity. We can understand how it was that Saint

Augustine, who had been a Manichean, became the sworn enemy of this doctrine which, in re-establishing graduated initiation, would despoil the Church of her uncontrolled power. The theories of Manicheism were gradually spread throughout the West. The Catharists propagated them in Hungary, the Albigenses in France, and the Templars, at the height of their power since the Crusades, disseminated them all through Europe, and even in the East. But the king of France and the Pope laid their heads together to destroy the Order of the Templars, and instigated the massacres that continued until every member of it had been exterminated, and all its archives and the accessories of its ritual burnt. The same rigorous methods were used to deal with the Albigenses. It was the Sicilian Vespers of absolute monarchy against independent chivalry, the Saint Bartholomew of the Papacy against Christian esotericism.

A more productive era for western occult science began with Christian Rosenkreuz, who founded the Rosicrucian Order in the fourteenth century. His genius foresaw the necessity for co-operation between Christian mysticism and nascent science, and for linking up western science with eastern wisdom, that the widening chasm in the human mind might be spanned, and a buffer prepared against the formidable shocks of the future. It may be said that the great occultists of the sixteenth century —Paracelsus, the alchemist, Jacob Boehme, the visionary cobbler, Cornelius Agrippa, the philosopher-magician—were all inspired by his regenerative spirit. The prevailing thought of these wise and fearless seekers is the absolute parallelism, the profound harmony, that obtains between the *microcosm* and the *macrocosm*, between man and the universe. The hierarchy of kingdoms in the constitution of the universe—mineral, vegetable, animal and human—corresponds to the hierarchy of forces in the constitution of man—the physical, etheric and astral bodies, and the conscious self. Man, being an epitome of the whole universe, thus becomes the image of God. This was a discovery of incalculable import, and the radiant centre of esoteric truth. It is certain that this truth is implicitly contained in the ancient mythologies, in symbol-ical form ; but the occultists of the sixteenth century were the first to reveal and demonstrate it scientifically. In them intuitive vision was combined with analytical knowledge.

The position of the occultists of the seventeenth, eighteenth and nineteenth centuries is very different. Less persecuted by the Church, which still fears them, but whose power is diminishing, they are more so by official science, whose credit is increasing, while it is gradually taking upon itself the task of intellectual and moral leadership, and confining itself more and more to the observation of material phenomena. Though the adepts of occult science can no longer be burned or hanged as demoniacs or heretics, it is sought to kill them by ridicule and by dwelling only upon their failings and excesses. Nevertheless they have made a valuable and indispensable contribution to esoteric wisdom through the work of such men as Court de Gébelin, the eighteenth-century theosophist, Claude Saint-Martin, Fabre d'Olivet, Eliphas Levi, Saint-Yves d'Alveydre, and many others. Upon the great human brotherhood, which is the Christian idea, they grafted the brotherhood of religions sprung from a common source and aspiring to a common end. So are the arms of the Christ opened widely to embrace all prophets and all initiates.

If, together with the actual occult tradition, we take into account the sub-influences which stir the deeper consciousness of humanity —and which are often the result of some influx from above—we must add to these manifestations the innumerable and marvellous intuitions of the nineteenth century poets. The truths of the Beyond gleam continually through their writings, as the sky through gaps in the clouds. Goethe's *Faust* is from this point of view a sort of encyclopedia of occultism. And what surprising glimpses there are in Byron's *Cain* and *Manfred*, and in Shelley's *Prometheus Unbound*! What a sheaf of esoteric thoughts one could gather from the works of Lamartine and Victor Hugo, and even from Alfred de Vigny who, amid his tranquil despair and stoic doubt, had fleeting visions of the most sublime truths! As to Richard Wagner, he is the greatest unconscious occultist who has ever lived. His Wotan, his Valkyries, his tetralogy, evoke all the Mysteries of the northern peoples in dazzling symbology. Lohengrin and Parsifal exalt Christian initiation. His music overflows with every kind of magic, and almost seems, like that of Beethoven, to have rediscovered the primordial and creative Word.

To complete the list, let us render homage to the professional philosophers who have adventured, voluntarily or otherwise, into occultism. Has not Schelling recognised, in somnambulic clair-voyance, the higher and immortal self of man? Has not Hegel, the idealist, seen in nature the involution of spirit into matter, and in history the evolution of matter towards spirit? Even the pessimistic Schopenhauer, defying all his contemporaries, dared to put intuition above logic as an instrument of knowledge. M. Bergson, adopting and defining this idea, has recently declared that " philosophy is nothing but a conscious and deliberate return to the principle of intuition." Nothing more was needed to cause the leaders of atheism to award him the label " clerical." M. Boutroux, for his part, has enraged many Positivist hedgehogs by announcing that the deeper hypnotic states, in which the self changes its personality and actually creates its own object, open the door to metaphysics, shamefully exiled from philosophy for half a century.

With so many openings made in the thick wall of materialism, we can to-day look forward to the future with more assurance.

Materialistic science, obstinately confined to the observation of visible phenomena, and the Church, entrenched among abstract rites and dogmas, whose deeper meaning is less and less understood, have certainly not yet fulfilled their missions. They are sufficient for the minds and souls of those who live more in the past than in the future. Moreover, they will inevitably be transformed, but only through conflict with newly organised powers which menace them from without. The religion, science and art of the future also have need of new groupings, which can only come about through crystallisation under the impulsion of a new principle.

It follows from the whole intellectual and spiritual history of the last two thousand years, which I have broadly outlined, that this crystallisation can only be made possible by *a synthesis of the Christian and Luciferian principles.*

Both of them have undergone transformation in the course of time, and only to-day do they reveal to us their inner mysteries. This is how the most illuminated theosophist of the present day defines the mysteries of Christianity. " The earth is a cosmos of wisdom, thanks to the cosmic powers that have formed its elements and constructed its organisms in skilful harmony. The actual earth is composed of these wisdom elements, and man is refinding them. But a new force has come into play which leads man to feel himself an independent member of a spiritual world. The Cosmos of Wisdom must be changed into a Cosmos of Love. All that the self can produce within itself must become Love, and the greatest and most comprehensive example of Love is the Christ, the sublime Solar Spirit. By Him the germ of Love has been deposited in the heart of the human being, and Love must be poured out thence over the whole world. Even as the primordial wisdom was expressed through the external forces of the world, so in the future *Love will be manifested as a natural force. This is the secret of all future evolution.* What man has to accomplish in conscious harmony with the whole of earthly evolution is the dissemination of Love. In its very essence spiritual knowledge will be changed into Love. . . . The exterior knowledge of the universe will be interiorised in man. Love is Wisdom reborn from the Self." [1]

---

[1] *Die Geheimwissenschaft*, Rudolf Steiner; p. 400 *et seq.*

The Christian principle, *Sacrifice to God*, thus leads to Knowledge through Love unlimited. The Luciferian principle, *Individuality and Power*, leads inversely to Love through Knowledge; for, pushed to its extreme, it attains to Sacrifice, by the supreme affirmation of Individuality and by the desire to create in its turn. Voluntary sacrifice, being always creation, means no longer death but resurrection. Thus these two principles, when united, complete and confirm one another. Their collaboration is the necessary condition for the future crystallisation.

With these premises we can foresee what Religion, Science and Art will be in the future. We can visualise them, not indeed in their outer physiognomy, which will be the work of human liberty and genius, aided by free nations and creative individuals, but in their spiritual, intellectual and moral aspects, which proceed logically from all former evolution.

It is my opinion that western esotericism must accentuate its Greco-Christian character, because Greece sums up all the East for us, and is moreover the inventor of Art and Science; and because the Christ is the highest and most synthetic religious manifestation known to the world.

Jesus Christ and the other *Messiahs* will then continue to have their sanctuaries more glorious than ever, and illuminated by divine love. *Lucifer*, as representative of the flower of ascending humanity, corresponds to the *Cult of Heroes*, the greatest of whom will have their temples in the religion of the future. Beyond the *Word*, the *Son*, and their highest manifestations, will be honoured and worshipped the Universal Spirit, the supreme Creator, the Unfathomable, Invisible and Eternal, the *Father* and His manifestive powers:—invisible Nature, the Virgin-Mother; Alma Mater, the uncreated Light; Cybele, mother of Demeter in the Orphic religion, the Holy Ghost in the Christian religion, symbolised by Iona the Dove, the feminine attribute of God. As to the Elohim with their hosts of Archangels, the devas of the Aryans and the gods of the Greeks—when their cosmic and psychic action is again recognised, their arts, their sciences, and their worship will be reinstated.

A new religion needs a new architecture to express its main trend of thought. The Greek temple, with its architrave and pediment above the colonnade, and its bare cella containing the statue of a god or goddess, represented admirably God dwelling upon earth and teaching men, but set apart, and inaccessible. The Gothic cathedral, the final expression of purely Christian art, with its ogives and its tapering spires, also represents marvellously the aspiration of the soul towards heaven, and the prayers of the faithful whose clasped hands are raised towards the saints and angels floating in the nave. The new temple will aim at representing the influx of divine powers to the earth and to the heart of man, and at expressing, in a sense, their reciprocal inter-penetration through an ascending and descending movement. For this purpose it will make use of slender rounded columns with skilfully decorated capitals, and elongated cupolas. The plan of the building will no longer be based on the square, like the Greek temple, or on the cross, like the Christian church, but on the circle, or several intersecting circles. The inner frieze will be ornamented with the symbols of the planets and the signs of the zodiac, indicating the past and future phases of earthly evolution.

This religion will be explained and supported by a new science, which might be called Theosophy—or better still, *the Science of Spirit*. Its aim will be to seek for the principles and causes that lie behind all phenomena, and to rise from the visible to the invisible, from the material to the spiritual. With this object in view, it will strive to build up a synthesis of the sciences of physical observation, by cultivating, through the discipline of graduated initiation, the faculties of vision, inspiration and intuition that are necessary for the exploration of the astral and spiritual worlds.

The principal apostle and preacher of these new forms of know-ledge will be *Art, the initiator and redeemer*. Art will in truth be the inspired interpreter, the hierophant and the torch-bearer of integral Science and universal Religion. Human language will once more become creative, and poetry a sacred thing. Poetry, read or spoken, in the family circle or in civic life, will, like the epic of olden times, revive the past and idealise the present. Lyric poetry will reappear, as in the heroic ages, as a revelation of the Immortal Soul to souls incarnate, a lamp of inspiration burning amid the shadows of life. Drama will again become the representative of the sacred Mysteries, and in it will be revealed the infinite perspectives of human destiny. The gods will appear in it in new forms, and the divine drama will shine through the human drama like the rays of a crimson and violet sunset piercing a bank of storm-clouds. No rules and no dogmas will be imposed, save nobleness and dignity. In the words of Christ, it is by their fruits that works and men shall be judged. That which is fruitful shall be judged to be true. Enlightened humanity will choose what beautifies the body, widens the mind, and illumines the spirit, while refusing all that might injure, contaminate or dis-sociate them.

In social organisation and in education, as also in religion and art, account will be taken of the *natural human ladder*, and of the *hierarchical principle* inherent in nature ; for humanity will always be divided into instinctive, passional, intellectual and spiritual types. Education and social selection can be based only on this principle. Men can raise themselves from a lower to a higher rung of the ladder, but only by observing the necessary stages.

The task of governing humanity belongs to the intellectuals, inspired by the spiritual types who guide it from above. Discord between them causes anarchy to rage in the social organism ; when they co-operate, all is peace and harmony.

So shall there be formed very gradually a new humanity, of which the spiritual sages will form the first rank, and the poets, artists, thinkers and scholars, the second. Woman, intuitive and endowed with spiritual sight, will have her place in the temples, under the control of the initiates. Disinterested love, expressed in action by the higher brotherhoods, will penetrate to the more developed souls and have its effects on the instinctive and passional types also. Love between man and woman will become deeper and more intense, through the more intimate fusion of soul and spirit. Perfectly mated couples will provide examples of the perfect union of the Eternal-Masculine and the Eternal-Feminine, which is a Divine Mystery manifested throughout the universe from above downwards. In them transfigured passion will become creative of life and beauty. Woman will play, in addition, a great and leading part in the education of the child and of the nation.

Such is, in its general outline, the ideal picture of the chosen humanity which will be evolved from the mass through individual effort and organic grouping. But let us not think that it will be formed or maintained without a struggle. The conflict of the forces of inertia, discord and destruction, with those of progress, harmony and creation, will be incessant and intense. It will even increase ; for in proportion as the forces of Good are combined and organised, the forces of Evil will be gathered together in greater numbers. This will result in a struggle of a different kind from the present class war, which is bitter enough, and may yet be more so, but is concerned only with economic interests and material possessions. The other will involve spiritual interests, transcendent truths, and the government of souls. On the one side will be ranged egoism, hatred, and the spirit of negation, armed with black magic (which will be widespread) ; on the other, love, wisdom and faith, armed with white magic (the royal art of initiates in all ages).

In this way will be fulfilled the words of the Christ, and of the Apocalypse, concerning the division of humanity into two camps,

between whom the Christ, again appearing spiritually, shall judge.[1]
There will be reproduced also, in new and more subtle forms, the
terrific struggle between white and black magic which prevailed
in the later Atlantean period, and which will be, as then, the fore-
runner of new world-cataclysms. The only weapons of the
chosen ones will be divine knowledge and divine love, and their
only ambition to save as many souls as possible from perversion,
destruction and death. In the time of Atlantis, black magic was
victorious. It drove its opponents into exile in other lands, and
triumphed upon the great continent of Atlantis, which later sank
beneath the ocean. In the future struggle victory will lie with
the divine science of white magic, which, whether visible or
invisible, acknowledged or denied, exalted or abused, has never
ceased to rule the world from the beginning of things—and a new
race will be born.

The first initiates of the Holy Grail cherished a remarkable
legend concerning Lucifer, and the Rosicrucians adopted it and
revealed its deeper meaning.

After his fall from the spheres of light to the darkness of earth,
the rebellious Archangel lost a precious stone which had shone
like a star in his crown. From this stone was carven the cup in
which Joseph of Arimathea received the blood of Christ. Even
so shall the human soul, to which Lucifer gave the unassuageable
thirst of the ' self,' the growing individuality, be filled, drop by
drop, with the Divine Love that flows from Christ. When the
meaning of his sacrifice is fully understood, and his mission
accomplished, the Archangel Lucifer, free, and more glorious
than before, will have become the God of the planet Venus, which
was originally destined for him, and for which he has always experienced an insatiable longing. By this time the Christ will be
completely identified with the earth and with humanity. The
black cross, symbolising sin, expiation, and death, will have become
the white cross, the Cross of Light, glorious symbol of Resurrection,
from which rain down roses of Eternal Love, living and fragrant
as the lips of angels.

---

[1] Those who talk of a new incarnation of Christ in the present age show that
they have not yet understood His true nature, or the mission of Christianity.
The Christ is a Being Who had to be incarnated once to prove to men that the
Word existed, and to impress humanity with a definite impulsion towards spirituality. But this phenomenon cannot be repeated, and if it were it would be a
backward move, not an advance. The Christ promised to come again, not in the
flesh but ' in the clouds '—that is, in the etheric body—' to judge both the quick
and the dead.' The ' quick ' are the live souls who will be able to see Him, and
who are progressing. The ' dead ' are the dead souls who dwell in darkness and
are retrogressing.

Lucifer, having regained his star and his diadem, will assemble his legions for new works of creation. Attracted by his flaming torch, celestial spirits will descend to bathe in the vaporous atmosphere of Venus, and he will send these messengers from unknown spheres to the men of earth. Then the torch of Lucifer will signal 'From Heaven to Earth!'—and the Cross of Christ will answer 'From Earth to Heaven!'

Our planet must go through many more metamorphoses, and humanity must experience many more phases, before the final transfiguration. But from the midst of present conflict we are allowed to contemplate this vision of the initiates as an inspiring symbol. May it shine like a star, far-off but fixed and luminous, above all our odysseys and tempests!